AFRICAN STUDIES SERIES
General Editor: J. R. GOODY

ISLAM AND TRIBAL ART IN WEST AFRICA

OTHER BOOKS IN THIS SERIES

ISLAM AND TRIBAL ART IN WEST AFRICA

RENÉ A. BRAVMANN

Associate Professor of Art History and Chairman of the
African Studies Program, University of Washington

CAMBRIDGE UNIVERSITY PRESS

Published by the Syndics of the Cambridge University Press
Bentley House, 200 Euston Road, London NW1 2DB
American Branch: 32 East 57th Street, New York, N.Y.10022

© Cambridge University Press 1974

Library of Congress Catalogue Card Number: 73-77262

ISBN: 0 521 20192 6

First published 1974

Composed in Great Britain
at the University Printing House, Cambridge
Printed in the United States of America

For Stevie

CONTENTS

MAPS

PLATES

ACKNOWLEDGEMENTS

The trail of indebtedness which I have left behind in the writing of this book has been enormous, and to thank all those who have had a part in its making would require a substantial work in itself. I wish, however, to acknowledge those without whose guidance and encouragement this task would have never been completed. My deepest thanks to the Foreign Area Fellowship Program and its members for their generous support of the research resulting in this volume. I am also indebted to the Indiana University Foundation for its loan of crucial field recording equipment. Of those persons who have helped in so many ways special acknowledgements are due Mr William B. Fagg, Keeper of Ethnography, the British Museum; Mr Richard B. Nunoo, Director of the National Museum of Ghana; and Dr A. A. Y. Kyerematen, former Director of the Ghana National Cultural Centre. The faculty and staff of the Institute of African Studies at the University of Ghana kindly extended to me every courtesy and their total assistance while I was in residence there. Professors Jack Goody and Ivor Wilks were particularly instrumental in guiding me along certain lines of inquiry which ultimately resulted in this publication. My sincerest appreciation goes to Bradford G. Martin for encouraging me to delve further into Islamic sources and for his counsel. I would also like to cite my colleagues Simon Ottenberg and Pierre van de Berghe, who kindly discussed various segments of this manuscript with me. Ultimately I would like to acknowledge an enormous intellectual and emotional debt to Roy Sieber, who kindled my interest in the arts of Africa and who directed me towards this particular theme.

Field research would not have been possible without supremely able interpreters: Kofi Ofori Ansong, Moro Bamba, and particularly Peter Kwesi Pipim. My deepest thanks, however, are reserved for the numerous informants in west central Ghana and the northeastern Ivory Coast who freely and openly shared their minds and hearts with me.

Many thanks are also due numerous persons who helped in the actual compilation of this manuscript. I am especially indebted to Eleanor Howard for her rigorous editorial assistance and for her careful preparation of the final draft of this work.

Finally I wish to express my deepest gratitude to my wife, Stevie, who shared in more ways than she will ever know in making this book a reality.

R. A. B.

August 1973

INTRODUCTION

Writers on the arts of sub-Saharan Africa have either ignored the influence of Islam or have treated the theme inaccurately. That they should ignore it is surprising, since Islam has for many centuries been one of the most pervasive factors affecting the arts and culture of West Africa. Many art historians, though they lament the paucity of historical documents and objects available to them in their attempts to reconstruct the history of African art, have avoided altogether this potentially valuable avenue of research. Others have presumed that Islam would be bent on the destruction of the masking and figurative traditions so integral to the indigenous cultures and have described the relationship between the religion and the arts as one that is invariably negative.

Typical of their commentary are the recent statements of several noted writers on the arts of sub-Saharan Africa. According to Trowell, "As far as sculpture was concerned, Moslem influence was merely negative, for the religion forbade the making of graven images."[1] Fagg, less given to sweeping generalities, is nevertheless equally pessimistic about the chances for the survival of tribal art in the face of Islamic expansion. Pointing to the early western Sudanic empires, he stresses the importance of Islam in this region and concludes that

These were not the conditions, material or philosophical, in which what we know as tribal or "primitive" sculpture can exist. Islam, of which iconoclasm is an essential tenet, is overtly inimical to representational art . . .[2]

For Bascom, many cultures that had artistic traditions in the past no longer retain them, because of the encroachments of Islam and its uncompromising iconoclastic stance:

Islam takes literally the prohibition of the First Commandment: "Thou shalt not carve thyself images, or fashion the likeness of anything in heaven above, or on the earth below, or in the waters at the root of the earth". . .[3]

[1] Margaret Trowell and Hans Nevermann, *African and Oceanic Art*, p. 13. Trowell's cliché-ridden comment lacks even the slightest evidence.
[2] Eliot Elisofon and W. B. Fagg, *The Sculpture of Africa*, p. 27. Fagg clearly overestimates the impact of Islam on the western Sudan, which causes him to overstate his case concerning the effects of the religion on the arts.
[3] William Russell Bascom, *African Arts*, p. 7. Although Bascom carried out extensive field work among the Yoruba, he seems not to have taken notice of the fact that artistic traditions have continued to flourish in northern Yorubaland, especially in Ilorin province, where Islam is very strong. Estimates in 1954 for Ilorin province indicate that

Even when accusations of the intolerance of Islam towards traditional art have been tempered, writers have tended to base their judgments about the impact of Islam on the arts on unproven assumptions. A notable example of such an assumption can be seen in Fagg's conjectures regarding the influence of the religion on the art styles of the western Sudan. According to Fagg, the non-Muslim populations of this region

accept or imitate some elements of the material culture of their Muslim neighbours, including, in the case of some pagan chiefs, their formal dress; and, in a more subtle way, their sculpture and its associated ritual seem to be modified (and often also concealed) in a way that might render them less objectionable to orthodox Mohammedans . . . It is difficult to say what may have been the motives behind this tempering of the outward forms of paganism – whether it was intended to render easier [the] necessary commercial contacts with Muslims, or to avoid provoking holy wars, or was simply partial imitation, more or less conscious, of the abstraction favoured by Islam, or indeed whether it is attributable to Muslim influence at all rather than to coincidence or to a common culture . . . It is suggested here that historical influences such as these may have had a greater part in determining the abstract tendencies in the art styles of the Sudanese pagans than is appreciated by those writers who are content to explain them solely in terms of the fashionable jargon of psychology.[4]

When Fagg refers to "this tempering of the outward forms of paganism" he fails to provide any evidence that there has in fact been tempering. He says only that "their sculpture and its associated ritual *seem* to be modified" (emphasis mine). "Abstract tendencies" are in fact apparent in Sudanese sculpture – that is, if one is willing to accept the terminology of twentieth-century Western art criticism; but these might well have been due to the very nature of the materials employed (e.g., soft woods, which invariably lend themselves to more schematic forms) or to deeply rooted stylistic traditions that pre-dated Muslim influence, rather than to the inroads of Islam. Certainly in the forest region of West Africa the majority of art traditions do not demonstrate such "abstract tendencies" as a result of the spread of Islam.

Michel Leiris and Jacqueline Delange have gone so far as to state that "the tenets of [the Islamic] faith have tended to prevent the making of anthropomorphic images [in the West African savannah]," but this clearly belies the countless examples of such forms from this region of Islamic penetration.[5]

Total indictments as well as more mildly couched negative assessments have been leveled repeatedly, but they have been based on only the barest

about 75 percent of the population is Muslim (J. Spencer Trimingham, *History of Islam in West Africa*, p. 230, note 2).

[4] Elisofon and Fagg, *The Sculpture of Africa*, p. 28.

[5] *African Art*, trans. by Michael Ross, p. 113.

shreds of evidence. René Gardi, in his very recent work *African Crafts and Craftsmen*, begins by decrying the forces of Westernization that have undermined African societies and their arts. He then shifts his attention to Islam, remarking that the spread of the faith and its attendant "iconoclasm . . . destroyed the postulates for the representation of holy pictures."[6] Although he specifically refers to "holy pictures," it seems clear that Gardi is condemning the influence of Islam on traditional figurative art in general. Curiously enough, however, his survey of the crafts in West Africa includes illustrations of figurative work by several artisans who are surely Muslim. In discussing the brass-casters and wood-carvers of Korhogo, he describes the work of Brahim and Sengi Kulibary and of Foley Kulibaly,[7] and his photographs reveal that these men are producing cast face masks, cast figurative containers, and what appears to be a female *dèblè*, a Senufo figurative type used by the Poro, a socio-religious control association. Gardi does not mention the ethnic origin of these artisans, but their family names strongly suggest they are members of two Mande clans.[8] The Mande in this area, as elsewhere, are almost totally Islamized. The Arabic first name of Brahim Kulibary is characteristic of many Islamized Mande, and the facial scarification pattern seen in the photograph of this artist is likewise typically Mande.[9] It is thus highly likely that Gardi was in fact interviewing Muslim artisans.

Only Frank Willett, in his recently published survey, *African Art*, has cast a more favorable light on the subject of Islamic influence on African art.[10] Although aware of the fact that Islam may discourage representational forms, his own research in Nigeria revealed that Islamization does not categorically mean the demise of figurative art. In Nupeland, for example, he notes that, "doors, although essentially ornamental, often include animals, while masked dancers are still alive . . ."[11] Furthermore, he goes on to relate that yet other Islamized peoples in West Africa have masquerades, but this statement unfortunately stands unsupported. Although clearly more sensitive and open to the apparent relationship of Islam and traditional art, he does not develop this idea with any real conviction. Willett, however, is the exception. All others have continued to decry the actions of this faith with respect to traditional life and the arts. Through constant reiteration, such comments as those already noted have

---

[6] p. 7.

[7] Ibid., pp. 63–5, 125–6.

[8] Quite probably they are members of the same clan. Gardi may well have recorded the same name with variant orthography as a result of hearing the semi-vowel imprecisely.

[9] Plate 42, p. 62.

[10] A panel devoted to the subject of Islamic influence on the arts was a part of the African Studies Association meeting in New York City in the fall of 1967. Exploratory papers clearly revealing a number of associations between Islam and indigenous art traditions were presented by Roy Sieber, Arnold Rubin, and La-Belle Prussin, but these works have not been published.   [11] p. 241.

come to constitute the "evidence" presented by scholars seeking to explain the relationship between Islam and the visual arts in Africa.

My field research on the visual arts in the regions of the Cercle de Bondoukou (Ivory Coast) and west central Ghana emphatically revealed that these pessimistic assumptions are not necessarily correct. In this heavily Islamized area – deeply influenced by the Muslim Mande Dyula, Ligbi, and Hwela since at least the seventeenth century – traditional life and the arts continue to flourish. Local cults, shrines, and rituals have not been attacked by the Mande, nor have the associated art forms been uprooted and destroyed. Quite the contrary: the Islamized Mande generally accept such aspects of "paganism" without question and in many instances even support and cooperate with their neighbors to ensure that these traditions remain vital and in full operation. Even more unusual, however, is the occurrence of two masquerades – the Gbain and the Do – controlled by the Dyula, Ligbi and Hwela. These cults, concerned with witchcraft and protection, are clearly Muslim, as will be described later. The entire situation here defies the dictum that Islam and "paganism" are incompatible and that the confrontation of Muslims and non-Muslims invariably results in conflict and the demise of the arts.

Was this simply an exception to the rule – a highly anomalous situation? Research on the secondary-source level indicates that it definitely is not exceptional. Comparative evidence for other parts of West Africa, found in historical and anthropological accounts, travel literature, social and historical studies of Islam, and Arabic documents suggests similar situations elsewhere. It is obvious that the entire issue of the relationship of Islam to the arts needs to be reassessed.

The reassessment will require examination of a number of deep-seated negative attitudes held about the relationship of Islam to traditional culture. Has Islam in fact been negative in effect, invariably weakening and undermining the foundations of tribal life? For many, the aniconic attitudes espoused by Islam (specifically those relating to representational imagery) are clearly responsible for the apparent scarcity or demise of the visual arts in areas of West Africa influenced by the faith. But did such elements of Islamic dogma actually have any appreciable impact on Muslims in West Africa? If so, where and how were they applied? In addition, Islam as a religion and culture in sub-Saharan Africa, specifically West Africa, has been held to be intolerant and uncompromising with respect to traditional societies. Universalistic in its orientation, it was and is fundamentally opposed to animism and tribalism. Could Islam, however, have succeeded in influencing such large portions of West Africa if this opposition had been strongly manifested? To account for the impressive gains made by the religion, we must assume that Muslims interacted with traditional societies in a very different manner.

4

A necessary first step in treating the relationship of Islam and traditional art is a reconsideration of Islam itself, based on a review of sources generally overlooked or ignored by art historians and museologists. The history of Islam in West Africa and the avenues by which the faith touched and affected indigenous societies must be restudied. The potential and actual influence of Islamic tenets concerning representational art must be evaluated. Particularly crucial are the questions of the nature of Islam in West Africa and the manner in which Muslims have interacted with non-Muslim cultures. So-called classical cases of Muslim destruction of tribal traditions must be reconsidered. It is also necessary to establish that Islam and local art traditions can be compatible, which I shall demonstrate by considering a variety of secondary sources and the masking traditions among the Mande elite of the fourteenth-century empire of Mali and among the present-day Mande Sanu of Bobo-Dioulasso (Upper Volta) and the Muslim Mande of Gonja (Ghana).

With the positive relations between Islam and such art forms established on a broad level, it becomes possible to treat this theme more intensively as it applies to the Islamized Mande Dyula, Ligbi and Hwela of the Cercle de Bondoukou and west central Ghana. This region clearly demonstrates the high degree of interaction which can exist among Muslims, non-Muslims, and traditional art forms. Such interchange is most dramatically expressed in the relationship of the Muslim Mande to the Bedu, Gbain, and Do masquerades, and I shall describe these in detail in order to underscore the extent to which Islam and traditional life can co-exist.

5

CHAPTER I

THE ISLAMIZATION OF WEST AFRICA

To deal with the subject of Muslim influence on the arts, one must begin at the beginning. It is necessary to look at the ways in which Islam succeeded in influencing such large portions of West Africa. I shall examine the process of Islamization by briefly considering the various channels or methods by which Islam has penetrated and affected West African societies. Long-held ideas of Islamic history suffer from two essentially negative (and usually mistaken) beliefs: that Islam has been unmerciful and unbending in its relationship to traditional cultures and that traditional societies were and are helpless in the face of such a monolithic and presumed "higher" force. These ideas must be refuted in order to demonstrate that the expansion of the faith was characterized by tolerance and a highly pragmatic approach to the problems associated with culture contact and change. The picture that emerges reveals that Islam interacted with traditional life in a highly positive and mutually beneficial manner.

A broad look at the historical currents of Islam in West Africa reveals a number of basic features governing the expansion of the faith. Certainly the oldest and most persistent feature was the continual operation of Muslim traders over vast sectors of West Africa. It was through the agency of individual merchants, small mercantile family groups, and highly dispersed trading corporations that the religion was first introduced into the western Sudan (probably as early as the eighth and ninth centuries A.D.), extended into the southern savannah and Guinea Coast forest, and diffused throughout northern and central Nigeria. Muslim North Africans and Berbers carried the religion into the Sudan, and subsequently Islamized West African trading groups pushed the limits of the faith further south. Indeed, prior to the jihāds (holy wars) of the eighteenth and nineteenth centuries, Muslim merchants were invariably responsible for introducing the religion into "pagan" territories. As Trimingham has noted, "Not only does Islam cast a long shadow before it, but also in order to be accepted in a free situation the ground must be prepared."[1] The role of preparing the ground fell to the trader, the first representative of Islam to cast the shadow of the faith into new regions. Everywhere in West Africa, it has been the Muslim

---

[1] J. Spencer Trimingham, *Islam in West Africa*, p. 28.

trader who has served as the advance agent of the faith, and it has been his lot to condition the new environment for deeper and more permanent religious and cultural penetration.

In a very real sense, this economic class could be described as a group of "merchant-clerics," for many of its members clearly served in a dual capacity. In general, their aims were twofold: the control of regional and interregional trade routes, especially to monopolize the distribution of luxury goods and necessary products that could not be obtained locally; and the introduction of superficial and material elements of Islamic culture to individuals or groups.

Though the trader has not always been given his due in the historical and ethnographic literature on West Africa, especially in acculturation studies, he can be neither slighted nor ignored when dealing with the phenomenon of Islam.[2] In villages and towns throughout this area, Muslim commercial activities were not sporadic but had a permanence established by centuries of contact. The vitality and growth of commercial emporia in the Sudan – for example, Ghāna, Takrūr, Jenne, Timbuktu, Gao – are directly attributable to the activities of Muslim traders. The opening up of the Senegambia, the Voltaic zone, and northern Nigeria to Islam was due to the movement of Malinke, Soninke, Tukulor, and other Islamized traders of the Mande family – such as the Dyula and Ligbi – who followed either pre-Islamic arteries of trade or new ones created by their own industry.

Yet this was not simply the commercial canvassing of broad regions by peripatetic merchants, for many of these traders created numerous settlements in the form of either independent communities or "stranger" quarters in predominantly non-Muslim towns along all the major trade routes they traversed. These settlements served primarily as local markets of exchange and stopping points for itinerant traders, but many quickly developed into important urban centers that were to attract other merchants and ultimately clerical families. The establishment or rapid growth of such impressive towns as Boron, Kong, Odienné, Bondoukou, Bouna, Bobo-Dioulasso, Salaga, Yendi, Kano, and many others, was directly due to the arrival of enterprising Muslim trading families.[3] Although constituting only

---

[2] The study of interregional, regional, and local trade patterns has not received the attention it deserves. Future research, however, should reveal the dimensions of this dynamic aspect of West African history. For a remarkable pioneering work on this subject, see Raymond Mauny, *Tableau Géographique de l'Ouest africain au Moyen Age.*

[3] Despite the importance of these Muslim commercial communities, relatively little study has been devoted to them. To date the best studies have focussed their attention on Kong, Bondoukou, and Salaga. For Kong, see Louis-Gustave Binger, *Du Niger au Golfe de Guinée*, vol. I, ch. 6, and Edmond Bernus, "Kong et sa région." For Bondoukou, see Louis Tauxier, *Le Noir de Bondoukou*, and R. Austin Freeman, *Travels and Life in Ashanti and Jaman*. For Salaga, see Nehemiah Levtzion, "Salaga: A Nineteenth-Century Trading Town in Ghana," and J. A. Braimah and J. R. Goody, *Salaga: The Struggle for Power.*

7

a small minority, these families were to have a substantial impact on the communities. This is clearly revealed by Ivor Wilks's studies of Ashanti, where a small but influential Muslim population played an important role in the political and economic life of this major forest state in the early nineteenth century.[4] The wide-ranging effects of Muslim commercial penetration have been assessed nicely by Lewis:

> By establishing trading colonies, and sometimes later states, these Muslim merchants created a wide-flung supra-tribal network of trade . . . Through their organization in dispersed corporations, or guilds, they were able to wield considerable economic influence within the various states and communities in which they operated. Thus, an eighteenth-century Dyula merchant in Timbuktu might well employ agents buying gold in Ashanti in the south, and others selling it in Fez in North Africa.[5]

An example of the way in which the pivotal role played by the Muslim traders has been seriously underrated can be seen in Trimingham's survey *History of Islam in West Africa*. As Wilks has observed elsewhere, Trimingham dismisses those regions which lie outside the Sudan, saying "The Guinea states in the south lie outside our sphere [the Sudanic zone, which is the focus of his survey of Islam in this book], since they were not in contact with the Sudan[ic] states and were uninfluenced by Islam."[6] Initially published in 1962 and then reprinted in 1963 and 1965, this statement has not been modified to take in the realities of Muslim trading enterprises. The evidence is plain that virtually all forest states came under the influence of Islam through the agency of traders. Their movements resulted not only in the creation of complex and active systems of trade but also in the continual advancement of Islam in West Africa.

There were yet other important avenues by which Islam succeeded in spreading across West Africa. The diffusion of the religion occurred through migrations or dispersals of large groups of Muslims, smaller family units, occupational classes, and individuals. Periods of conflict and decline, such as the gradual demise of the medieval Sudanic kingdoms of Ghāna, Mali, and Songhay, or the fall in the fortunes in the eighteenth century of market towns like Begho and "Old Bima," on the fringes of the forest in west central Ghana, led to the movement of Muslim urban dwellers and a variety of specialist groups.[7] The defeat of Bouna in the early nineteenth century

---

[4] *The Northern Factor in Ashanti History* and "The Position of Muslims in Metropolitan Ashanti in the Early Nineteenth Century."

[5] I. M. Lewis, ed., *Islam in Tropical Africa*, p. 25.

[6] Ivor Wilks, "The Growth of Islamic Learning in Ghana," p. 410. The reference is to Trimingham's *History of Islam in West Africa*, p. 7.

[7] For a discussion of the migrations from Begho, see Tauxier, *Le Noir de Bondoukou*, and Wilks, *The Northern Factor in Ashanti History*, part 1: Begho and Mande. For "Old Bima," see René A. Bravmann and R. D. Mathewson, "A Note on the History and Archaeology of 'Old Bima.'"

by Adinkra, the king of Gyaman, led to the movement of the sizable Muslim Dyula population of that town to Kong, further west, and elsewhere.[8] Family disputes also prompted the dispersal of members over a wide area of West Africa. An instance of this sort of movement comes from the auto-biography of Abū Bakr al-Siddiq, when he describes the history of his family in the late eighteenth century:

After [my grandfather's] death, there was dissension between them and their families, and they separated and went into different countries of the Sudan. Idrīs went to the country of Massina, where he dwelt in Diawara, and married a daughter of *Mār, al-qa'id* Abū Bakr: her name was Ummuyu. 'Abd ar-Raḥmān travelled as far as the land of Kong. He married the daughter of Abū Thaūmā Alī . . ., lord of that country, and dwelt there. The name of his wife was Sārah. Mahmūd travelled to the city of Bouna, and settled there . . . His wife's name was Zuhrā. Abū Bakr remained at Timbuktu with the rest of the family. He was not married at the time I left our country.

Before all these things happened, my father used to travel about. He went into the land of Katsina and Bornu. There he married my mother, and then returned to Timbuktu, to which place my mother followed him.[9]

But it is not necessary to see such mobility as the result of familial dissen-sion or conflict between states, for it was characteristic of Muslim popula-tions to be mobile. Perhaps the most dramatic example of the peaceful expansion of Islam can be seen in the movements of the Fulani, who originated in the Futa Toro of Senegal and between the thirteenth and late fifteenth centuries gradually migrated across the Sudanic region and into northern and eastern Nigeria, where they had a considerable impact upon the future of Islam.[10]

A particularly important feature of Islamic expansion is seen in the roles played by individual scholars and clerical families. Ivor Wilks has recently reconstructed the impressive range of the Saghanughu, a Mande clerical family, whose religious training and teaching abilities formed generations of students throughout the western Sudan.[11] The origins of this family can be traced back to the sixteenth century (and Wilks points out that there is fragmentary evidence for the existence of the Saghanughu dating back to the apogee of Mali in the fourteenth century and possibly earlier), and to the area of Kangaba on the Upper Niger.[12] From this base, successive generations of Saghanughu scholars and their students estab-lished Qur'ānic schools throughout the savannah regions of Guinea, the Ivory Coast, Upper Volta, and Ghana, many of which are still active today.

---

[8] Wilks, "Abū Bakr al-Siddiq of Timbuktu," pp. 161–2.   [9] Ibid., p. 158.
[10] For the most recent and thorough study of Islamic movements into Nigeria, see Muḥammad Al-Ḥājj, "A Seventeenth-Century Chronicle on the Origins and Mis-sionary Activities of the Wangarawa."
[11] "The Transmission of Islamic Learning in the Western Sudan," pp. 162–97.
[12] Ibid., p. 177.

9

The Aqīt of Timbuktu, a prominent medieval scholarly family, appear to have played a similar role in the transmission of Islamic knowledge.[13] Much of the eighteenth- and nineteenth-century literature from both Nigeria and Ghana demonstrates a strong intellectual connection with the writings of this school.[14]

Individual scholars (marabouts) were also responsible for the dissemination of Islam. The life of Al-Maghīlī is a remarkable example of the influence of a single Muslim scholar and reformer. His periods of residence in Takedda, Gao, and Katsina were to leave an impress on the quality of Muslim life in these areas.[15] Scholars from the western Sudan making the pilgrimage to Mecca often stopped in Hausaland and Bornu to visit teachers and rulers.

Aïda-Aḥmad al-Tāzakhtī, a pupil of Al-Maghīlī, for example, settled at Katsina and taught, was made *qāḍī* and remained there for fifteen years until his death in 1529. Another scholar, Makhlūf al-Bilbālī (d. 1533), also taught for a while in Kano and Katsina. Aḥmad Bāba's own grandfather, Aḥmad b. 'Umar b. Muḥammad Aqīt, had also taught in Kano on his return from the pilgrimage around 1487 A.D.[16]

Such movements of scholars have been a constant factor in Islam in West Africa, ensuring the circulation of ideas and the availability of Islamic religious education.

The continual advance of Islam was also encouraged by its literate character, for as a religion with a book, it demanded a basic level of literacy from its adherents. Thus, as Hunwick observes,

wherever Islam spread, encouragement was given to the learning of Arabic and to the foundation of both small schools for teaching the reading of the Koran and higher schools for deeper study of the Arabic language and the literature of Muslim peoples – more especially the theological and legal literature which was to form the basis of both the spiritual and temporal life of the new converts. Once established in an area as the language of religion, Arabic was soon put to other more worldly ends, for purposes of trade, politics and dynastic and family records.[17]

The importance of Arabic in the medieval Sudanic states, for example, was undeniable, for the records and dispatches kept by Muslims who served as court secretaries and advisors were instrumental in the consolidation and

[13] John O. Hunwick, "A New Source for the Biography of Ahmad Bāba al-Tinbuktī (1556–1627)."
[14] For two generalized accounts of the impact of the Aqīt family and the Timbuktu school on scholars in Ghana and Nigeria, see Thomas Hodgkin, "The Islamic Literary Tradition in Ghana," and Hunwick, "The Influence of Arabic in West Africa."
[15] Hunwick, "The Influence of Arabic," pp. 28–9.
[16] Ibid., p. 31.
[17] Ibid., p. 24.

administration of these far-flung domains. Furthermore, knowledge of Arabic allowed for an international system of communications tying various portions of West Africa to the North African Muslim world. The many uses that Arabic served may be seen in the variety of literary forms employed by religious and political leaders in eighteenth- and nineteenth-century Nigeria. These included governmental and administrative correspondence and directives, books and pamphlets of a political and propagandistic nature, historical and biographic treatises, poetry, and a wide range of religious and didactic literature.[18] The spread of Arabic and the later development in the eighteenth and nineteenth centuries of vernacular Islamic literature in such languages as Kanembu, Fulbe, and Hausa ensured the success of Islam.

The frontiers of Islam were also expanded through the dispersion of Muslim specialists – artisans plying their skills as ironworkers, goldsmiths, bead-makers, weavers, and so on – into regions where such services were highly prized. The virtual monopoly held by the Mande and Hausa in the making of beads and glassware and in the dyeing industry (described by R. Austin Freeman, who resided at Bondoukou in the Ivory Coast at the end of the nineteenth century[19]) is an early and telling instance of Muslim domination of certain important areas of technical and artistic expertise. Oral traditions that I collected about eighty years later from dyers in the same town and in the surrounding countryside indicate that many of these families of specialists moved into the area at a relatively early date, possibly the beginning of the eighteenth century.[20] They claim to have introduced the dyeing technique and have maintained exclusive control over this craft to the present day. Non-Muslim weavers in the region depend on both the Mande and Hausa for this service and must either carry their spun cotton to the nearest dyeing center or await the arrival of itinerant Muslim dyers, who collect the cotton in various villages and then take it to their base of operation. Activities such as this, related to a variety of artistic skills, undoubtedly occurred quite broadly throughout West Africa, and the potential influence of these groups or individuals as diffusers of the faith must have been considerable. As Lewis points out,

Being less mobile, these small immigrant craft communities tended to settle more permanently among non-Muslim populations, and marrying with their hosts, or certain classes of them at least, must often have produced a more enduring impression.[21]

[18] Ibid., pp. 38–41.
[19] *Travels and Life in Ashanti and Jaman*, ch. 8.
[20] Traditions collected from Dyula dyers of the Makara quarter of Bondoukou, November 1966; from itinerant Dyula dyers at the Nafana village of Kabre, December 14, 1966; in the Dyula/Ligbi village of Jinini, March 4, 1967; and at Bondakele, a Degha pottery center, on March 10, 1967.
[21] *Islam in Tropical Africa*, p. 26.

Physical proximity of Muslim and non-Muslim peoples also operated as a factor in the dissemination of the religion. Close contact between these two groups was common throughout West Africa, both in urban contexts and in the rural countryside. Under these circumstances the possibilities for cultural and religious interaction and change must have been significant, for even where Muslims resided in their own wards or sectors of towns and villages (a residence pattern generally of their own choosing), they were not cordoned off from their neighbors. In some areas, it is clear that various degrees of Islamic influence filtered into "pagan" life despite little overt proselytism or economic interchange. This seems to have been true of the Wolof of Senegal, who did not come under intensive Islamic influence until the nineteenth century. Casa da Mosto's late-fifteenth-century account reveals that some Wolof chiefs worshipped Muḥammad but points out that these rulers were simply imitating the behavior of Muslim Soninke groups in the interior.[22] Mimicry of Muslim ways probably occurred even under minimal culture contact, since Islam, as a religion and a culture, always carried with it a high degree of prestige. An instance of such minimal contact has been cited by Goody in his study of Islam in Gonja and other sectors of northern Ghana, where aspects of the religion have filtered down into traditional life despite the lack of intense Islamization.[23] Elements alien to traditional societies, or those which could not be reconciled with these cultures, were probably rejected, but certain aspects of Islam – especially material objects such as Qur'ānic charms, clothing, prestige goods, and a host of magical elements – were readily accepted.[24]

Even the most intransigent cultures were influenced at one level or another through this non-aggressive but very persistent channel of transculturation. The Nafana, a Senufo sub-group residing in the Banda district of west central Ghana and the Cercle de Bondoukou in the northeastern Ivory Coast, have resisted Muslim proselytism for nearly three hundred years. Mande clerics have had virtually no success in their attempts at conversion, but the Nafana have adopted a number of Muslim material traits. The paramount chief of Banda, the Mgono, considers his Muslim cloth, a white linen wrapper with Qur'ānic inscriptions, to be the most

[22] *Voyages in Western Africa*, p. 31.
[23] J. R. Goody, "Restricted Literacy in Northern Ghana."
[24] The importance of Islamic magic for non-Muslim societies has been amply documented by many European travelers in West Africa. T. E. Bowdich (*A Mission from Cape Coast Castle to Ashantee*) and Joseph Dupuis (*Journal of a Residence in Ashantee*) both commented on the use of Qur'ānic charms and talismans among the Ashanti, where such items were highly prized by the Asantehene and members of his court. Goody ("Restricted Literacy in Northern Ghana") has recently revealed the ready acceptance of such elements among various culture groups in northern Ghana. A particularly interesting dimension to the use of Islamic magic should be revealed in Bradford G. Martin's projected paper "West African Magic and Its Origins," a work based on some twenty-five pieces of magical material collected from Ashanti in the first quarter of the nineteenth century and now in Copenhagen.

efficacious and powerful of his royal gowns. Qur'ānic charms are tied not only to the state stools but to virtually all items of royal regalia: white stools, *assipim* chairs, *akonkromfi* seats, and state swords. The present Mgono, Kofi Dwuru, like his predecessors, is clearly a "pagan" but has availed himself of those aspects of Muslim culture which are easily acceptable but do not require a commitment to the faith.[25]

Yet another tactic followed by Muslims in advancing the faith has been to attempt to influence and convert the ruling elite within local cultures. Indeed, this has been a Muslim tactic throughout the history of Islam in West Africa. It was certainly the case prior to the religious revolutions of the eighteenth and nineteenth centuries in both the Sudanic and Guinea Coast forest zones. This is not to claim, however, that Islam became the guiding force in the states it influenced, for it was at best simply another religious element grafted onto them. The work of Muslim clergymen, poets, scholars, and architects in such Sudanic states as Mali and Songhay could be impressive, yet their efforts did not succeed in changing the fundamental structures and beliefs of these societies. Such states did not simply substitute Qur'ānic prescriptions and Muslim legal statutes for traditional political and religious sanctions, a fact substantiated by the writings of Al-Maghīlī and Al-Lamtūnī in the cases of Songhay and Takrūr.[26] Many rulers leaned toward Islam; some, like Muḥammad Askia, converted to the faith. Nevertheless, the influence of Islam was restricted in both scope and depth. The policy of introducing the religion at the top, of fostering traditional elites, did, however, result in new gains for the faith, since it invariably exerted at least some measure of influence on all the courts in which it was acknowledged.

It seems clear that the manner in which Islam expanded and sought to affect indigenous West African societies was highly varied and essentially non-disruptive in nature. For the most part, Islam pursued the paths of least resistance, dissemination of the faith being marked by slow and steady advances that did not disturb the cultures it came to influence. The only aggressive channel of advance – jihād or holy war – was also the least followed. And it is important to note that of all the avenues of expansion, only this one (described by Trimingham as "religious imperialism") was sporadic and short-lived. The jihād, followed by the imposition of Muslim rule and an attempt to establish a theocratic state guided by Islamic religious, administrative, and legal precepts, was restricted to the eighteenth and nineteenth centuries, and although this period has been regarded as one of decided Muslim intolerance to "pagan" and quasi-Islamized

---

[25] The subject of Islamic features among the Nafana of Banda is further explored in Chapter 3.

[26] For the comments of Al-Maghīlī and Al-Lamtūnī, see Hunwick, "Religion and State in the Songhay Empire, 1464–1591" and "Notes on a Late Fifteenth-Century Document Concerning 'Al-Takrūr.'"

cultures, it is evident that even the most zealous Muslim reformers did not succeed in shattering the traditional pillars of West African societies. In fact, only a few of the theocratic states established during this era survived for any significant period of time. Most of these states deteriorated quickly, either through a lack of any clear and organized system of succession or through internal disputes and conflicts between the leaders. Marginal conquests, combined with rapid and superficial conversions, characterized much of the effort of the reformers. Even where such revolutions were most successful, as in the case of the northern Nigerian emirates, traditional life survived and remained vigorous.

There is no denying that this was a period of religious zeal, doctrinal rigor, and a sincere attempt to improve the quality of Muslim life in West Africa. The sincerity of the Mujāhidūn is obvious from their writings, but it is also clear from their works that they were cautious in the application of jihād. The question of who could be called an unbeliever or a quasi-Muslim was a serious one, and such charges were not leveled casually.[27] Thus the use of force was not indiscriminate. Furthermore, it is evident that even after military successes, religious leaders often compromised their position in the formation of their caliphates. 'Abd al-Salām ruthlessly destroyed Nupe idols during his conquest of this area, but his ultimate control of the region was based not only on Muslim administrative procedures but also on such traditional regulatory modes as cults.[28] 'Uthmān dan Fodio was perfectly aware that such compromises were often made, for his *Kitāb al-Farq* was a warning to his compatriots (the future emirs of those areas subdued by the Fulani) not to compromise their principles by following or even allowing traditional local practices.[29] Religious fervor could reach very high peaks, but such flushes of enthusiasm often dissipated in the face of contacts between Muslims and non-Muslims.

Whereas religious zeal accompanied by intolerance did exist in Islamic history in West Africa, it was infrequent and sporadic. The overwhelming weight of evidence indicates that Muslims were quite willing to make concessions and to align themselves with local cultures in order to propagate the faith.

[27] For a carefully argued treatment of this problem, see Martin, "Unbelief in the Western Sudan: 'Uthmān dan Fodio's 'Ta'lim al-Ikhwān.'"

[28] Personal communication from Bradford G. Martin, June 1971. Also see Peter Morton-Williams, "The Fulani Penetration into Nupe and Yoruba in the Nineteenth Century," pp. 18–20.

[29] D. M. Last and M. A. Al-Ḥājj, "Attempts at Defining a Muslim in Nineteenth-Century Hausaland and Bornu," p. 239.

MUSLIM DOGMA CONCERNING
REPRESENTATIONAL ART

Islam's prohibitions against imagery and idols have heretofore been accepted at face value and have been cited by art historians and museologists to strengthen discussions of the destructive nature of the religion with respect to tribal art in West Africa. For most, the aniconic stance of Islam could have no effect but a negative one. There has not been, however, an attempt to deal with the problem of *precisely* what Islam has had to say on the subject of the visual arts, nor has there been a real consideration of the actual effect of official dogma on Muslims at large and specifically in West Africa. The orthodox Islamic world has held a decidedly negative attitude on the subject; even the most cursory look at the body of religious literature – i.e., the Qur'ān, the ḥadīth, and the source books of Muslim law – substantiates this fundamental assumption. Yet one must seriously ask if this literature had any appreciable impact on Muslims in West Africa. Did official dogma influence or regulate the thoughts and actions of either the religious leaders or the majority of the faithful? Were orthodox tenets seriously applied in this area?

The doctrinal injunctions against the fashioning and using of "idols" and the abhorrence of pictorial imagery are recurrent themes in classical Islamic literature. For the most part, such prohibitions are directly expressed and thus provide a clearcut guide for members of the faith. There are also a number of oblique references to the subject, and these too have helped define orthodox thinking. The Qur'ān, viewed by the faithful as the eternal word of God and the ultimate source of doctrinal authority and religious conduct, does not expressly forbid the making of images,[1] although it is clear that the spirit of the Qur'ān and of numerous references in it do in fact express a negative attitude towards representational art. Numerous statements in the Qur'ān imply that the creative efforts of the artist or sculptor may be unlawful if there is an attempt to imitate God's creative powers. Wensinck maintains that the concept "to fashion" or "to create" is legally restricted by the Qur'ān to Allāh. He claims, for example, that

[1] Thomas W. Arnold, *Painting in Islam*, pp. 4–5.

In Kur'ānic linguistic usage *ṣawwara* "to fashion" or "form" is synonymous with *bara'a* "to create": Sūra, vii. 10, "and we have created you, then we have fashioned you, then we have said to the angels, etc." Sūra, iii. 4: "It is he who forms you in the mother's womb as he will." Sūra, xl. 66: "It is Allāh who has made the earth for a home for you and the heavens for a vault above you, shaped you and formed you beautiful" (cf. Sūra, lxiv. 3). Sūra, lix. 24 Allāh is called al-khaliḳ, al bāri', al-muṣawwir.[2]

Any attempted usurpation by mere men of God's powers to fashion or create is therefore an obviously unlawful and blasphemous act.

Although the Qur'ān is indirect on this subject, the ḥadīth are not. This collection of thoughts and sayings ascribed to Muḥammad, which was amassed and compiled by Muslim scholars after his death, plainly reveals Islamic attitudes with regard to imagery. Theologically the ḥadīth are considered by the 'ulamā', the learned class, to be a body of knowledge almost equal in prominence and stature to the Qur'ān itself. Its influence on the faithful is undeniable, and it has shaped Muslim doctrinal and legal thinking on a wide variety of subjects. In the ḥadīth literature many comments are found concerning the position of the arts, the character and status of the artist, artistic creativity, and so forth. In virtually all instances the statements are negative. The writings of Al-Bukhārī, Muslim, and Al-Tirmidhī, as noted by Wensinck, are laden with injunctions and warnings regarding the arts.[3] For example, Al-Bukhārī's warning that Muḥammad curses those who make images appears in several places – e.g., *Buyū'*, bāb 25, 113; *Ṭalāq*, bāb 51; and *Libas*, bāb 96.[4] Virtually all compilers of the ḥadīth underscore the injunction that those who make images or idols will be punished by Muḥammad and Allāh.[5] In addition the faithful are admonished to avoid any place in which images are housed.[6] For Al-Tirmidhī, those who make images are clearly polytheists and must be shunned by the faithful.[7] The ḥadīth literature is uncompromising on the subject of representational art, and its judgments are leveled not only at image-makers – that is, painters and sculptors – but also at all types of artistic creativity in which representational forms are possible. As Arnold has stressed, such artisans are described in the orthodox literature by the Arabic term *muṣawwir*, literally meaning "creator" or "fashioner." Since this word is reserved to the great creator himself, its application to the human creator is an abomination.[8] Thus, as Arnold so aptly expresses it,

. . . the highest term of praise which in the Christian world can be bestowed upon the artist, in calling him a creator, in the Muslim world serves to emphasize the most damning evidence of his guilt.[9]

[2] A. J. Wensinck, "Sūra," p. 561.
[3] Wensinck, *A Handbook of Early Muhammadan Tradition*, p. 108 (images).   [4] Ibid.
[5] Ibid. The writers prohibiting the making of idols include Al-Bukhārī, Muslim, Al-Tirmidhī, Al-Nasā'ī, Mālik ibn Anas, and Al-Ṭayālisī.   [6] Ibid.
[7] Wensinck, "Sūra," p. 561.   [8] Arnold, *Painting in Islam*, p. 6.   [9] Ibid.

CHAPTER 2

Exceptions to these severe injunctions do exist in the corpus of the ḥadīth literature, but they are minor. Al-Bukhārī, for example, notes that the making of images without souls (*ruḥ*) is not forbidden (*ḥarīm*).[10] Furthermore, nearly all collections of the ḥadīth concede that figural decoration on such items as cushions and rugs is legal.[11] Nevertheless, the weight of orthodox opinion clearly supports an iconoclastic view, and concessions such as these merely emphasize the basically negative dictates of the classical authors.

With the completion of the ḥadīth by the early fourth century A.H. (tenth century A.D.), orthodox opinion was clearly established in this direction. Such views received further support from many legal interpretations by various jurists throughout the Islamic world. Islamic law (*fiqh*) is strongly dependent on the theoretical principles set forth by the Qur'an and the ḥadīth; it is a sacred law (*sharī'a*) incorporating principles desired by God. Hence Muslim legal texts are essentially extrapolations of the principles of the *sharī'a*. Although they may take into account local circumstances or individual opinions, they remain for the most part faithful to the guidelines set forth in the Qur'ān and the ḥadīth. This is true of all four of the orthodox schools of law (the Madhāhib), which were established in the ninth century. Although the four schools (Ḥanafī, Mālikī, Shāfi'ī, and Ḥanbalī) do display some differences in doctrine, judicial methods, and legal interpretations, they have preserved to a great extent in their books of *fiqh* the attitudes of the ḥadīth, including those concerning imagery.

The authority of these various orthodox schools gradually spread across the entire Muslim world, each one becoming prominent in certain sectors of Muslim influence. The Mālikī school of law, founded by Mālik ibn Anas (d. 795), the Imām of Madina (Medina), came to dominate the North African area, specifically the region of the Maghreb, and ultimately spread to West Africa.[12] It was from this school that the first compendium of Islamic law was created – the *Muwaṭṭa'* of Imām Mālik. The work is a juxtaposition and combination of the reasoning of individual scholars, local consensus, and numerous precedents gleaned from the traditions of Muḥammad. It is a long text that has served as the source of inspiration of all later Mālikī treatises. As in the case of other schools, the spread of the Mālikī doctrine resulted in a proliferation of yet other legal treatises, abridgements, and more concise manuals that summarized the regulations in the *Muwaṭṭa'*. Two of the most important works of North African authorship – works that became classics and so exercised enormous influence in this area, demonstrate a heavy dependence on Mālik's *Muwaṭṭa'*.

---

10 Wensinck, *Handbook*, p. 108. The reference is to the *Buyū'*, bāb 104.
11 Ibid. ("Images on cushions and the like allowed").
12 This discussion of *fiqh* sources on imagery will be confined almost entirely to the Mālikī school because of its overriding authority in West Africa.

These are the *Risāla* of Ibn Abī Zayd al-Qayrawānī (922–96) and the celebrated *Mukhtaṣar*, the Mālikī legal treatise of the Egyptian Khalīl ibn Isḥaq al-Jundī (d. 1365). Although there are other important North African Mālikī texts, it is these two manuals of Mālikī law that have dominated the thinking of the orthodox.[13]

It is significant that in these two works the subject of imagery is not nearly so prominent a theme as in the ḥadīth. The *Mukhtaṣar* of Sīdī Khalīl, although a drastic abridgement of the *Muwaṭṭa'*, is still a substantial work, consisting of sixty-one chapters governing various aspects of religious life: ritual, prayer, fasting, the pilgrimage to Mecca, holy wars, proper food and drink, the personal status of individuals, economic transactions, marriage, divorce – in fact, every aspect of human behaviour. Within this long and detailed treatise, the subject of idols and images is treated in a peripheral manner – if, indeed, the subject can be said to be treated at all. The most direct comment made on the entire subject of imagery is buried in a rather long section concerning the wedding feast. In five paragraphs dealing with various regulations governing the banquet, we find the following:

You are obliged to accept a personal invitation, even when fasting, provided that: 1) there is no one present who can cause you detriment from the point of view of religious law, nor is there present any blameworthy or forbidden thing from that point of view, such as silken rugs, silver or gold vases, or figurative representations placed, for example, against a wall; but it is not lawful to refuse the invitation if permissible games are played ... even if you are a person of high regard according to established opinion; 2) there is not too big a crowd; 3) the door of the banquet room is not closed to you when you arrive.[14]

Nowhere in this entire work is there a clearcut statement of the illegality of representation. Even in Chapter 50, which deals with apostasy and blasphemous behaviour – where one would certainly expect to find artistic creativity outlawed, judging from the ḥadīth – the subject is ignored. Only a brief reference to the abandoning of oneself to magical practices, considered to be a blasphemous act, could possibly be construed as a vague reference to idolatry, and this is still a far cry from proscribing representational art.[15] Section 6 of Chapter 2, which deals with Islamic prayers, does note that it is illegal to decorate the *qibla* in a mosque, but again there is no elaboration on the subject.[16] The interdiction here is quite general,

---

[13] The prominence of the *Risāla* and the *Mukhtaṣar* in North Africa, especially the Maghreb – and its importance even today – has been noted by a number of French scholars. See especially Georges H. Bousquet's *L'Islam maghrebin* and *Précis de droit musulman*.

[14] Khalīl ibn Isḥāq [Khalil ben Ish'āq], *Abrégé de la loi musulmane suivant le rite de l'Imâm Mâlek*, vol. 2: *Le Statut personnel*, p. 62. English translation mine.

[15] Ibid., vol. 4: *Judicature, Droit pénal, Affranchissements, Statut successoral*, p. 43.

[16] Ibid., vol. 1: *Le Rituel*, p. 56.

for it does not specify a particular kind of decoration. Section 3 of Chapter 1 concludes with proscriptions concerning ornaments of precious stones and metals, but here what is *ḥarīm* is the material and not a particular subject matter for the ornaments.[17]

Al-Qayrawānī's *Risāla*, the other major compendium of Mālikī law and one nearly as detailed and even more comprehensive, devotes equally little space to the subject of figural imagery. The most direct comments in this work are found in the section entitled "[Religious] Duties and Proper Conduct." According to Al-Qayrawānī, the representation of animals on chairs, domes or canopies, walls, and seals, is a blameworthy practice. He does not condemn figural representations on fabrics, although he does advise the faithful that they are better avoided.[18] Comments regarding the appropriateness of gold and silver for decorative purposes also occur in this portion of the *Risāla*. The use of gold is prohibited, for as Al-Qayrawānī notes, this is a directive from Allāh. The use of silver, however, is permitted for decorating weapons, seals, and even the holy book.[19] One would assume from the succeeding remarks on figural representation that figures could not be portrayed in silver, but this is not made clear. The directives in the *Risāla* concerning representational art are therefore neither more clearcut nor more confining than those in the *Makhtaṣar*.

Despite the cursory treatment in these two important Mālikī texts from North Africa, it is plain that the weight of Mālikī opinion followed that expressed earlier in the ḥadīth. Comments by other Mālikī jurists (*Fuqaha'*) and commentators on the Qur'ān and the ḥadīth often show considerably more emphasis on this theme. The *Shifa'* of Qāḍī 'Iyaḍ al-Andalusī (1083–1149) is a case in point. The *Shifa'* is an outspoken Mālikī source on the question of the creation of idols and their use for worship. For Qāḍī 'Iyaḍ, such acts are blasphemous and are performed only by un-believers.[20] His views on certain aspects of imagery in general are more lenient, yet they clearly follow the dominant strain of Mālikī thinking. 'Iyaḍ allows for the representations of trees and other natural things that do not have a spirit – indeed, they may even be bought and sold. Even an image like a doll – which has a shadow and is therefore, strictly speaking, forbidden – is permitted by 'Iyaḍ.[21] Discussion and differences of opinion were registered by various members of the Mālikī 'ulamā', especially on such points as what natural objects had or did not have *rūḥ* or what kinds of images cast shadows and therefore could not be reproduced. Despite these differences, the vast majority remained faithful to the spirit and dictates of the ḥadīth and the Qur'ān.

---

[17] Ibid., p. 22.
[18] Ibn Abī Zayd al-Qayrawānī [Ibn Aboû Zaîd el Kayrawâni], *Risâla ou traité abrégé de droit malékite et morale musulmane*, p. 27. [19] Ibid.
[20] The comments on idols by 'Iyaḍ appear in Bradford G. Martin's translation of 'Uthman dan Fodio's "Ta'lim al-Ikhwān," p. 82. [21] Wensinck, "Sūra," p. 562.

Nevertheless, unanimity concerning the position of the pictorial arts was clearly not achieved even at this early period. In a series of important articles, Bishr Farīs cites a heated controversy regarding the legitimacy of *taṣwīr* – figurative art.[22] In his appendix "La Querelle des Images" in "Philosophie et jurisprudence," he refers to a commentary on the Qur'ān by Al-Qurṭūbī (d. A.D. 1273), which reveals a major dispute among scholars in the tenth through twelfth centuries. These included Abu 'Alī al-Fārisī (d. 987), Makkī al-Qayrawānī (d. 1045), and Aḥmad ibn Muḥammad al-Naḥḥās (d. 948), all of whom regarded *taṣwīr* as legitimate.[23] All three were prominent North African scholars, and their positive stance on this subject was thus a major statement. They all supported their views by referring to the Ṣūra of Saba', xxxiv. 13, which deals with the fashioning of statues (*tamāthīl*) for King Solomon.[24] Fārisī makes the strongest statement in favor of representation, going so far as to say that only the corporeal representation of Allāh is prohibited.[25] Al-Qurṭūbī notes that these comments did not go unchallenged, citing Ibn 'Atīyah (d. 1147) of Andalusia, who strongly opposed these radical opinions.[26] Subsequent interpretations by North African jurists were to further submerge the strong pro-*taṣwīr* views of these men.

Yet other dissenting views on *taṣwīr* were voiced at later periods and from other areas of the Islamic world:

The 13th-century Persian poet Sa'dī thought God to be the source and inspiration of everything, including the visual arts; one of his contemporaries, the mystic Jalāl ad-Dīn Rūmī, upheld the value of painting for didactic purposes, that is, paintings of beautiful and ugly creatures might afford an appropriate explanation of how evil can emanate from God.[27]

In the eastern portions of the Muslim world far more positive endorsements of the arts were expressed. Perhaps the most notable example comes from the Persian judge and historian Khwāndamīr, whose collection of early sixteenth-century writings, the *Nāmah-i-Nāmī*, is filled with praise for the artist.

Here, God Himself was depicted as a painter, and the efforts of the human artist to follow Him were no longer regarded as mockery but as noble emulation, so that realism was deserving of the highest praise.[28]

Controversy over the legality of *taṣwīr* continues today. The antitraditional attitude is expressed in contemporary debate by Aḥmad Muḥammad 'Isā, writing in the journal of the theological University of Al-Azhar. 'Isā clearly rejects the traditional stance and criticizes the Al-

[22] Bishr Farīs [Farès], "De la figuration en Islam," "Essai sur l'esprit de la décoration islamique," "Philosophie et jurisprudence illustrées par les Arabes."
[23] Farīs, "Philosophie et jurisprudence," pp. 100–4.   [24] Ibid., p. 104.
[25] Ibid., p. 100.   [26] Ibid., p. 101.
[27] Richard Ettinghausen, "Images and Iconoclasm: Islam," p. 817.   [28] Ibid.

Azhar Committee on Fatwas – a group rendering decisions on points of Islamic law – for its conservatism in upholding the opinions on *taṣwīr* shared by those members of the 'ulamā' who "blindly" follow and support the tenets of the ḥadīth. He charges that

> The Committee in its fatwas has not progressed beyond the view that the making of representations is absolutely prohibited, as held by its predecessors, even though some of the Ulamā have held that "photographic representations for use" are permitted. The significance of the reliance of these fatwas on repeating the opinions of practitioners of jurisprudence and ḥadīth as recorded in the works of old authors is that we still need a fatwa which in its essence relies on reason and not on tradition. This is especially so since the ḥadīths which we have on the making of representations contain many contradictions and differences which cause some people to hesitate to regard them as being explicit on the subject of the tabuing of representations.[29]

He attempts to bolster his own "liberal" views by drawing on the writings of Muḥammad 'Abduh (1849–1905), a modernist scholar and reformer who stated that Islamic law did not prohibit the making but simply the worshipping of images.[30] He goes on to note the statement of Fārisī and the variety of legal interpretations that have existed on *taṣwīr*.[31] He concludes by observing that the very monuments of the history of Islamic art plainly refute the proscriptions of the ḥadīth as promulgated by Muslim theologians and lawyers. For Aḥmad 'Isā, such monuments were not created by transgressors of the faith or by apostates; rather they stand as testaments to Muslims who were concerned not "with verbiage," but with "the general law of life which sweeps aside those who do not go along with it."[32] There is no doubt that 'Isā's views are untenable for the majority of modern-day members of the 'ulamā', yet his opinions are important, since they are representative of the controversy that still exists.

If scholarly opinion did not always conform to official doctrine on the subject of *taṣwīr*, this is even more true of actual practice. Monuments based on figurative traditions, whether wholly Muslim in inspiration or derived from pre-Islamic prototypes, appear through much of the history of Islam and in virtually all areas encompassed by the faith. This is true whether one looks at regions dominated by the Sunnī or by the Shī'ī – the two major sects of Islam. For some writers, such as Kremitske, the more rigorous and traditional Sunnī practices were responsible for a decided lack of figurative art in the areas dominated by this sect.[33] Yet as Arnold has noted, this is a fundamental error that has persisted despite a multitude of evidence to the contrary. According to him,

---

[29] "Muslims and Taswīr," p. 265.
[30] Ibid., pp. 263–4. 'Isa does not cite the particular work by Muḥammad 'Abduh that he quotes so extensively. His entire article (in translation) is remiss in this way.
[31] Ibid., pp. 252–7, 265–6.   [32] Ibid., p. 263.   [33] John Kremitske, "Islam," p. 332.

The fact is that the Shiah theologians condemned the representation of living objects just as severely as ever their Sunni co-religionists did. The Shiahs possess collections of the Traditions of the Prophet of their own, and in these the art of the painter is unhesitatingly and uncompromisingly condemned. They warn him, as in the Sunni traditions quoted above, of the manner in which he will be convicted of the enormity of his offence by being bidden on the Day of Judgement to breathe life into the objects of his creation: "but he will not be able to breathe life into them."[34]

There are numerous examples of figurative art from the Sunni-influenced portions of the Muslim world. The many depictions of animal form, nude human figures, dancers, and even a portrait of perhaps Umayyad Caliph Walīd I (reigned 705–715) in a sumptuous "pleasure house" of the caliph's, are dramatic and early instances of pictorial imagery. From the style of the figures, it is apparent that these depictions were by "foreign painters."[35] Yet without the patronage of the local caliphate, they would have been impossible. Six years after the reign of Walīd I, Caliph Yazīd II issued in 721 an iconoclastic edict that was carried out with considerable rigor.[36] The shift of emphasis in dogmatic thinking could be dramatic. Even the Abbasid caliphs, as Arnold remarks, although "careful to avoid shocking the feelings of the orthodox inhabitants of their capital . . . frequently employed figures for the internal decoration of their palaces, as is revealed by the frescos at Sāmarrā."[37] At a later period, the historian Al-Maqrīzī described in some detail a number of dazzling works in precious materials – including representations of animals – owned by the Fatimids of Egypt.[38]

Spanish soil was a particularly fertile area for figurative art, as the lion images in the courtyard of the Alhambra and the frescos of its Torre de las Damas clearly show.[39] The tradition of ivory-carving flourished under the patronage of Muslim Cordovan kings, and according to Arnold, a variety "of mechanical devices, such as water clocks, musical instruments, etc., were also manufactured in the shape of human figures or had little figures attached to them."[40] It is important to note that Spain was strongly influenced by the Mālikī school of law.

The extent to which imagery was used can be seen in the comments of Qalqashandī and Maqrīzī related by Arnold:

Sweetmeats were also fashioned in the shape of human beings and animals, and were distributed during the public feasts given on festival occasions by the Fatimid caliphs of Egypt, but out of respect for the exponents of the sacred law, such objects were not placed before the chief qāḍī and his assessors.[41]

---

[34] *Painting in Islam*, p. 12.   [35] Ibid., p. 30.
[36] Alexander A. Vasilev, "The Iconoclastic Edict of Caliph Yazīd II, A.D. 721."
[37] *Painting in Islam*, p. 20.   [38] Ibid., p. 22.   [39] Ibid., p. 23.
[40] Ibid.   [41] Ibid., pp. 23–4.

Even statues of reigning monarchs were created both in Egypt and Spain during the ninth and tenth centuries A.D.

Arnold underplays the evidence provided by such examples when he says:

Such are the scanty records, scattered throughout the literature of more than a thousand years, of the encouragement that Muhammadan monarchs and nobles gave to workers in the pictorial and plastic arts, despite the disapprobation which their theologians expressed for all representations of living beings. Most of these works of art have perished; but a certain number of the carpets, ivories, crystals, metal-work, and wood-carving have survived the various cataclysms that from time to time have swept over the Muhammadan world, and they are now safely guarded fron iconoclastic zeal in public museums, private collections, and – strangest fate of all – in the sacristies of Christian churches and cathedrals.[42]

It is obvious then that the gulf between dogma and actual conduct could be considerable, even where the ḥadīth literature and its most rigid interpreters dominated Muslim thinking. These examples, however, neither indicate that Islam was on the wane nor indict the individuals responsible for them. They reflect what Kenneth Cragg has so succinctly described as the conflict "between the stuff of events and the dictates of the spirit"[43] – the age-old problem of relating the realms of the ideal and the real. They demonstrate a fundamental truth common to all faiths: a gap invariably exists between dogma and practical observance. To label the evidence of the gaps as "aberrant tendencies" or "discrepancies," or to sit in judgment on the producers and patrons of these monuments, is to miss the point completely. Theologians and jurists could rail against those caliphs who adorned their public residences, and they could denounce members of the religious elite who commissioned beautifully decorated manuscripts, but most clerics were acutely conscious of the limits of their influence and power and were aware of the delicate balance between dogma and action.

What was the impact of this body of dogma on the faithful in West Africa? If the assessments of art historians and museologists are correct, it follows that these orthodox texts were both known and applied by Muslim religious leaders in West Africa. Within the last fifteen years, a number of Islamicists working in West Africa have uncovered a veritable mine of data on the position of Islam in the area. Beginning with the works of Bivar and Hiskett and continuing to the present with the writings of Martin, Hunwick, and Al-Ḥajj, scholars have begun to shed light on the strong historical and intellectual connections that have long existed between West Africa, the Maghreb, and other portions of North Africa. The data are impressive, and it is clear that Qur'ānic commentaries, the ḥadīth, and Mālikī works of law made a considerable impression on Muslims south of the Sahara. This

---

[42] Ibid., p. 29.
[43] *Counsels in Contemporary Islam*, p. xi.

intellectual and historical connection was clearly recorded as early as the fifteenth century. The writings of Hunwick on the life, education, teachings, and influence of Aḥmad Bābā al-Tinbuktī (1556–1627) and his predecessors at Timbuktu confirm the vitality of Muslim scholarship and its connections with the orthodox 'ulamā' of North Africa during this early period.[44] Earlier data undoubtedly exist, but they have not yet come to light. The writings of Aḥmad Bābā are numerous – indeed, forty-one works are attributed to him – and according to Hunwick, they evince a strong dependence on and "adherence to the dictates of the Mālikī *Madhab*."[45] His single most important contribution is his compendium of Mālikī jurists – the *Nayl al-ibtihāj bi-taṭrīz al-dībāj* – which is a major source of data for both Maghrebi and West African scholars.[46] The strength of his intellectual ties with the Mālikī school is something that he himself confessed: "We are Kalīlites [referring to Khalīl ibn Isḥāq, author of the *Mukhtaṣar*]; if he erred, we err with him.[47]"

There is additional evidence to indicate the close connections between the western Sudan and North Africa. There was constant intercourse between Muslim scholars from the Sudan and North Africa during the medieval period. Even earlier, in the thirteenth century, Muslims from Kanem in the central Sudan had established a Mālikī college – the Madrasat ibn Rashīq – in Cairo.[48] Correspondence between Sudanic scholars and those in the Maghreb and Egypt occurred but is still a relatively unexplored area of research. This is particularly true of the Istiftā' literature (letters asking for rulings – *fatwa* – on various points of law). One instance of Istiftā' literature described by Hunwick dates from 1493; this is the letter of Muḥammad al-Lamtūnī to the famous fifteenth-century Egyptian jurist Jalāl ad-Dīn al-Suyūtī asking his opinions on a variety of practices followed by Muslims in Takrūr.[49] Furthermore, the entire corpus of eighteenth- and nineteenth-century Arabic literature from West Africa shows a strong dependence on Andalusian, Maghrebi, and Egyptian authorities. The legal opinions of North African scholars are constantly cited in the various writings of the Muslim reformers of West Africa.[50]

---

[44] John O. Hunwick, "Ahmad Bābā and the Moroccan Invasion of the Sudan," "A New Source for the Biography of Ahmad Bābā al-Tinbuktī (1556–1627)," "Further Light on Ahmad Bābā al-Tinbuktī."

[45] Hunwick, "A New Source," p. 570.   [46] Ibid.   [47] Ibid., note 1.

[48] Hunwick, "The Influence of Arabic in West Africa," p. 27.

[49] Hunwick, "Notes on a Late Fifteenth-Century Document Concerning 'al-Takrūr.'"

[50] The strong intellectual ties with North Africa noticeable in the writings of eighteenth- and nineteenth-century West African authors are cited in A. H. D. Bivar and M. Hiskett, "The Arabic Literature of Nigeria to 1804"; M. Hiskett, "An Islamic Tradition of Reform in the Western Sudan from the Sixteenth to the Eighteenth Century"; D. M. Last and M. A. Al-Ḥājj, "Attempts at Defining a Muslim in Nineteenth-Century Hausaland and Bornu"; Bradford G. Martin, "Unbelief in the Western Sudan."

The intellectual ties can also be seen in the education of Muslims in West Africa. Ivor Wilks's recent study of education among the Islamized Dyula clearly corroborates the connections.[51] For any Dyula to attain the position of *karamoko* (teacher), it is essential that he study the *Tafsīr al-Jalālayn*, a commentary on the Qur'ān by Al-Maḥallī (d. 1459) and Al-Suyūtī (d. 1505), as well as the Shifā' of Qāḍī 'Iyaḍ and the *Muwaṭṭa'* of Mālik ibn Anas.[52] *Karamokos* who hope to attain a position within the 'ulamā' must continue their studies, especially on works of Mālikī law. Among the Dyula, the most oft-read Mālikī tracts at this level are the *Risāla* of Al-Qayrawānī and the *Mukhtaṣar* of Sīdī Khalīl. Furthermore, it is absolutely essential that a systematic study of the ḥadīth literature, especially the commentaries of Al-Bukhārī and Muslim, be undertaken.[53] The pattern among the Dyula is thus to cover the major orthodox literature. It is significant that all thirty-four *isnads* (diplomas) collected by Wilks in the Ivory Coast, Upper Volta, and Ghana between the late fifties and mid-sixties were awarded for the study of the *Tafsīr*, and *Shifā'*, and the *Muwaṭṭa'*.[54]

It is clear that the major texts on orthodox behaviour were known in West Africa. Yet one must still determine the impact of this knowledge. It is obvious from Wilks's fieldwork that the Dyula 'ulamā' has in general been a very well-read religious leadership. But as Wilks points out, it is not enough simply to have a scholarly elite. There must be a literate majority to respond to such a leadership. Without a literate dialogue between the leaders and the faithful, the ability to maintain the Muslim way of life is severely curbed; and the ideal, as Wilks himself notes, has not always been attained or maintained by the Dyula.[55] Wilks makes it plain that higher learning among the Dyula is decidedly restricted, and this is probably even more true of other Muslim groups in West Africa. In some instances, according to Goody, the general level of religious literacy is very low.[56] It is therefore quite likely that the impact of the orthodox texts in West Africa was, as it still is, decidedly restricted when compared with areas closer to the homeland of Islam.

Beyond the question of the level of literacy is the more practical one of whether the teachings and tenets of the essential texts were followed. Considerable evidence indicates that they were often ignored. The 'ulamā' of Takrūr closed their eyes to many illegal actions carried out by the faithful in their region: Al-Lamtūnī of Takrūr upbraids the local 'ulamā' for not following the Qur'ān and ḥadīth:

51 "The Transmission of Islamic Learning in the Western Sudan."
52 Ibid., p. 168.
53 Ibid., p. 169.
54 Ibid., p. 172.
55 Ibid., p. 192.
56 J. R. Goody, "Restricted Literacy in Northern Ghana."

. . . some of their *fuqaha'* leave aside the Qur'ān and Sunna and stick to the *Risāla*, the *lesser Mudawwana*, Ibn Jallāb, al-Ṭulaiṭilī and Ibn al-Ḥājib, to the point where they show hostility to whoever comments on the Qur'ān and they flee from *tafsīr*.[57]

In Songhay, Al-Maghīlī points to the many examples of syncretism between Islam and indigenous religion and to the way of life established by the Songhay rulers utilizing the two faiths.[58] Even during periods of religious fervor and doctrinal rigor – for example, during the early-nineteenth-century jihāds – orthodoxy was easily compromised. The Fulani administrations established by Abd al-Salām in Ilorin and by Usman Zaki and Masaba in Nupe compromised their orthodox principles in the actual governing of their territories.[59] The correspondence between Al-Kanemi and 'Uthmān dan Fodio lays bare the syncretism between Islam and animism in Bornu.[60] Everywhere and at all times, Islam and its adherents conceded to local tradition and made compromises.

The central issue – the following of local religious practices and the worshipping of idols (and by extension, use of representational imagery) – is also a prominent theme in the literature of Muslim West Africa. The degree to which orthodox tenets prohibiting such behaviour were flouted is widely documented in Arabic manuscripts from this area. A lucid description of the syncretism prevalent in Songhay was provided by Askia Muḥammad of Songhay (1493–1528) and noted by Al-Maghīlī:

They have idols and they say "the fox has said so and so and thus it will be so and so" and "if the thing is so and so, then it will be so and so." They venerate certain trees and make sacrifices to them . . . They have their shrines . . . and they do not appoint a ruler or undertake any matter great or small except at the command of the custodians of their shrines.[61]

Nearly every piece of jihādi literature contains at least one reference to idolatry and other syncretic practices. Indeed, for Last and Al-Ḥājj, the strongest charges made by the nineteenth-century Fulani reformers were against the polytheism practiced by Muslims in Gobir and Bornu – in their case, the veneration of rocks and trees.[62]

The essential guides for right conduct were therefore generally available to members of the faith in West Africa: Islamic texts including books of law, a well-developed religious educational system, and a knowledgeable

[57] Hunwick, "Notes on a Late Fifteenth-Century Document," p. 17.
[58] Hunwick, "Religion and State in the Songhay Empire, 1464–1591," pp. 307–8.
[59] Peter Morton-Williams, "The Fulani Penetration into Nupe and Yoruba in the Nineteenth Century," p. 19.
[60] Last and Al-Ḥājj, "Attempts at Defining," p. 235.
[61] From a portion of Al-Maghīlī's work, the translation of which was kindly made available to me by John O. Hunwick, letter of May 23, 1971.
[62] "Attempts at Defining," p. 234.

clerical leadership were often present. Yet Muslims were apt to stray from the strict principles of Islam. This was true not only during non-revolutionary periods of Islamic expansion but also during periods dominated by jihād. The inquiries and concerns expressed over the centuries by local religious leaders and reformers in their letters to Muslim legal experts make it plain that their followers clung to traditional beliefs and behavior. In the light of this evidence, there is no reason to conclude that traditional art forms alone would have been destroyed as a result of Islamic teachings.

CHAPTER 3

THE SYNCRETIC NATURE OF ISLAM:
THE SURVIVAL OF TRADITIONAL
ART FORMS

The nature of Islam as a religious and cultural phenomenon in West Africa has not been previously appreciated by those writing on the arts. The religion has been dealt with as an extension through time and space of the orthodox theology of Mecca. And yet West African Islam is clearly not a pure or parent type but a religious culture that has undergone continuous modification. Indeed, wherever the faith has spread, and West Africa is no exception, it has pragmatically combined religious ideals with numerous concessions in order to adjust to local circumstances. Geertz emphasizes this basic feature in discussing the spread of Islam in Morocco and Indonesia, but his words are equally applicable to the area under consideration here:

. . . Islamization has been a two-sided process. On the one hand, it has consisted of an effort to adapt a universal, in theory standardized and essentially unchangeable, and unusually well-integrated system of ritual and belief to the realities of local, even individual, moral and metaphysical perception. On the other, it has consisted of a struggle to maintain, in the face of this adaptive flexibility, the identity of Islam not just as a religion in general but as the particular directives communicated by God to mankind through the peremptory prophecies of Muhammed.[1]

In no area of West Africa, including the most heavily Islamized portions of the western Sudan, has "classical" Islam taken root; instead, one finds a mosaic of Islamic communities that demonstrate a wide range of compromises between doctrine and the demands of culture contact. Needless to say, some areas are quantitatively and qualitatively more thoroughly Islamized than others, but even in these cases the religious culture is a syncretized phenomenon. Indeed, one could argue that it is precisely its adaptability that has enabled the religion to play such a vital role in the history of West Africa.

[1] Clifford Geertz, *Islam Observed: Religious Development in Morocco and Indonesia*, pp. 14–15.

28

In two studies, *Islam in West Africa* and *The Influence of Islam upon Africa*, J. Spencer Trimingham outlines the many steps by which Islam succeeded in adapting to West African cultures.[2] Throughout his analyses, he reiterates that it was the flexibility with which the religion responded to traditional cultures that ultimately accounted for its impressive success. Confronted with well-integrated indigenous societies, Islam had to accommodate itself to the realities of cultural reciprocity, not only during its initial stages of penetration but even when more fully established. Trimingham recognizes this crucial point, observing that

Islam has become an African religion. The changes that ensue from the meeting of cultures are dynamic in character. Islam and African cultures have a reciprocal influence. As it spread among Africans Islam was conditioned by their outlook and customs. Consequently every Muslim society varies in its understanding and practice of Islam. In adopting it[,] people reject no more of their inheritance than is absolutely necessary.[3]

What Islamic culture assimilates from animist culture is transformed in the process, for it is assimilated, not adopted, into Islam; at the same time Islam is affected by what it assimilates. The result is not a fusion but a synthesis.[4]

This give and take between Muslim and traditional cultures, each conditioning the other, has governed – has indeed characterized – the entire history of the religion in West Africa. It is a fact of life persisting in even the most heavily Islamized sectors. It seems clear that indigenous societies did not commit cultural suicide in the wake of Islamization, regardless of the pressures brought to bear on them, but evolved into new societal orders exhibiting features derived from both ways of life.

The syncretic nature of Islam in West Africa is based not only on the exigencies of time and place but also on the very make-up of the religion. In many respects Islam, as a religion and as a culture, has been particularly well suited to the problems confronting an expansionary faith in this area. Inherent in Islam are beliefs that allow an unusual measure of tolerance toward traditional culture. Islam makes few demands on the mass of its believers, asking only that the five pillars of the faith be observed: professing the faith, daily prayers, fasting, almsgiving, and the pilgrimage. And even these minimal requirements are viewed as ideals, so that deviations from such practices occur widely.[5] To stray from such observances does not exclude an individual from the community of believers, for in the end the crucial factor is that he recognize the existence of Allāh. Beyond this most basic commitment, a wide degree of latitude is allowed.

Given the minimal requirements of Islam for the majority of the faithful,

---

[2] *Islam in West Africa*, pp. 24–33, and *The Influence of Islam upon Africa*, pp. 37–42.
[3] *Islam in West Africa*, p. 40.
[4] Ibid., p. 41.
[5] I. M. Lewis, *Islam in Tropical Africa*, p. 40.

29

it is not surprising to find either individuals or whole communities retaining and incorporating into their new faith varying degrees of traditional life. For the average Muslim, traditional institutions and modes of behavior persist; and this proves to be a point of contention in virtually all Islamic communities between the 'ulamā' and the mass of believers. Members of the 'ulamā' are aware that Islam must accommodate itself to local circumstances if it is to attract converts, but they are also concerned that at least the doctrinal core of the religion be maintained so that Islam will not wither and die.[6]

It is precisely this issue – the conflict between the application of doctrine by the 'ulamā' and the possibilities for a wide range of accommodation available to any Muslim society – which Ivor Wilks stresses in his study of Islamic scholarship among the Mande Dyula.

This tendency towards assimilation [the adoption of aspects of traditional life by various Dyula communities], however, is usually counteracted by a constant and conscious concern for the renewal and reinvigoration of the Muslim content of Dyula culture – a process described by the Arabic term *tajdīd*.[7]

Those making up the religious elite must serve as the guardians of Muslim values, a role that may prove exceedingly difficult or altogether impossible, depending on the inherent vitality of the particular Islamized culture. Any weakening of the Muslim way of life is directly attributable to a breakdown of those controls normally regulated by the 'ulamā'. According to Wilks,

The Dyula measure failure in leadership in terms of regression through *ihmāl*, non-observance or "backsliding," to ultimate *kufr*, unbelief. The symptoms are unmistakable. The field of application of Muslim law, particularly on marriage, divorce and inheritance, shrinks and local customary procedures take its place (Anderson 1954: 266–7) . . . A qur'ān may become regarded as a sacred object in its own right, no longer read but worshipped and perhaps, as among the Kamara of Larabanga in Northern Ghana, only exposed to public view once a year, or an *imām*'s staff of office may be enshrined and periodically purified and sacrificed to, as among the Sanu of Bobo-Dioulasso.[8]

Religious leaders in all Muslim communities, whether in complete control or clearly losing ground to regressive tendencies, must strike some pragmatic balance between Islamic ideals and those concessions invariably made to traditional practices. The need for balance will prove highly significant when I discuss the impact of Islam on the visual arts.

Other features of Islam have allowed, and at times have required, the religion to be unusually tolerant of various aspects of indigenous life. Lewis observes that, as a comprehensive theology with an emphasis on

[6] Ibid., p. 59.
[7] "Transmission of Islamic Learning," p. 165.
[8] Ibid., pp. 192–3.

the afterlife, Islam is far removed from the spirit and immediacy of traditional beliefs. He makes this crucial distinction, one that has rarely been noted by writers on Islam:

Traditional moral powers are normally believed to sustain a moral order in which the just prosper and the good are rewarded, not so much in some nebulous after life but within the society itself . . .

All this is evidently antithetical to the universalistic spirit of Islam, its concern with eternity rather than today, and in the religious context opposed to Muslim eschatology, with its fatalistic acceptance of divine reward and retribution in the after life rather than in this.[9]

By its very nature, then, Islam cannot convey the sense of immediate relief, the concern for the here and now, that is so important a part of local religions. Traditional religious cults, their priests, and the paraphernalia so necessary to their workings are therefore far more resilient in the face of Islam than has generally been acknowledged. Even Trimingham, who is at times pessimistic about the possibilities that traditional institutions can resist the pressures of Islamization, concedes that

. . . most people are cultivators and every village has its cycle of animistic observance to ensure the falling of the rain and the fertility of the soil. Old functionaries, heads of family or village, rain-makers, masters of the soil or water, continue to perform their rites. No cleric would think of questioning them. They change like everything else, some are discontinued, others survive, some take on Islamic symbols, but propitiation in some form or another continues as before.[10]

Masked cults and shrines housing figurative art furnish the means by which the pressing problems of existence can be comprehended and resolved. They continue to play pragmatic roles even when modified by Islam, for they are highly resistant to destruction. In long- and well-established Muslim communities, masking and figurative traditions persist either because they function at a number of levels not treated by Islamic ritual or because they have proved more effective.[11] Local procedures may also be retained because they offer traditionally tested solutions to particular problems; although Muslim clerics may be capable of offering answers to the same problems, they are fully aware that indigenous methods continue to exercise a strong appeal because they are trusted modes of behavior. The acceptance of masking and figurative rituals in an Islamic context therefore cannot be construed simply as a case of massive backsliding or apostasy, but should be viewed as a reflection of the pragmatic results of the confrontation of Islam and traditional cultures. Aspects of indigenous life are retained everywhere precisely because they provide solutions that lie outside the universalistic realm of Islam.[12]

[9] *Islam in Tropical Africa*, p. 59. [10] *Islam in West Africa*, p. 59. [11] Ibid., pp. 103–4.
[12] It is important to note that traditional cultures and practices have not only withstood the advances of Islam but have also successfully resisted the manifold pressures and

Lewis goes on to point out that many aspects of traditional life are maintained because the theology of Islam permits local practices and beliefs.[13] Islam is pervaded by a host of spiritual forces, such as the jinn, which have become totally accepted and rationalized aspects of the religion. The world of the jinn within Islamic demonology is well developed, consisting not only of many beliefs and practices derived from Arabic native religion but also of numerous spirits that were incorporated into Islam during its long period of expansion. The Qur'ān and the ḥadīth both recognize the existence of heathen gods and spirits, but most of them are classified as demons and belong to the category of the disbelieving jinn. However, some of the pagan jinn converted by Muḥammad to Islam are believed to carry out their practices in the service of Allāh.[14] Within the West African context Trimingham states that,

... following its practice of ideological antithesis[,] Islam splits them [indigenous spirit forces] into categories of good and bad. In fact, the distinction is between pagan spirits regarded as inimical to man and Islamic spirits who are neutral.[15]

Trimingham's clearcut divisions, whereby all non-Muslim spirits are necessarily classified as reprehensible, appear on the basis of recent research to be far too inflexibly drawn. Local spirit forces may exist side by side with the world of the jinn and thereby constitute positive alternatives to the Muslim spirit world. In general, belief in the Bori cult among the Islamized Hausa is hardly viewed as unlawful behavior, for it is acknowledged as another avenue by which communication with the spirit world can be attained. The co-existence of both spirit categories in any Muslim community, therefore, does not necessarily imply a state of spiritual ambiguity or ambivalence (referred to by some writers as dualism), for as Baba of Karo relates, each ultimately contributes to the success of the culture:

The work of *malams* is one thing, the work of *bori* experts is another, each has his own kind of work and they must not be mixed up. There is the work of *malams*, of *bori*, of magicians, of witches; they are all different but at heart everyone loves the spirits.[16]

forces of Westernization. Even the most positive aspects of Western culture – more productive agricultural techniques, new medicines, the establishment of clinics and hospitals – have failed to supplant local procedures. The contributions of Western science and technology may be enthusiastically received and accepted, but they are generally viewed as simply other avenues to security and success. They rarely supplant traditional ways but are pragmatically syncretized with pre-existing patterns, values, and beliefs.

[13] *Islam in Tropical Africa*, p. 60.
[14] D. B. MacDonald and H. Massé, "Djinn," pp. 547–8.
[15] *Islam in West Africa*, p. 54.
[16] Mary F. Smith, *Baba of Karo*, p. 22. This very personal account of Baba, an elderly Islamized Hausa woman, dramatically reveals the easy juxtaposition in Hausa life of non-Muslim and Muslim spirits as well as other religious and cultural features.

In my area of fieldwork (the southeastern Mande region) there was certainly no unanimity of attitude regarding non-Muslim spirit forces. The responses by Muslim Mande to the question of the legitimacy of particular spirits ranged from total acceptance to utter rejection. Feelings expressed about the Gbain masking cult, for example, were very mixed, depending on which segment of a Muslim community was being interviewed. Numerous members of the 'ulamā' classified the Gbain as an "unbelieving" jinni, but for the majority of Muslims, including a sizable number of learned *karamokos*, the Gbain was clearly a converted spirit. There seemed to be no other way of explaining its contributions against witchcraft in various Muslim villages. A few individuals suggested that the Gbain ultimately came under the protection and authority of Allāh, thereby extending a measure of legitimacy to the cult, but they maintained that the tradition was pagan in its inspiration and orientation. For this small group, the Gbain was not a Muslim jinni but could be used because it performed in the service of Allāh by protecting his believers. Trimingham's claim that Islam takes an automatic and blanket view of non-Muslim spirits as "bad" simply did not hold in this instance. Among the many Muslims questioned about the Gbain controversy was rampant, and some individuals even changed their attitudes depending on whether they were interviewed publicly or privately.[17]

Not only is orthodox Islam filled with an elaborate spirit world of its own, but as Lewis acknowledges there exists within the religion a strong belief in mystical powers, and this too is sanctioned by the Qur'ān. Thus, Islam has been able to accommodate many spirit forces found within West African cultures, for "many of these traditional powers find a hospitable home; and passages from the Qur'ān are cited to justify their existence as real phenomen[a]."[18] It must be re-emphasized that not all spirits are legitimate according to the Qur'ān and that discussion exists at all levels in all Muslim communities as to what types of spirits may be included within the Muslim classification. For the Imām of Bondoukou, the spiritual

[17] Many Muslim Dyula informants at Bandakani Soukoura (a small village approximately fifty-five miles west of Bondoukou), where the Gbain tradition had once flourished, reacted in such a manner. One notable example was Saidu Wattara, an elder of some standing, who was publicly adamant about the Gbain. When interviewed privately, however, he admitted that his earlier stance was taken so as not to offend members of the 'ulamā' who were present at the meeting and who he knew opposed the use of the Gbain. Free from such restraints, Saidu Wattara talked easily about the Gbain mask. He claimed that it had existed in the village but had been destroyed some ten years earlier by the 'ulamā'. According to him, the general fortunes of Bandakani Soukoura began to decline shortly after the destruction of the mask; he attributed the present depressed state of the community to the fact that the tradition had not been revived. Although he and others clearly favor a revival of the Gbain cult, they have been unable to convince the 'ulamā' (some of whom were responsible for the demise of the tradition and are still opposed to it) of its necessity for the well-being of the community.
[18] Lewis, *Islam in Tropical Africa*, p. 60.

33

leader of all Muslims in the Cercle de Bondoukou and western Brong-Ahafo, the Gbain was unacceptable as a Muslim jinni because it smacked of paganism. He applied the concept of *najwā* or secret counsel to the Gbain, for it was the harbinger of knowledge and ritual processes that were not ultimately under the control of Allāh, and this is condemned by the Qur'ān.[19] Others, such as Mustapha Kamagate, a highly learned and respected *karamoko* from Jinini, expressed a contrary opinion, claiming that the strong Muslim content of the Gbain tradition clearly marked this spirit as a worthy servant of Allāh.[20]

Other traditional practices that incorporate the use of figurative art – and that are viewed by Western art historians as inimical to the functionings of an Islamic community – are in fact recognized by Muslim doctrine. Lewis states that divination, magic, and witchcraft are all notable features of Islam, and members of the 'ulamā' may attempt to replace local rituals dealing with these concerns with Qur'ānic ones.[21] They are rarely successful in eradicating the traditional practices, however, and in many communities both Islamic and traditional techniques are employed.

Clergy have introduced new techniques into the general body of magical practice, but it is simply an addition or substitution of written amulets for old, hence the Fulbe saying "those who write are no better than magicians." Pagans are ready to put any new technique to the test. They readily believe that the "word" possesses power and written amulets captivate them. But they are not prepared to rely on one method. A Temne Muslim house visited had symbols of three religions on the lintel of the doorway: at the top a printed Temne Christian text, underneath a cloth on which was tied a metal symbol, and beneath that a paper printed with Islamic texts, designs, and cabalistic signs.[22]

In some areas the Muslim clergy lack the training to employ Qur'ānic techniques to solve certain problems, and traditional practices therefore continue to dominate.

In many places when asked what were the functions of the medicine-man the first given was "to counteract witches," followed by to heal, administer swear-medicine, interpret dreams, and the like. Clerics, however, are unable to do this[;] consequently the medicine-man is a necessity for Muslim society ... Some Hausa regions still have a sarakin māyū (chief of witches) whose function is that of detection. In Futas Jalon and Toro the bilēdyo ... is the counter-agent. He is the general medicine-man who continues to function, even in these deeply Islamized regions, as exorcist, rain-maker, diviner, herbalist, and if necessary, black magician.[23]

Even in those societies where traditional anti-witchcraft cults have been displaced by Islamic practices, the possibility of reviving such an important

[19] The Qur'ân, pp. 271–2.
[20] Interview at Jinini, May 1967.
[21] *Islam in Tropical Africa*, pp. 60–1.
[22] Trimingham, *Islam in West Africa*, p. 113.
[23] Ibid., pp. 118–19.

force for social control is strong. In my fieldwork, I found an example of such a revival at Sandheui, a Dyula village to the west of Bondoukou where the Gbain mask had been destroyed and later replaced.[24]

Since Islam itself recognizes witchcraft and magic, it should not be surprising that many clerics will allow the faithful to resort to traditional methods of control when Muslim methods fail.[25] When protection is sought and help required, the line between Muslim and traditional life is easy to cross.

Given the history of marked accommodation that has typified Islam in West Africa and its theologic potential to accept and tolerate so many aspects of traditional culture, one might well expect the visual arts, including masking and figurative traditions, to survive within a Muslim context. This should be especially true for a masked cult that functioned more effectively than available Islamic methods or that dealt with a problem for which there was no Qur'ānic solution at all. Local practices and cults that have operated successfully against a wide array of societal ills are highly resistant to external pressures, for they are associated with the very survival of the group. To abandon a proven masking or figurative tradition related to agricultural or human fertility in favor of unproven Islamic procedures might well invite disaster. Yet specialists on Islam in Africa, not to mention art historians and museologists, seem to feel that representational art, especially in the form of masks or figurative traditions, could not and so did not survive in the face of Islam. Lewis, who is particularly sensitive to the syncretic nature of Islam, while pointing to the widespread popularity of spirit-possession cults among Muslim groups, remarks that

Despite the distaste with which they are almost universally regarded by the pious, these cults, particularly those which do not employ physical images and masks, have not only shown considerable powers of survival in their own local situation but have also sometimes succeeded in spreading.[26]

Trimingham thought that masks and figurative art, both symbols and accoutrements of the old pagan order, were either uprooted or left to rot through disuse: "Ancestor houses gradually disintegrate under wind and rain and are not renewed[,] while masks are sold to visiting anthropologists."[27]

Certainly evidence exists in support of Trimingham's contention that Islam was destructive to indigenous art. Such data, however, are decidedly fragmentary. Substantially more information can be found to demonstrate the opposite claim: that a high degree of compatibility, ranging from quiet

[24] Here I was told by the Muslim Dyula inhabitants that some fifty years earlier a Gbain mask had been destroyed by two elders who had returned from the Ḥājj. However, the mask was replaced shortly thereafter, and the tradition continues to operate. Interview at Sandheui, January 3, 1968.

[25] Trimingham, *Islam in West Africa*, p. 103.

[26] *Islam in Tropical Africa*, p. 64.   [27] *Islam in West Africa*, p. 38.

tolerance to total acceptance, has often characterized the relationship between Islam and local art traditions in West Africa.

Neither Lewis nor Trimingham deals effectively with the subject of Islam and the arts. Although clearly stating that "pagan" cults may persist within a Muslim environment, Lewis does not believe that this is likely in the case of those using masks. He does not explain why this is necessarily so, and one can only assume that he is prejudiced by the old anti-art clichés about Islam. Trimingham is even more pessimistic in his assessment, claiming that "although the mask [and by extension figurative art] may continue to operate in Islamized societies, it has lost its former socio-religious function and may degenerate into a form of clowning."[28] His pessimism about the arts is difficult to comprehend especially when contrasted to his frequent recognition of the survival powers of so many other aspects of traditional life in the face of Islamization. Both writers are fully aware of the cultural and religious syncretism that has resulted from the spread of Islam south of the Sahara, and yet they are loath to extend this syncretism to the arts. Surely art types and forms are subject to the same principles of culture contact that govern all other societal features: the same resiliency so characteristic of other traditional institutions in contact with Islam should logically exist in the visual arts. By the same token, the pragmatism displayed by Islam towards non-Muslim life in general can be expected to govern the behavior of the faithful towards the arts.

It must be mentioned that Trimingham is far from consistent in his comments on the arts. Though he generally views art as no more than symbolism, he sometimes acknowledges its crucial role in West African societies.[29] Such inconsistency is unwarranted, however, for the visual arts are clearly far more than mere representations. They are in virtually all cases intimately associated with the essence of traditional institutions, thought, and life and therefore are less subject to change, destruction, or abandonment than purely esthetic expressions of a culture. In sum, Trimingham, like Lewis, is guilty of underestimating the position of the arts in African cultures. They both view art as a peripheral element of society, a trapping easily pushed aside and discarded during acculturation. They fail to appreciate the fact that the visual arts are not cultural baggage but lie very close to or form a part of the heart of these cultures.

Before dealing with examples from the Mande region of West Africa that clearly demonstrate compatibility between Islam and figurative art, an instance of so-called Muslim intolerance towards such art often cited by art historians and museologists should be analyzed. An almost classic case crediting Islam with a totally destructive effect on the arts comes from

---

[28] Ibid., p. 37.
[29] Ibid., pp. 37, 199. Here his inconsistent attitudes regarding art are most clearly expressed.

Nupe. Six Elo cult face masks collected by the German ethnographer Leo Frobenius at Mokwa in 1910–11 constitute the entire corpus of mask types from this culture in museum collections. (Five of the masks are of the female Elo type, with two graceful curved horns, and the sixth is an example of a *gara*, the robber or rogue, with a single straight horn surmounting the mask.) For Fagg, this paucity of objects is directly attributable to the intensive jihād leveled against Nupeland in the second quarter of the nineteenth century.

The Nupe were converted to Islam by force of arms about 1830 when the great Fulani warrior Mallam Dendo subdued the kingdom; apart from some relief carving on doors, these few masks are almost the sole evidence of the survival of representational art there.[30]

The assumption made by Fagg and others is that with the conversion of the Nupe their art forms were undermined and so virtually died out. Masks and figurative art were especially hard hit once the word of Allāh had been embraced. The fact that Frobenius collected his six Elo masks some eighty years after Dendo's jihād and the supposed mass conversion of the Nupe is not even questioned.

Even the most cursory look at the ethnographic literature pertaining to the Nupe indicates that Islam did not in fact obliterate traditional art forms. Numerous masking traditions continued well into this century, based on the evidence recorded by Nadel in the early 1930s and 1940s, and many of them exist today. According to Nadel, the Elo cult (restricted in its distribution to western Nupeland, where it was found among the Gbedegi, a Nupe "sub-tribe") still employed carved wooden masks during the period of his fieldwork. He noted Elo in three Gbedegi centers: the riverain community of Rabah, some fifteen miles down the Niger from the important village of Jebba; Mokwa on the Jebba–Bida road, a town of 2,000 inhabitants and eight mosques; and Gbajibo, twenty miles upstream from Jebba. Although he found Elo masks in only three Gbedegi villages, they were used much more broadly, for "smaller villages and hamlets in the neighbourhood, which did not themselves possess the *elo* masks, perform the dance annually with masks borrowed from Mokwa."[31]

A photograph (plate 1) taken by Nadel of an Elo-type mask, an Elokô or "Great Elo," depicts an example virtually identical to one of the female

---

[30] W. B. Fagg and Margaret Plass, *African Sculpture: An Anthology*, p. 12. Fagg underestimates the period of Islamic influence on the Nupe. The earliest encroachments of Islam in Nupeland occurred through the agency of Fulani traders and clerics and antedate Mallam Dendo's jihād by nearly a century. It was adopted as the official state religion as early as 1770, when Etsu Jibiri converted to the faith. For the best account of Islamic impact on Nupe, see Siegfried Frederick Nadel, *A Black Byzantium*, pp. 76–86.

[31] Nadel, *Nupe Religion*, p. 214.

1. Nupe mask of the Great Elo.

Elo collected by Frobenius (plate 2) almost twenty-five years earlier and now in the British Museum.[32] The similarities between the two masks are striking; they extend from the total configuration to the smallest of details. Both examples consist of a smooth oval convex face with two antelope horns meeting at their tips and projecting gracefully from the top of the human heads. Within the open ovoid space formed by the joining of the horns is a figure complex consisting of three schematically treated motifs. At the bottom is a small animal; surmounting this is what appears to be a dance staff; and at the top is a human figure with flexed arms and clasped hands. The raised and incised carvings and the painted motifs on these two

[32] Ibid., p. 28; Fagg and Plass, *African Sculpture*, p. 12. Although Nadel does not specify, it is very likely that he photographed this Elokô at Mokwa, the same village in which Frobenius collected the British Museum specimen.

2. Nupe Elo mask; wood, white clay; h. 25.5".

masks are absolutely consonant. A slender projecting nose is flanked by two slightly raised ears that visually serve as parenthetical borders to the design of the upper face. An open mouth and small beard – the latter having a functional purpose, since it is gripped by the dancer in order to stabilize the mask during its use – round out the surface carving devoted to the face of the mask. Incised chevron patterns are worked along the outside perimeter of the horns, forming a continuous fret-like pattern. White clay paint is applied to the chevrons on the horns and on the facial scarification patterns. These patterns include a line running obliquely from the middle of the nose to each cheek (the typical and traditional Gbedegi facial marking), three small vertical marks to the outside of each nostril, and three flaring cat's whiskers at each corner of the mouth. The last two patterns were noted by Nadel as being modern markings very popular in and around the capital town of Bida.[33]

Nadel encountered not only carved wooden masks of the Elo but also a number of mask types woven out of grasses or fabricated from cotton cloth. One type – the Egugun, consisting of a fabric costume and a cloth mask with sewn cowrie-shell designs – was clearly an import, occurring only among the immigrant Yoruba groups known locally as Konu.[34] The Nupe referred to the cult as "Gugu," and although completely tolerant of it, they had not incorporated the tradition into their cycle of rituals. Even Muslim Nupe living in such mixed Nupe–Yoruba communities as Shonga, Shari, and Mokwa, who had witnessed Gugu performances regularly, did not seem to be concerned or upset about such blatantly non-Muslim displays.

Quite different in appearance was a second mask type noted by Nadel, the Mamma. This was a purely Nupe cult that occurred only among the Gbedegi, the "sub-tribe" where the Elo was found.[35] Performances of the cult were highlighted by masked dancers (*nagbe*) whose costumes consisted of skirts and large veils, the latter separate pieces enveloping the heads and upper torsos of the dancers. The entire ritual garment was made of sun-dried and bleached grasses ingeniously tied and knotted in such a way as to produce a highly functional dance costume.

The most spectacular mask type witnessed by Nadel was the Ndako Gboya (plate 3), a local tradition found among all Nupe groups except the Dibo and Ebe (who are located on the southeastern and northwestern frontiers of Nupe country). Although generally not given to describing the arts in detail, Nadel was so impressed with these masks that he left a vivid account of them:

The masks of the *ndako gboya* are unlike any other masks used in the cults of Nigerian peoples . . . each consists of a long tube made of white cotton cloth, just wide enough for a man to stand inside, which is suspended from a wheel-

[33] *A Black Byzantium*, p. 405.   [34] *Nupe Religion*, p. 213.   [35] Ibid.

3. "The appearance of the *ndako gboya*."

shaped bamboo frame fixed to the top of a tall pole, about twelve feet in length. The man representing the spirit stands inside the cloth tube[,] which comes down to the ground, holding the pole in his hands. He will move about with varying speed, occasionally jumping and running, and lift and lower the pole or incline it this way or that, making the cloth tube swing and sway ... There are two small slits at eye-height in the cloth; but the dancer can see little through them, and depends on the help of assistants ... who lead him along and clear the way for him, carrying sticks to drive back the onlookers. In large ceremonials up to ten masks may be employed, though normally there will be two or three, or even one only.[36]

The wide range of functions represented by the three Nupe mask types – the Elo, Mamma, and Ndako Gboya – is indeed interesting, considering the degree of Islamization in Nupe country. The Elo cult and its wooden masks represent the most secular tradition of the three, for although it is tied to the Nupe ritual calendar, governed by acts of secrecy, and controlled by elderly titled officials (as are all Nupe cults), it is not considered by locals to be a sacred ceremony. According to Nadel,

The dance seems to contain the remnants of some plot or dramatic theme ... But again, the people deny that there is such a plot or that these "roles" have any meaning.

In a sense, the *elo* is a mixture of ritual and entertainment. But unlike the usual Nupe ceremonial, in which the ritual part precedes the "play," the *elo* involves ritual only ... in its administration ...; the rest is pure entertainment. Perhaps, in its original form, the *elo* was more fully a ceremonial with some religious purpose as well as a plot.[37]

The Elo masquerade appears to operate primarily for entertainment, but this is certainly not true of the Mamma ritual, for the masks employed in this rite are considered to be powerful enough to kill women and strangers who happen to see them. Nadel mentions, for example, that the District Head of Mokwa, a Muslim Fulani, fled in terror after having glanced momentarily at a Mamma dance held at the village of Jebba. Members of the cult who witnessed this spectacle claimed that his fear was quite genuine and that his reaction to the mask was typical of strangers.[38] The purpose of Mamma is to cleanse the village of evil forces other than witchcraft and may range from curbing an epidemic of smallpox to frightening and apprehending petty thieves.[39]

It is the Ndako Gboya, or anti-witchcraft cult, however, that is clearly the most powerful and influential of the three masking associations. In most sectors of Nupeland it is considered an essential organization, since its duty is to seek out witches, who must be found and punished before their victims can be helped.[40] When the British administration banned this cult

---

[36] Ibid., p. 190.   [37] Ibid., p. 216.   [38] Ibid., p. 91.
[39] Ibid., pp. 84–93.   [40] Nadel, *A Black Byzantium*, p. 24.

in the Bida district because cult members were extorting large sums of money from villages, a great feeling of distress arose: "there was no means of fighting witches and no protection 'save God' who, as we know, is inscrutable, idle, far away."[41] In 1910–11 Frobenius noted a similar attitude of helplessness and despair among the inhabitants of Mokwa when their Ndako Gboya mask was burned by British missionaries.[42]

Nearly contemporary evidence reveals that virtually all the masquerades cited by Nadel in the thirties and forties still form a prominent aspect of Nupe life. The Elo is still danced with at the important Nupe town of Mokwa, according to Phillips Stevens.[43] In the Emirate of Pategi, opposite the confluence of the Kaduna and Niger rivers, Gugu masks are carried by the Nupe in order to commune with ancestors, while five anti-witchcraft masks of the Ndako Gboya cult were still in existence as recently as 1956.[44] Such data are unfortunately fragmentary, but they suggest quite plainly that even today the Islamized Nupe have not given up these important features of their culture.

Why should these traditions have persisted in an Islamized culture like the Nupe? In some cases, as Nadel indicates, the cults even derived their support from Muslims. The secularly oriented Elo cult survived, despite its use of wooden face masks with stylized human heads, because the tradition itself appears not to have been objectionable to Muslims. At the time of Nadel's research, the Nupe did not attach any sacred significance to the Elo rite. The reason offered for its existence was a purely esthetic one: the cult performed for the enjoyment of the community. "It is without sacrifice, esoteric phase or prayer; nor is it (today at least) credited with any aim beyond dzodzo, 'play.'"[45] According to Nadel, the Elo served as a necessary counterpoise to other Nupe rituals characterized by "sober esoteric sacrifices, unaccompanied by music, dancing, and public 'merry-making.'"[46]

Nadel, however, may well have underestimated the functional importance of the Elo and its relationship to the Islamized Nupe. Recent data from Phillips Stevens indicate that the Elo is now performed at the town of Mokwa only on the Prophet's birthday.[47] Since Nadel's research the tradition, at least at Mokwa, has obviously somehow become tied to one of the major Islamic festivals.

The Mamma cult is of a totally different order. Muslim Nupe are interested in the Mamma masks but, as mentioned above, are fearful of

[41] Nadel, *Nupe Religion*, p. 200.
[42] Leo Frobenius, *The Voice of Africa*, vol. 2, p. 393.
[43] Frank Willett, *African Art*, p. 273, note 199.
[44] "The Nupe of Pategi," pp. 275–7.
[45] *Nupe Religion*, p. 107.
[46] Ibid., p. 225.
[47] Willett, *African Art*, p. 273, note 199.

them. Despite the esoteric nature of the cult and its ritual performances, which lie outside the domain of Islam, it has not been attacked by the Muslim population. In part this might be explained by the fact that there were very few Mamma masks in use during the 1930s and 1940s, and perhaps such localized distribution presented little threat to Muslims.[48] Another reason for its survival is its function of curbing the numerous evil forces that plague man's existence. This is especially important for the Nupe, who believe that man does not have recourse for such problems to either Soko, the traditional high god, or to Allāh, since they are too far removed from the affairs of the world and man.

The most noteworthy example of a masking tradition surviving within this Islamized context is the Ndako Gboya cult. Not only is the Ndako Gboya tolerated by Muslim Nupe, but many of them actually participate in it, for the masked society has proved a far more effective deterrent to witchcraft than have Qur'ānic remedies. Nadel noted that the historical associations between the cult and Islam were intimate, for it has operated as a royal cult under the ultimate authority of the *etsu* or king of Nupe ever since the mid-nineteenth century.

. . . under Etsu Masaba [the youngest son of the Fulani Emir Mallam Dendo] the head of this order, the grandfather of the present head of the *ndako gboya* society, was invested with the pompous title of Majī Dodo, Master of the Monster, and with this royal recognition the organization of the society was made subservient to Nupe kingship. One after the other the heads of the society received their titles from the Etsu Nupe. Villages and districts which sought the help of the *ndako gboya* against witches had to apply first to the king. This new royal prerogative also entailed a considerable economic benefit: for the king shared in the income of the order which was derived from the gifts collected in the villages which had called in the *ndako gboya* . . . This powerful prerogative of the king was, in fact, maintained by the Mohammedan Fulani Emirs till very recently.[49]

Although the British ban of Ndako Gboya in 1921 broke down the economic and political collusion that had developed between the cult and the Fulani emirs (a situation that had led to unveiled and unbridled extortion), the cult retained much of its vitality and maintained its association with the Islamic elite. Some twenty-five years later, at the time of Nadel's research, the leaders of various chapters of Ndako Gboya still "received their rank from Moslem Emirs, and the present incumbents, at least, consider themselves good Mohammedans."[50] Despite the fact that the cult was based on non-Muslim spirits, it did not incur Muslim censure, since it was subsumed under the authority of the *etsu*. Beyond the realm of politics,

[48] Nadel, *Nupe Religion*, p. 84.
[49] *A Black Byzantium*, pp. 141–2.
[50] *Nupe Religion*, p. 119.

however, it must be stressed that if Islam had succeeded in destroying the cult, both Muslim and "pagan" Nupe would have lost their primary defense against one of the most pressing problems confronting any African society – witchcraft.

The traditional argument that the Nupe are a people devoid of art, representational or otherwise, as a result of Islamic pressures and conversion simply does not hold up in the light of available evidence.[51] Incorrect assessments of the nature and depth of Islamic impact on the Nupe have grossly exaggerated Islam's effects on the arts. Although Islam has been a long-standing force within Nupe society, the region is still far from being Dar al-Islām. Even today Islam, in a highly syncretized form, is concentrated primarily within the towns and larger villages of Nupeland, whereas the countryside is dominated by traditional religious controls. Elements of Islam have certainly filtered down into village life, but pre-existing cults with their complexes of masks, costumes, and so forth continue to survive.

Since Islam has not had a destructive effect on Nupe art traditions, how then does one explain the decided paucity of objects from this region? One possible answer is that it is geographically outside the areas ravaged by treasure hunters, art dealers, and collectors, and thus has been shielded by the art-rich Yoruba, who have for years sated the appetites of such persons. Nupe country might well be far richer artistically than is suggested by its representation in Western collections. Moreover, the region's artistic reputation would obviously be quite different if Western museums and other collections included non-sculptural creations such as the long and impressive white cloth Ndako Gboya masks and the intricate grass costumes of the Mamma society.

Another explanation comes from the observations of Nadel, who found relatively few cult objects such as figures and masks during his many years in Nupeland. For the most part, he found that the accoutrements of spirits and shrines consisted of leaves, twigs, clay bowls, and pots.[52] The materialization of the spirit world was generally in the form of utilitarian objects and not a profusion of masks or figures. This very low density of "art" types might well have existed even in pre-Fulani times, an assumption that gains strength from the fact that certain sections of Nupeland, marginally touched or totally unaffected by Islam, display no greater wealth

---

[51] Whether Islamization adversely affected the "royal arts" (regalia) is not certain, for Nadel's data are both fragmentary and unclear. At the village level, the various objects associated with kingship – the iron bells, fetters, and chains introduced by Tsoede – apparently have been retained and continue to function as the primary symbols of political validation. This seems not to have been the case in respect of the etsu's court: although Nadel mentions that Usman Zaki, the second son of Mallam Dendo, appropriated the regalia of the etsu when he became king of Nupe, he later states that the royal emblems disappeared from the court (*A Black Byzantium*, pp. 73–5, 80, 88).

[52] *Nupe Religion*, p. 16.

45

of art objects. Nadel's point is important not only for the additional light it sheds on the theme of Islam and its compatibility with masking traditions in Nupe, but also because it hints at a possible explanation of why some African cultures (given an equal availability of materials and so forth) produced so little in the way of "art."

Although it has just been demonstrated that the classic example of how Islam caused the demise of art among the Nupe is but another misinterpretation, one cannot infer from this that Islam has always displayed such tolerance towards non-Muslim practices. Recorded instances do exist of Muslim intolerance to local institutions and a concomitant destruction of art forms, but these are quite rare and even then not fully documented. Delafosse records an occurrence in the 1860s when Ba-Lobbo successfully converted the Samono, a non-Muslim fishing population inhabiting the banks of the Niger: "les Somono . . ., dont beaucoup étaient encore païens, brûlèrent leurs idoles, se convertirent en masse à l'Islam et bâtirent des mosquées . . ."[53] On a less spectacular scale and without the threat of arms, there have been occasional fulminations and uprisings led by Muslim clerics against local shrines, such as the campaigns leveled against the Nama and Komo cults in the area of Segu in 1945 and 1947.[54] Other instances have been recorded from Konodimini, Tintam, and Borko, also in Bambara country, and in the Dogon region near Sanga in the Cercle de Bandiagara.[55] The available data, however, seem to indicate that such moments of religious fervor were sporadic and thereby heighten the impression that Islam has been basically accommodating to and tolerant of local conditions and institutions, including representational art.

As a prelude to an intensive look at the phenomenon of compatibility between Islam and representational art in the area of my field research, it is instructive to touch on this topic briefly with reference to the greater Mande area. This casts the net wide, but the need for a broader look at the Islamized Mande and art traditions is essential for two reasons. The specific groups that I dealt with in the field are simply the southeasternmost extension of a very important historical, religious, and economic dispersal. The Mande in the Cercle de Bondoukou and western Brong-Ahafo cannot be treated in isolation, for their connections with Mande peoples to the north and west are intimate. Thus the same relationship between the visual arts and Islam noted in the field might well exist for other segments of the great Mande family.

In addition, although the dispersion of the Mande has been one of the primary forces leading to the expansion and consolidation of Islam in West Africa, it seems clear that the manner in which they were able to establish their religion varied considerably with circumstances. Muslim Mande com-

---

[53] Maurice Delafosse, *Haut-Sénégal – Niger*, vol. 2, p. 295.
[54] Trimingham, *Islam in West Africa*, p. 108, note 2.   [55] Ibid.

munities differ considerably in their organization, their commitment to the faith, and their relationships with non-Muslim peoples, yet there is ample evidence to indicate that the arts have survived Islamization in many of these communities. I have therefore selected examples of the visual arts from three distinctive Mande Muslim contexts in order to emphasize that masking and figurative traditions can survive and remain vigorous in a variety of Islamic settings. The first example is from the medieval empire of Mali during that early period of Islamic influence in the western Sudan when the religion was adopted solely as an additional and superficial imperial cult by the ruling estates and foreign mercantile classes of various Sudanic kingdoms. A second example, an unusual occurrence in the history of the Mande, comes from Dafina, in Upper Volta, an area revolutionized by jihād and dominated by the nineteenth-century Mande state of Wahabu. Finally, attention will be focussed on the state of Gonja in the northern region of Ghana, specifically the Bole division, where the Mande have played an important role in the creation and development of the kingdom while displaying great tolerance toward such local practices as the Simma masking tradition.

The earliest document on the Islamized Mande and the visual arts is the fourteenth-century account of Ibn Battuta, the ubiquitous Maghrebian traveler who visited the medieval empire of Mali and resided at the court of its ruler, Mansa Sulaiman ibn Abi Bakr. For the most part, Ibn Battuta, like other North African chroniclers who visited the Sudan during this period, focussed his attention on such questions as the status of Islam and the activity of Sudanese markets. Fortunately, Ibn Battuta was able to remain in Mali for a considerable time, and he recorded in some detail the pomp and pageantry that dominated court life. As a "good" North African Muslim he was appalled by the strange mutation of Islamic and non-Muslim rituals he witnessed. (Maghrebian assessments at that time regarding the quality of Islam in the Sudan were invariably quite low.) Luckily for us, he was disturbed enough by such practices to leave us the earliest description of a masked ritual from any area of sub-Saharan Africa.

According to Ibn Battuta, the court griots (*julā*) who performed in honor of the king dressed in feather costumes and wore wooden masks carved in the shape of a bird with a painted red beak. These masked dancers sat in front of Mansa Sulaiman reciting and singing poems of praise, exhorting him to perform noble deeds as long as he occupied the dais of the kingdom. After the recitation, each masked dancer placed his head on the lap and on each shoulder of the Mansa, obviously as a sign of deference.[56] Ibn Battuta was told that this custom pre-dated the introduction of Islam in Mali and that it had persisted despite the fact that Islam had been adopted by the Mande royal family as the official religion of the state.

[56] Ibn Battuta, *Voyages*, pp. 413–14.

47

A particularly interesting aspect of this account is the question of the actual timing of the masked ritual referred to by Ibn Battuta. He visited Mali in 1352–3 and states that he remained there long enough to witness the two major Islamic festivals, the *īd al-fiṭr* and the *īd al-adha*, which occur roughly four months apart.[57] The former is the feast of rejoicing following Ramadhan; the latter is the festival of the sacrifice occurring on the tenth day of the Muslim month of Dhū'l Ḥijja (the pilgrimage). Ibn Battuta mentions that the masked griots performed their recitations and masked dance at the court of Mansa Sulaiman on the day of the *īd*, which in Arabic simply means "festival." Did he mean that the masked performance occurred at the *īd* of the pilgrimage or at the one after Ramadhan or at both? These festivals are celebrated widely throughout Muslim West Africa as important state occasions, and prominent political individuals such as the griots might well have appeared at both of them. It is noteworthy that the performance of these masquerades coincided with at least one, and possibly two, of the most important and public of Muslim holidays, a feature that I observed among the Mande Dyula, Ligbi, and "Mandeized" Hwela in west central Ghana and the northeastern Ivory Coast.

Ibn Battuta's description of this courtly masking tradition clearly points to the co-existence of figurative art and Islam in an early Mande context. He goes on to note the gamut of regalia used at the court of the Mansa. Especially interesting is the reference to a gold-leafed bird figure surmounting a silken parasol held by a Turkish Mameluk attendant on Sulaiman sitting in state.[58] Islam among the ruling elite of Mali obviously did not destroy representational art. Yet even D. F. McCall, who grants that masking and figurative traditions continued among the Bambara and other non-Muslim cultures within the kingdom, feels that the occurrence of such art forms within the Islamized Sudanese ruling elite would have been highly unlikely. He says, "the rulers of Mali . . . were almost certainly anti-art and exerted pressure to relinquish the worship of idols . . ."[59] The available evidence, however, points to a very different situation.

Indeed, the historical interconnections between the Muslim elite and masking traditions might well be even more intimate than Ibn Battuta's description indicates. Father Henry noted that there is a Bambara tradition of origin (and it must be stressed that the Bambara were a major cultural component of the Mali empire) for the Komo society that credits the introduction of the cult to the Islamized ruling elite. This legend claims that certain important accoutrements of Komo were acquired by Mansa Mūsā, the older brother of Sulaiman, while on his famous pilgrimage to Mecca in 1324. The tradition credits Mūsā with having traded one of his magical

[57] Ibid., pp. 409–13.
[58] Ibid., pp. 403–8.
[59] *Africa in Time Perspective*, p. 115.

48

robes for the spirit of Komo and numerous *boli*, the altars that are a necessary feature of all Komo shrines and vital to the very functioning of the
cult.[60] Whether or not the details related in this tradition are actually true
cannot be verified, but what is pertinent is that some historical connection
or association between Komo and the Muslim ruling estate is clearly
implied in the legend.

That Ibn Battuta should have recorded the use of masks and figurative
art forms among the Islamized Mande elite of Mali is hardly surprising,
given the limited role that the religion enjoyed in the Sudanic state system.
Trimingham assessed the shallowness of Islamic penetration well:

> The introduction of Islam did not upset the equilibrium of the Sudan states
> nor provide them with a new basis of authority. Mansas of Mali, *jās* and *sīs* of
> Songhay, *mais* of Bornu, and chiefs of all lesser states, adopted Islam as the
> imperial cult without disturbance to the mythic basis of their authority. They
> did not attempt to spread it among subjects other than state servants, for that
> would have meant their downfall. Village life followed the same pattern as
> before. Rulers, though calling themselves Muslims and often reinforcing their
> authority by going on pilgrimage to the sacred house to acquire power, performed
> all traditional religious functions their position required for ensuring the welfare
> of the state.[61]

Individual rulers of Mali might well have demonstrated a strong attach-
ment to Islam because of the economic benefits derived from professing
the faith (for example, the profits of long-distance trade monopolized by
Muslim mercantile interests), but their religious and political positions
were ultimately based on allegiances to both Muslim and local standards of
life. Given these circumstances – and the fact of their existence is based on
a considerable body of evidence – Fagg's comment that "It is improbable,
then, that the Sudanese empires practised any but the geometric art of
Islamic cultures" is both contradictory and wholly unfounded.[62]

The compatibility of Islam and art within the Mande empire of Mali is
derived from a very early period of Islamic influence in the western Sudan,
a time when the impact of the religion on the Mande was decidedly restricted in scope and superficial in nature. Would the same results have
occurred under differing circumstances – for example, where jihād was
practiced and Islamic tenets prevailed? The answer is clearly yes, as will be
seen in the case of the Dafing of Upper Volta, a Mande people who
established an Islamic state in the heart of the Bobo country.

The Muslim Dafing, alternately known as the Bobo-Dyula, are another

[60] Joseph Henry, *L'Ame d'un peuple africain: les Bambara*, pp. 130–4. Other legends
dealing with the origins of the Komo are to be found in Charles Victor Monteil, *Les
Bambara du Segou et du Kaarta*, p. 270.
[61] *Islam in West Africa*, p. 139.
[62] Eliot Elisofon and Fagg, *The Sculpture of Africa*, p. 27.

segment of the great Mande family whose origins lie in the upper Niger region. They inhabit the area of Dafina, a region circumscribed by the northern bend of the Black Volta River. They appear to have arrived in this region as early as the fifteenth century, a period coinciding with other intensive Mande efforts towards the commercial colonization of the Volta basin.[63] The influx of Mande traders during this period led to the creation of a number of Dafing communities – e.g., Safane, Douroula, Boromo – amidst the decentralized non-Muslim Bobo and Nounouma. Although nothing is known of the relationship forged between these Muslim immigrants and the local populations, it seems probable, judging by the character of Mande intrusive settlements elsewhere, that a rough balance of power was maintained between the two groups.

By 1750, however, Dafina had experienced a second and more massive infusion of Mande traders and clerics from the heavily Islamized region of Jenne, and within the next seventy years the existing order was upset. In 1774–5 Sa'id ben Muḥammad al-Mustafā succeeded in creating the Saghanughu Imāmate at Bobo-Dioulasso,[64] and Safane developed into a famous Muslim town of learning.[65] Some thirty years later Al-Ḥājjī Mahmūd, the son of a cleric of Douroula, returned from his pilgrimage to Mecca, assumed the role of reformer, proclaimed a holy war against the inhabitants of Boromo, and established the state of Wahabu.[66] Mahmūd's goal was to create the foundations of a state worthy of the appellation Dar al-Islām, but his dream was only partially realized within his lifetime. He was succeeded by his nephew Karamoro Mukhtār who managed to maintain control of the state, despite numerous uprisings, until the arrival of the French.[67]

Although a true Islamic theocracy based solely on Qur'ānic legal and administrative precepts was never fully realized in Dafina, Al-Ḥājjī Mahmūd and his nephew managed to develop a small and vigorous political and religious entity in Wahabu. Wahabu was clearly based on a non-Muslim substratum, yet Islam flourished in the major Dafing communities. A level of Dar al-Islām was certainly attained in such towns as Safane, Douroula, and Bobo-Dioulasso, for their fame as centers of Islamic learning spread throughout the Voltaic region in the nineteenth century. These same Muslim communities, because of their far-flung reputations, also served as important stopovers for pilgrims traveling the southern

[63] Louis Tauxier, *Le Noir du Soudan*, p. 410.
[64] Wilks, "The Saghanughu and the Spread of Maliki Law," p. 72.
[65] Joseph Dupuis, *Journal of Residence in Ashantee*, Ms. no. 8. By 1825 the fame of Safane was considerable, being noted by Dupuis while he was at Kumasi.
[66] Elements of three Mande Muslim groups joined in the jihād of Al-Ḥājjī Mahmūd: Yarse-Mossi from Ouahigouya, Dagara-Dyula from Tessalima, and the local Marka-Dafing (Nehemiah Levtzion, *Muslims and Chiefs in West Africa*, pp. 150–1).
[67] Ibid., p. 149.

4. Do masqueraders at Kotedougou.

savannah Ḥajj route extending through the northern Ivory Coast and southern Upper Volta.[68]

It is precisely from what was and still is the nerve center of Islam in Dafina, the region between Safane and Bobo-Dioulasso, that evidence for the compatibility of Islam and another masking tradition, the Bobo Do or Dou cult, is derived. In 1888 the French explorer Louis-Gustave Binger recorded a Dou masquerade at Kotedougou (plate 4), a village inhabited by Bobo-Fing, Bobo-Dyula (Dafing), and Fulbe and situated some twenty miles east-northeast of Bobo-Dioulasso.

En approchant du village, je fus frappé de l'animation qui régnait aux abords . . .

Il y en avait, en effet, partout, autour des cases, sous les arbres, dans les champs, dansant, faisant la roue, marchant sur les mains, et courant de temps à autre après les spectateurs . . .

Les *dou* sont des individus ridiculement déguisés, portant des vêtements sur lesquels on a cousu du *dafou* (chanvre indigène), des fibres et des feuilles de palmier ban; comme coiffure, ils ont un bonnet ou une callotte également en *dafou*, surmonté d'un cimier en bois rougi à l'ocre, ou quelquefois muni d'un bec d'oiseau également en bois. Deux trous sont ménagés dans la callotte pour les yeux.[69]

[68] René Caillie, *Travels through Central Africa*, vol. 1, p. 259.
[69] *Du Niger au Golfe de Guinée*, vol. 1, pp. 378–9.

Although the Dou cult at Kotedougou was obviously controlled by the Bobo-Fing, it is worth noting that in this large village (Binger thought it had roughly 1,000 inhabitants) almost one-quarter of the population consisted of Muslim Dafing. According to Binger, the Mande of Kotedougou did not observe the Dou and in fact could not tell him anything relating to the tradition, but apparently they were not hostile to such ritual displays.[70] What is particularly surprising is that Binger witnessed a similar masked dance, for which he gives no details, at Bobo-Dioulasso, the Dafing center influenced by Mahmūd's jihād and dominated by the Saghanughu Imāmate.[71] He does not indicate who was in control of the Dou at Bobo-Dioulasso, but if it was in the hands of the Bobo, it had managed to survive and was operating in a most heavily Islamized environment.

Almost eighty years later, in 1966, Ivor Wilks witnessed a similar dance in Bobo-Dioulasso. The masquerade was held at night and was conducted by the Dafing (specifically the Sanu) in a funerary context.[72] The Sanu are one of the many Mande Dafing patronymic clans in Bobo country with a history of settlement dating back to the initial arrival of Mande immigrants in this region. According to Wilks, they have had a record of backsliding or apostasy but were reconverted in the mid-nineteenth century through Mahmūd's jihād and the religious activities of the Saghanughu.[73] The success with which they were brought back into the religious fold is revealed by the fact that at Bobo-Dioulasso "The Sanu . . . began a return to orthodoxy in the later nineteenth century, and in this century have taken over from the Saghanughu the imāmate of the central mosque."[74] Today they are clearly Muslim, although as Wilks points out, most Sanu are certainly not to be classified with the scholarly religious elite.[75] The majority of the Sanu are representative of the overwhelming percentage of Muslims in this area, indeed in West Africa, who are guided by the ideals of the five pillars of the faith and who thus qualify as Muslim.

Wilks's evidence for the Sanu masked funerary ritual is fragmentary, but he was able to record a number of tantalizing details. Since the masks were carried and no lights could be used visibility was poor, but it was clear that the masks were vertically oriented. The cult involved was referred to by the Sanu as Do and was certainly the same tradition Binger recorded at a much earlier date among the Bobo-Fing of Kotedougou. This masking association is found widely among the Bobo where it operates at a number of levels including the funerary context in which the Sanu were utilizing the masks. Like the masks witnessed by Wilks, Bobo Do masks are generally

[70] Ibid., p. 379. [71] Ibid., p. 378.
[72] My thanks to Ivor Wilks for data concerning the use of the Do masks by the Muslim Sanu of Bobo-Dioulasso. [73] Letter to the author, July 25, 1969.
[74] Wilks, "Transmission of Islamic Learning," p. 193, note 2.
[75] Letter of July 25, 1969.

surmounted by a large vertical superstructure.[76] This might well indicate that the Sanu pieces were either acquired from the Bobo or that this Muslim group had adopted the types and styles of such masks from their non-Muslim neighbors. Like their non-Muslim counterparts, all the Sanu masqueraders were totally enveloped in raffia to keep their identity secret.

An important aspect of the data communicated by Wilks deals with the attitudes held by the Islamic elite toward such a masking tradition and its use by fellow Muslims. (The views held by the more learned Sanu, such as those associated with the central mosque, were not obtained.) The Saghanughu clerics of Bobo-Dioulasso feel such Sanu practices are clearly unlawful and therefore will take no part in them. Wilks mentioned that the Saghanughu would not even direct him to the part of the town where the ritual was to take place. He was taken to the Sanu quarter by the mufti's son, but his guide would not remain to watch the proceedings.[77] Yet the Saghanughu, like so many Muslim religious leaders, realize that little can be done to suppress or destroy such a cult, for it does provide a measure of security for the mass of believers that has proven at least as effective as the measures ordained by Islamic scripture. Wilks underlines the point that, although members of the clergy are very sensitive about the persistence of such "pagan" practices within their domains, they are pragmatic enough to realize that Islam has been and must continue to be accommodating if it is to remain strong and expand.[78]

Our final example comes from the Bole division of Gonja in north-western Ghana where yet other Mande patronymic clans have constituted one of the important elements of this conquest state ever since its foundation in the sixteenth century. Unlike their fellow Muslims in Dafina, the Mande in Gonja neither attempted to establish their own authority through the creation of an Islamic theocratic state nor pursued the course of jihād in order to expand the boundaries of the faith. Levtzion recognizes this feature of Muslim settlement in Gonja as being broadly characteristic of Islamic (both Mande and Hausa) penetration throughout much of the middle Volta region, including the states of Wa, Mamprussi, and Dagomba.

Muslims in the Middle Volta states became integrated into the social and political system, identifying themselves as members of these states. Though in personal conduct they endeavoured to observe the rules of Islam as much as

---

[76] The woodblock print of the Do masquerade at Kotedougou by Riou, who accompanied Binger on his expedition, reveals Do masks in two very different styles. One consists of a small straight wooden crest resting on top of the dancer's head; the other is a somewhat more typical Bobo bird-faced mask with a strong projecting beak but without the superstructure above the mask itself. These masks seem to represent style variations within the Do tradition that differ considerably from the usual examples encountered in Western museums, private collections, and surveys on African art. They may, however, also be a product of Riou's artistic imagination, for many of his sketches go beyond the realm of pure documentation. (Binger, *Du Niger au Golfe de Guinée*, vol. 1, p. 379.) [77] Letter of July 25, 1969. [78] Ibid.

possible, they presented Islam to their chiefs in mild and diluted forms. In this way they were able to build up communication with the chiefs, winning their sympathy towards Islam and preparing the way for further Islamic influence.[79]

In Gonja the Mande maintained themselves as a cohesive unit within a tightly stratified society consisting of three major social groupings. The Ngbanya, or ruling elite, are the unilineal descendants of the non-Muslim Mande invader and founder of Gonja, Ndewura Jakpa. The Karamo, or Muslims, are referred to by Goody as "a kind of deuxième état" and include numerous Mande clans, the most important being the Sakpare, who are the only Muslims eligible for the position of Imām in Gonja divisions, their claim resting on their descent from the Mallam who assisted Jakpa in his conquest by supplying him with a variety of spiritual services.[80] The third group is the Nyamase, the non-Muslim commoners, who are either autochthonous to the area or immigrants, some having arrived shortly before the invading Mande, others after.[81]

Social differentiation was and continues to be clearly defined not only through the entire state but in all of the divisions of the realm. Each division, in fact, is simply a small-scale reflection of the total configuration of Gonja, with the three social estates represented in all of them. In the Bole division, centered in the capital town of Bole where the royal court is located, leadership is vested in the Bolewura, a direct descendant of the fifth son of Jakpa. He is aided in his administrative duties by a host of subordinate officials, all Ngbanya, who are attached to the court and serve as chiefs in the various villages of the division.[82] The Muslims in the town of Bole form a sizable community, the most important elements being the Sakpare and Dabo, both hereditary Mande clans exempt from paying tribute because of their historical associations with Jakpa. Two other Muslim groups are also resident in the town: the Mbontisuwa or "Akan Muslims," who are descendants of Mande from the Techiman area of western Brong-Ahafo, and various Muslim trading families, Mande and Hausa, who settled in the town of Bole after the conquest.[83] Both the Mbontisuwa and the newest trading families are considered strangers and thus are required to pay tribute to the Ngbanya. The Sakpare Imām serves as both head of the entire community of believers and an important advisor to the Bolewura; the Nso'owura, or chief of the Muslims, is the Muslims' representative to the royal court and head of the *dogtes* or court heralds. Commoners occupy various wards within the town of Bole itself, these being based on tribal affiliation, but the large majority live in their own

[79] *Muslims and Chiefs in West Africa*, p. 192.
[80] J. R. Goody, "The Over-Kingdom of Gonja," pp. 186–7.
[81] Interview at Bole, August 9 and 10, 1967.
[82] Levtzion, *Muslims and Chiefs in West Africa*, pp. 55–6.
[83] Goody, "The Over-Kingdom of Gonja," p. 200.

villages, which are scattered throughout the division. Nyamase villages are governed by an earthpriest, who is himself a Nyamase and is considered to be both the political and religious head, and by a Ngbanya chief representing the Bolewura and the ruling elite.

The highly stratified nature of Gonja society clearly evident in the Bole division is counterbalanced, according to Goody, by a set of unifying factors that are political, religious, and social in nature. The most important integrative force is based on the very history of the state:

> What [gave] massive support to national unity [and a feeling of cohesion within the divisions] was the ideology of common descent held by all members of the widely dispersed ruling estate who regarded themselves as the offspring of Ndewura Jakpa. Not only members of the ruling estate but also the local Muslims stressed the Jakpa legend and provided it with the sanction of literacy and of a world religion. Even the commoners constantly placed themselves in relation to the coming of the conqueror.[84]

Underlying this binding historical ideology are numerous rituals, deriving from all three estates, which further unify the social groups in each of the divisions and throughout the state. Dynastic shrines associated with the Ngbanya occur throughout Gonja; these are invariably in the hands of either Muslims or commoners, who are thus given access to and privileges regarding the maintenance of these historical centers. At the village of Mankuma, just north of the town of Bole, for example, is the royal burial ground of past Yagbumwura, the paramount chiefs of all Gonja; this site is controlled by Nyamase.[85] The cycle of Gonja state festivals is based largely on the Muslim calendar, and the holiday of Damba (Muḥammad's circumcision) is the most critical time of the year, for it is then that all estates come together to reconfirm their allegiance to one another.[86] Earth and medicine shrines controlled by the Nyamase are considered essential to the well-being of the state and are consulted by members of both the royal and Muslim estates. The annual purification rites for these shrines, for example Senyon-Kupo in the village of Senyon east of Bole, are attended by all three classes and by the reigning Yagbumwura.[87] In these ways, each social group contributes to the ultimate cohesion of Gonja society and expresses itself within the total body politic.

It is against this backdrop of social interaction and cooperation that the Simma society, a masking tradition associated with certain Nyamase groups of the Bole division, is best understood. The distribution of Simma

---

[84] Ibid., p. 201.
[85] Interview at Bole, August 16, 1967.
[86] A detailed description of the Bole Damba ceremony appears in H. H. Tomlinson, "The Customs, Constitution, and History of the Gonja People," pp. 13–15. I witnessed the Damba at Bole in 1967.
[87] Interview at Senyon, August 17, 1967.

is quite broad, occurring among the Vagala and Tampolense (Gur-Grusi speakers), and the Nome and Batige (Gur-Mossi), who inhabit a number of small villages north and east of the town of Bole.[88] Only one historical source exists for the Simma – that of H. H. Tomlinson, who recorded the tradition in 1953 at the Tampolense village of Sala. Although he does not clearly describe the function of the cult, his description of Simma, or Sigma as he calls it, is valuable.

The Sigma Fetish originated in the Tampluma area, but now has followers in many villages of North Western Gonja. Sigma is a secret society. Any member who has a complaint to make may go to the Fetish hut, don his vestments and thus disguised go round the village voicing his complaint. His anonymity is protected by the Fetish. When a prominent man dies, provided he has not offended the Fetish, the members of the Fetish, in his village, will put on their costumes and caper round the town . . .

The vestments of this society, which are kept in a small thatched hut set apart from the village, consist of small black fibre skirts extending into pantallettes and made in one piece, [and] a fuzzy wuzzy head-dress the front of which is formed by a wooden mask carved and painted in the likeness of a face. Each of the Fetish villages has a different face carving. At Kunfosi it is a bush cow or a child; at Sala a herte beast.[89]

My own research revealed a far greater range of activities for Simma: the masks (plates 5, 6) were said to be used during the dry season to help bring rain; they performed at the funerals of elderly members of the cult; and they could be called upon to perform at the interment of Ngbanya chiefs and Muslims if their families so desired. All Nyamase associated with Simma conceded, however, that it was most often used to counteract the evil effects of witches. Although owned and controlled by the non-Muslim commoners, the society was open to and performed for the benefit of the people of all three estates. Muslims did not join Simma but consulted the cult elders of various villages; the powerful Simma at the Batige village of Kunfosi was often consulted for remedies against witchcraft.[90]

The powers of Simma are acknowledged by members of all three social groups in the Bole division and even by the Imām of Bole and the Bolewura. According to local tradition, the authority of the paramount chief is such that anything he seizes with his right hand becomes his personal property, but this prerogative does not extend to the Simma. The Bolewura has no jurisdiction over the society, and its masqueraders may in principle even go so far as to ridicule and physically abuse him.[91] Since this is a recognized

---

88 I recorded Simma society masks in these villages: two in the Vagala village of Jentilepe; four at Jang (Vagala); two at Nahari (Nome); two at Kulmasa (Nome); three at Ypala (Nome); and two at Kunfosi (Batige).
89 "The Customs, Constitution, and History of the Gonja People," pp. 11–12.
90 Interview at Kunfosi, August 14, 1967.
91 Interview at Bole, August 16, 1967.

5. Simma masks; wood; black, white, ochre paint. Female (left) l. 22″; male l. 27″. Vagala village of Jang.

6. Simma mask, male; wood; ochre, white, black paint; l. 28″. Batige village of Kunfosi.

assertion of the society's strength and independence, the Bolewura cannot take action against its members – individuals who, when Simma is not operating, pay proper obeisance to their paramount chief.[92]

Among the Muslims of Bole, including Imām Abdulai, Simma is regarded as the third most powerful Nyamase cult in the division, its strength and reputation being eclipsed only by that of Senyon Kupo and Tigare. The cult has not been censured by the Sakpare, the Dabo, or other Muslims for two reasons: it has served as an effective deterrent to the potentially overriding power and authority of the Ngbanya, and it has worked effectively for those Muslims who have sought additional or alternative means to combat a variety of problems – witchcraft, crop failure, disease, and so forth.[93] The functioning of the cult was generally viewed not as a threat to the authority and the role of clerics but as the representation of another means by which Muslims could achieve a feeling of security. Muslim attitudes concerning Simma were similar to those expressed about other non-Muslim shrines in the division – they were not necessarily pernicious or evil, for they operated in most instances in a positive manner and hence as integrative features that helped to bind the various groups of the Bole division.

These three examples from the greater Mande region, based on very different Islamized Mande contexts, reveal some of the positive associations that can exist between Muslim peoples and traditional art forms. As such, these instances indicate not only the flexibility with which Muslims have adapted themselves to local cultural situations but also the tenacity of indigenous art traditions.

[92] At Kunfosi I was told that all Nyamase must prostrate themselves before the Bolewura but that this was not necessary for those dressed in the costumes of Simma, although they generally did so anyway. Interview, August 14, 1967.
[93] Interview at Bole, August 18, 1967.

CHAPTER 4

HISTORY OF THE MUSLIM MANDE IN THE CERCLE DE BONDOUKOU AND WEST CENTRAL GHANA

The features described for the movement of Islam throughout West Africa are characteristic of the history of Islam among the great Mande families who were responsible for carrying the religion from the borders of the sahel to the savannah and the Guinea Coast forest. Attention will be focussed primarily on two Mande groups, the Dyula and Ligbi, for these mobile merchants and clerics were intimately associated with the spread of Islam into the Volta basin, the upper Sassandra and Comoe river valleys of the Ivory Coast, and ultimately into the Cercle de Bondoukou and west central Ghana.

Almost twenty years ago, J. R. Goody lamented the fact that almost no study, with the exception of the works of early French writers, had been devoted to the position of the Mande throughout this area.

The extent of Mande influence in the Western Sudan has not been fully appreciated, particularly by historians of the Gold Coast. Meyerowitz, concentrating upon the "dia," overlooks or misinterprets much of the evidence; Rattray is skeptical concerning the claims of the Wa Moslems to have come from Mande. French authors, and especially Binger, Delafosse and Labouret, all *Mande* scholars, have been much more conscious of this influence . . .[1]

Two works by Goody, "A Note on the Penetration of Islam into the West of the Northern Territories of the Gold Coast" and *The Ethnography of the Northern Territories of the Gold Coast West of the White Volta*, initiated further studies dealing with the Muslim Mande. They were followed by a number of pioneering works by Ivor Wilks, who over the last ten years has contributed significantly to our knowledge of the Mande not only in such savannah states as Dagomba, Gonja, and Mamprusi but also in the forest-based Ashanti confederacy. More recently Nehemiah Levtzion's study of Islamization in the middle Volta basin has helped to place the larger Voltaic region within the overall perspective of West African Islam and

[1] *The Ethnography of the Northern Territories of the Gold Coast West of the White Volta*, p. 17.

has underscored the broad-ranging effects of Mande colonization through-out much of this region.[2] Thanks to the efforts of these and other research-ers, a sizable body of evidence has been gathered on the historical influence of the Mande Dyula and Ligbi.

Goody has found further evidence in the linguistic maps of West Africa for the depth to which these two Mande peoples penetrated the savannah country of the Ivory Coast and the Volta basin.

As can be seen from the map in "The Languages of West Africa," languages of the *Mande* family are distributed right along the great trade route which led from the Niger bend down to the Begho–Bondoukou area.

A second tongue of *Mande-Tan* languages, mainly Dyula, extends into the Voltaic area in the direction of Bobo-Dioulasso and Boromo, another region in which gold was obtained, "en grande quantité" according to Binger.[3]

Similar extensions of Mande-Tan languages, especially Dyula, are found in the Ivory Coast in the areas of Man, Odienné, Seguela within the area of the upper Sassandra River, throughout the Senufo region, and parti-cularly in the southern stretches of Jimini, along the Bondoukou–Dabakala–Kong axis, and in Bouna.[4] As Goody stresses, purely linguistic evidence for the distribution of the Mande can be deceiving:

The influence of the *Mande*-speaking peoples cannot be judged only by the present distribution of the various dialects and languages. For in many areas such as Wa (the Dagaa-Dyula), Mossi (the Yarse, specialized traders of Dyula origin) and Gonja (the ruling lineages of Bambara or Malinke descent), the Mande immigrants, entering as traders or as conquerors, adopted the language of the indigenes . . . Even where they did not form a substantial proportion of the population their influence was great. The association of the founders of the Mamprusi group of states, namely Mamprusi, Mossi (of Yatenga and Wagadugu), Gurma, Dagomba, Wa and Nanumba, with Mande is explicit in the "drum histories."[5]

But even where Mande peoples have not retained their original languages and dialects – as occurs east of the Black Volta River, where they were integrated far more completely into traditional state structures than were Mande groups west of this boundary – other evidence exists that allows us to identify Mande movements and reconstruct their prominent role in the Voltaic basin.

To this day, Dyula and Ligbi settlers throughout this vast sector of West Africa have maintained traditions of origin that associate them with

[2] *Muslims and Chiefs in West Africa.*
[3] Goody, *Ethnography of the Northern Territories*, p. 17, referring to Diedrich Westermann and M. A. Bryan, *Languages of West Africa*, pp. 33–6.
[4] Westermann and Bryan, *Languages of West Africa*, pp. 33–6.
[5] Goody, *Ethnography of the Northern Territories*, p. 19.

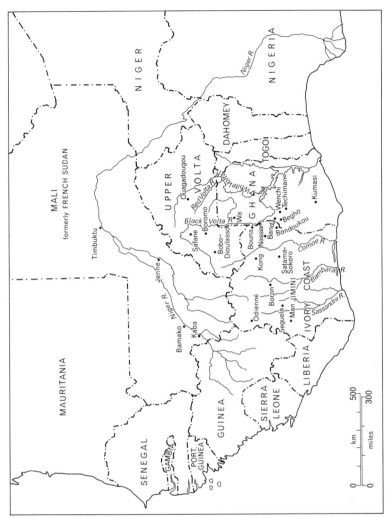

1. The Mande Dyula and Ligbi zone, West Africa.

the heartland of Mande country. Like all other highly dispersed Mande peoples, be they non-Muslim or Muslim, the Islamized Dyula and Ligbi trace their histories back to Kaba (O.S. Kangaba), which is approximately 120 miles southwest of Bamako on the left bank of the upper Niger River (map 1). Though a small village, Kaba is an important ritual center, for every seven years local Mande inhabitants, under the supervision of the royal Keita clan, re-enact in dramatic fashion the creation myth of the Mande people.[6] Even the most far-flung and historically isolated of Mande

---

[6] Germaine Dieterlen, "The Mande Creation Myth," pp. 124–5.

communities acknowledge Kaba as their home and as the heartland of Mande culture. Dyula and Ligbi groups in the Cercle de Bondoukou and west central Ghana, for example, generally maintain a strong sense of their historical past, but even when details concerning their migration from the area of the upper Niger to their present locations are forgotten they continue to retain traditions regarding Kaba. For them the memory of Kaba is critical, since it preserves their historical identity and integrity as an immigrant population; they refer to this small village with enthusiasm and pride.

In addition to preserving historical traditions that reveal their Mande origins, the Dyula and Ligbi continue to refer to themselves by their Mande patronymic clan names. According to Ivor Wilks, even though some Dyula groups have lost their original language through centuries of assimilation, "All Dyula persist in the use of Malinke and Soninke [Mande] salutation names: Tarawiri (Fr. Traoré), Sissay (Cissé), Kunatay (Konaté), Kamaghatay, Jabaghatay, and the rest."[7] The retention of these patronymics has been crucial in preserving the overall unity of the clans, for there is little organization to the clans themselves. A common name obligates every individual within a clan to offer aid and hospitality to fellow members, and this creates a feeling of community among even the most widely dispersed Mande groups. One's name thus serves as a passbook, for any Dyula or Ligbi knows that he will find lodging, companionship, and help wherever fellow clan members reside.[8] Mande cultural identity is maintained through the use of these names, but in certain instances, as Goody cautions,

The presence of these clan names is not in itself a reliable indication of Mande origin, as we have seen in the case of the Senufo and the ruling lineages of Buna; the prestige of the Mande, and in particular of the Moslem Dyulas, was such that others tended to adopt their clan names as well as their religion and their dress.[9]

He goes on to emphasize, however, that the appearance of clan names, when found in conjunction with Mande traditions of origin and linguistic evidence, allows the researcher to gauge the impact of the Mande throughout the region.

The penetration of the Islamized Mande, specifically the Dyula and Ligbi, into the Voltaic region and ultimately to the forest fringes of the Ivory Coast and present-day Ghana, is one of considerable antiquity.

---

[7] "Transmission of Islamic Learning," p. 163.
[8] Goody feels that there is some similarity between the Mande clan or *diammu* and the clan system as found among the Ashanti. In both cases "There is no internal organization above this lineage level nor is the unity of the group ever expressed in any joint meeting or ceremony. Common descent carries with it a common name and a common avoidance; it is associated with the obligation to marry out and with the idea of joint rights over property . . ." *Ethnography of the Northern Territories*, p. 19, note 4.
[9] Ibid., p. 19.

Although there is a good deal of controversy over when such movements began, Wilks's arguments for an early-fifteenth-century dating (based on oral traditions, the marked development of Jenne during this period as a major entrepot for gold-trading activities to the south, and increased European demands for this precious metal) are indeed convincing.[10] Furthermore, Levtzion points out that it was approximately at this time that the earliest known instances of state development within the Volta basin occurred, these being Bono-Mansu in the Bron forest country and the Mossi-Dagomba states in the savannah.

All these states were associated with the trade-route from the Niger to the forest. The states offered security to the trade, and the benefit their rulers derived from controlling the routes helped them in consolidating their authority.[11]

Some time during this period, then, dynamic Mande trading families were led by their commercial instincts beyond the borders of the Malian empire and towards the south in an attempt to forge closer trading links with the gold- and kola-producing areas of the Volta basin.

The earliest of these conscious Mande movements towards the gold-bearing regions of the south appears to have occurred in the Bobo country of Upper Volta. It was into the region of the upper Black Volta River, the area known as Dafina, that Dyula traders came during the fifteenth century in an attempt to create trading colonies that would tap the fabulous gold reserves of Poura, Baporo, Filampou, Soumbo, and Diensi.[12] All these gold centers lay astride the upper Black Volta, and it is significant that Dyula settlement during this period, and even later, occurred in Dafina, just to the west and northwest of this river. Each Dyula market town – Boromo, Wahabu (O.S. Ouahabou), Safane, and Bobo-Dioulasso – was established close to an auriferous field and along a major artery of trade leading to the gold emporium of Jenne. Ideally located, these towns eventually mono-polized the gold trade between Dafina and the Niger River.

Other Dyula and Ligbi groups extended their activities even deeper into the Voltaic region during this period. The earliest Islamized Mande Dyula element in Mossi country, known locally as the Yarse, probably arrived at the end of the fifteenth or in the early part of the sixteenth century, settling in Ouagadougou, where it created its own ward.[13] Subsequent waves of Yarse traders settled both to the north and south of Ouagadougou, their communities to the south (such as Kombissiri and Dakaye) again being crucially located in relation to the Mossi–Gourounsi gold areas lying between

[10] *The Northern Factor in Ashanti History*, pp. 5–7.
[11] *Muslims and Chiefs in West Africa*, pp. 5–6.
[12] Louis Tauxier, *Le Noir du Soudan*, p. 410. The gold fields along the upper Black Volta are clearly seen in Raymond Mauny's *Tableau Géographique*, pp. 293–7. P. 295 includes a useful map of the major gold-bearing regions of West Africa.
[13] Tauxier, *Le Noir du Soudan*, pp. 464–6.

the confluence of the Red and White Voltas.[14] Further south and to the southwest, a small group of Mande Ligbi had already moved across the Lobi gold fields and taken up residence at the Kulango town of Bouna in the northeastern corner of the present-day Ivory Coast. They claim to have arrived at Bouna before the coming of the Dagomba, who established the Bouna dynasty in the mid-sixteenth century, and well before fellow Ligbi traders joined them in the early eighteenth century after the collapse of Begho.[15] Just to the east of the Lobi gold fields, near the town of Wa, other Islamized Dyula appear to have settled three trading villages – Nasa, Vise, and Palwogho – at some time during the sixteenth century.[16] There is, moreover, evidence to indicate that some Mande elements penetrated even further south during the fifteenth century – that is, to the very fringes of the Voltaic forest zone. The fifteenth-century Bron state of Bono-Mansu, for example, appears to have been involved with the gold and kola trade to the Niger, and according to local traditions its capital town had a sizable complement of Muslim traders who resided there in their own quarters.[17] To the north and east of Bono-Mansu, at Buipe and Jakpawause in the area of the confluence of the Black and White Voltas, archeological research has revealed early habitation sites and painted ceramic traditions that seem to be associated with Mande trading activities and may well derive from this same period.[18] Northwest of Bono-Mansu, in the Banda district of west central Ghana, the town of "Old Bima" was probably colonized by Mande Dyula and Ligbi traders at this early date.[19]

The most important southern Mande commercial center established during the fifteenth century seems to have been Begho or Be'o, which was some twenty miles west-northwest of Bono-Mansu. It was at Begho that Islamized Ligbi and Dyula traders, accompanied by non-Muslin black-smiths of the Mande clan known as Numu, met and created not only a highly active gold and kola market but also the most vital Muslim community of the southern savannah. Two separate migrations of these Mande traders occurred: the Ligbi arrived from the west, the area of Boron and the Jimini sector of the Ivory Coast; the Dyula moved into the region from the north, possibly from the gold centers of Bouna and Wa.[20] The develop-

---

[14] Levtzion, *Muslims and Chiefs in West Africa*, p. 165.
[15] Ibid., pp. 201–2 and interview at the Ligbi quarter of Bouna.
[16] Levtzion, *Muslims and Chiefs in West Africa*, p. 139. Indeed, the early arrival of the Ligbi and Dyula both at Bouna and in the area of Wa might well have prompted the Dagomba, as Levtzion suggests, to bring both gold-laden regions under their control during the sixteenth century.
[17] Eva L. R. Meyerowitz, *The Akan of Ghana*, pp. 106–22.
[18] René A. Bravmann and R. D. Mathewson, "History and Archaeology of 'Old Bima,'" pp. 146–7.
[19] Ibid., pp. 136–9. For possible Mande influence at Ahwene Koko, the predecessor to the state of Wenchi, see Paul Ozanne, "Seventeenth-Century Wenchi."
[20] Levtzion, *Muslims and Chiefs in West Africa*, pp. 8–9, and Yves Person, "En quête d'une chronologie ivoirienne," pp. 326–9.

ment of Begho on the very edge of the Akan forest enabled the Dyula and Ligbi to control the flow of gold stemming from the deposits of Banda and the Tain basin and placed them in an ideal position with respect to the highly productive kola-nut forest country to the south. Although Begho was probably only a small local market consisting of Bron, Hwela, and Guang inhabitants prior to the arrival of the Mande, it was to become the southern terminus for the important Mande trade route connecting Jenne, Bobo-Dioulasso, Kong, and Bouna with the country of the Akan.[21]

Somewhat later, in the sixteenth and seventeenth centuries, other Dyula and Ligbi trading families established themselves further west in the southern savannah country of the Ivory Coast. Their movements into Barabo, the area just west of Bondoukou, resulted in the foundation of such important trading centers as Yerebodi, Sandhuei, and Bandakiani-Sokoro during the late sixteenth century.[22] Like Begho and Bono-Mansu, these towns were located just north of the forest and controlled the flow of gold and kola, in this case coming from the area of Anno and the southeastern Ivory Coast, which came under Agni control in the early eighteenth century. Even farther west, across the Comoe River and north of what was to become the Baule-dominated forest zone, yet other Dyula families settled in the southern Senufo country of Jimini. Even today many of the mixed Dyula–Senufo towns in Jimini, for example, Satama-Sokoro and Mborla-Dioulasso, trace their origins back to the first appearances of the Mande in southern Jimini.[23] In the savannah country between the Bandama and Sassandra rivers, additional Dyula and Ligbi groups established the important entrepots of Boron and Seguela, which tied the western Ivory Coast forest region with Mande commercial communities upstream from Jenne.[24] Thus by the beginning of the eighteenth century, Dyula and Ligbi traders had succeeded in establishing a continuous line of southern markets stretching from the modern-day border between Guinea and the Ivory Coast to the confluence of the Black and White Voltas.

Although this impressive southerly expansion of Dyula, Ligbi, and other Mande trading elements was clearly predicated on economic desires, an important corollary to these movements is the early spread of Islamic agents into the same regions. Little is known of the religious impact of the Dyula and Ligbi at this early period, but it is safe to assume that their influence in general was distinctly limited, for their primary aim was the control of trade and markets. The famous center of Begho, however, appears to have been an exception, for it was here that the earliest proselytizing success of the Mande occurred: the Ligbi conversion of the indigenous Hwela.

[21] Wilks, *The Northern Factor*, p. 8.
[22] Paul Marty, *Etudes sur l'Islam en Côte d'Ivoire*, pp. 220–33, and interviews with the Timitay 'ulamā' of Bondoukou, January 24 and 25, 1968.
[23] Marty, *L'Islam en Côte d'Ivoire*, pp. 80–1, 205–13.
[24] Person, "En quête d'une chronologie ivoirienne," pp. 326–8.

Be'o accommodated, therefore, two autochthonous groups: Hwela and Brong. The earth-priest of the ritual area around Namasa [the Hwela village built shortly after the destruction of Begho and located very near the old site of this famous trading center] is a Hwela. This suggests that the Hwela were the earlier residents in the area. It is likely that the chiefs of old Be'o were Hwela because the Hwela, rather than the Brong, came under the religious and cultural influence of the Ligby. Generally speaking, when Muslims come to settle in a pagan state their close relations are with the chiefly estate rather than with the commoners; the chiefs adopt Islamic customs and beliefs while the subjects remain far longer untouched by Islam.

The Ligby must have lived in Be'o for quite a long time to allow the decisive impact they had over the Hwela. About half of the Hwela adopted Islam and the Ligby language.[25]

The Hwela were not only culturally "Mande-ized" and converted by the Ligbi but apparently were also heavily influenced by the Dyula. Hwela tradition acknowledges that since the acceptance of Islam, the Imāms of Namasa have all borne the name Kamaghatay, a Dyula patronymic.[26] It is clear, however, that the religious influence of the Ligbi and Dyula did not stop at Begho itself, for evidence cited by Wilks from the Gonja chronicle strongly suggests that Islam was introduced from Begho into the Gonja state in the seventeenth century by Muslim clerics, also of the Kamaghatay clan.

At that time the Begho *Shaykh* Ismā'īl, and his son Muhammad al-Abyad, converted to the faith the Malinke-Bambara ruling aristocracy of Gonja, then the rising power in northern Ghana.[27]

Levtzion places this important event – the dissemination of Islam from Begho across the Black Volta River and into Gonja – in perspective when he observes that,

Considering the impact of the Gonja Islam on neighbouring states, in particular Dagomba, one should underline the significance of Be'o in initiating the process of Islamization in this region.[28]

Elsewhere, however, early Dyula and Ligbi settlement led to only minimal gains for the religion. Mande infiltration of Barabo and southern Jimini, for example, left little impression on the indigenous Kulango and Senufo inhabitants. A few Senufo villages in Jimini, such as Ouandarama and Tintinkam-Dioulasso, received Dyula settlers in the seventeenth century from the important Mande-dominated community of Satama-Sokoro, but only a small number of Senufo families were converted to the

[25] Levtzion, *Muslims and Chiefs in West Africa*, p. 10.
[26] Ibid.
[27] Wilks, "Ghana," p. 1003.
[28] *Muslims and Chiefs in West Africa*, p. 10.

faith.[29] In Barabo, where Dyula and Ligbi traders achieved a clear commercial dominance over the autochthonous population (in this case the Kulango), they had even less religious effect on their neighbors.[30] Thus by the end of the seventeenth century Islam was still for the most part professed only by the immigrant Dyula and Ligbi. Its influence was limited to the numerous Mande communities that had been created between the Comoe River and the Volta confluence, and only in the exceptional case of the Hwela of Begho and the Gbanya rulers of Gonja did the religion make any appreciable inroads into the neighboring non-Muslim societies.

With the turn of the eighteenth century came a series of events that resulted in the decline of the most important of the Mande centers (Begho, Bono-Mansu, "Old Wenchi," and "Old Bima") and a major population shift of their Dyula and Ligbi inhabitants. Several factors, internal and external, appear to have precipitated this. The vital commercial arteries that had tied these flourishing markets to the trading emporia of the middle Niger River had slowly fallen into chaos, especially along their northern terminals, as a result of the instabilities wrought by the Moroccan conquest of Songhay. Furthermore, increased European activity on the Gold Coast diverted much of the gold trade to the south and away from the hands of Mande merchants in these trading communities. But it was the gradual expansion of Ashanti towards the rich gold fields of the northwest and her ultimate victories over Bono-Mansu and Begho by 1725 that finally brought about the eclipse of Mande fortunes throughout the area.[31] The oral traditions of Dyula and Ligbi groups who trace their histories back to Begho maintain that the town was not destroyed by external forces but by internal conflicts between the non-Muslims and the Islamized Mande inhabitants. Such a tradition may well be founded on historical truth, as Levtzion suggests, but the primary reasons for the collapse of Begho and other Mande markets were probably external rather than internal.[32]

The collapse of Begho and the other Mande communities and the subsequent dispersal of the Ligbi, Dyula, and Hwela had important repercussions for the future of Islam throughout west central Ghana and the northeastern Ivory Coast. Abandoning their old markets, these dynamic Muslim traders and clerics went north and west, settling in pre-existing non-Muslim villages or founding new communities. Most of the Ligbi moved first to Banda, the Nafana-dominated state just to the north of the

[29] Marty, *L'Islam en Côte d'Ivoire*, pp. 200–1.
[30] Conversion of the rural-based Kulango has not met with any real success, and even today very few have adopted Islam. Some take on the outward appearances of being Muslim by wearing long gowns, carrying Qur'ānic amulets, and abstaining from intoxicating beverages, but beyond these superficial concessions they remain attached to their traditional ways.
[31] Levtzion, *Muslims and Chiefs in West Africa*, pp. 10–11.
[32] Ibid.

deserted site of Begho, and here established the village of Jinini on the
very western border of that state. Others located themselves at the capital
town of Banda-Ahenkro, creating their own wards of Sase and Kankan.[33]
Another Ligbi segment, under the leadership of Al-Ḥājjī Moro Bamba,
moved beyond Banda to the northwest and into the Cercle de Bondoukou,
settling at what is today the important village of Bondo (O.S. Bondo-
Dyoula).[34] Yet others pushed as far north as Bouna, where they joined
Ligbi families who had controlled the gold trade of this town ever since
the late fifteenth century.

Mobile Dyula clans followed their commercial instincts even farther
afield. Many settled at Bondoukou, a rather small and commercially
insignificant Bron town in the early eighteenth century that through their
efforts was to become the economic heir to Begho in the succeeding two
centuries. Others traveled west of Bondoukou into the Mande-dominated
region of Barabo, where they augmented virtually all of the older Dyula
colonies that had been founded there during the initial stages of Mande
penetration.[35] Certain Dyula groups took up residence at Kong and Bouna
and were instrumental in the ultimate development of these two vital
centers of Islamic trade and learning.

For the most part, the "Mande-ized" Hwela remained in the area
immediately adjacent to the ruins of Begho, resettling at the village of
Namasa, although a few families did relocate farther west. Those who left
made their new homes in Sorhobango, a prominent Kulango village twelve
miles north of Bondoukou, and at Nassian, an important subsidiary commercial center also under the control of the Kulango and on the
Boudoukou–Dabakala road.

The impact of the commercially inclined Mande on the numerous towns
and villages of the northeastern Ivory Coast and west central Ghana was
profound. A measure of their influence is gained from Bowdich's early-
nineteenth-century map of Ashanti and her possessions, in which he
enumerates what were acknowledged at the time to be the most important
markets lying to the northwest of greater Ashanti. In every instance, the
towns cited are those which were directly affected by the Mande dispersal
from Begho, Bono-Mansu, and elsewhere: Bundoo (which undoubtedly
refers to the Ligbi center of Bondo), Nessea (Nessian), Buntookoo (Bondoukou), Kong, and Namasa.[36] It is important to note, however, that this

[33] Traditions collected from the Bamba 'ulamā' of Sase and Jinini indicate that the Bamba
left Begho because of a civil war and that they came to settle in Banda because of their
earlier contacts with the Nafana. Before the downfall of Begho the Ligbi had already
been active gold agents for the Nafana, and their move here was a logical choice.
[34] Al-Ḥājjī Moro Bamba is acknowledged by the Ligbi of Bondo as one of the great
Bamba scholars and religious leaders. His grave, which is located between Bondo and
its sister village Bondo-Koulango (a predominantly Kulango village), is still an important local pilgrimage site.   [35] Tauxier, *Le Noir de Bondoukou*, pp. 212–15.
[36] T. E. Bowdich, *A Mission from Cape Coast Castle to Ashantee*, p. 483.

development was not the result of a large-scale dispersal of Mande immigrants but represented the efforts of a limited number of traders, clerics, and their families. Although few in number, they left a decided imprint on this region within less than a century after their arrival.

How could a numerically insignificant immigrant Muslim population achieve and maintain such prominence in an overwhelmingly non-Muslim environment? In part by the very manner in which the Mande settled the region. Like other immigrant Mande peoples scattered throughout the western Sudan, the Dyula, Ligbi, and Hwela sought to locate themselves in the political and economic nerve centers of the cultures. Being an essentially urban population devoted to commerce, these dynamic clans concentrated on moving to the market towns of Bondoukou, Kong, Banda, Bouna, and others or to smaller villages that were economically dependent on the larger urban centers. In these large and prosperous towns, they created their own wards or quarters, and such Mande sectors came to represent a significant percentage of the total population. Indeed, at Bondoukou and Kong they were not only economically but numerically dominant, and these market towns were regarded as Muslim Mande communities in the eighteenth and nineteenth centuries.[37] Mande settlement of this region resulted in what Wilks defined in his work on religious education among the Dyula as a "marked opposition between town and countryside" and "the basic correlation between urban and Muslim, rural and non-Muslim."[38]

There are other factors, beyond residence patterns and economic vitality, that account for the impressive role played by the Mande in the history of the Cercle de Bondoukou and west central Ghana. Given their limited numbers, one might well expect that these peoples would not have been able to maintain their religious and cultural identities, that they would have succumbed gradually to pressures exerted on them by their non-Muslim neighbors. But in this area, as elsewhere, this did not happen. Indeed, the Dyula, Ligbi and Hwela have not only resisted such forces but have maintained their religious and cultural integrity in the face of such non-Muslim groups as the Nafana, Degha, and Kulango. This is true even with respect to the Bron, the dominant political and state-building power in the area.

[37] Population statistics recorded by Tauxier for Bondoukou and Marty for Kong indicate that the Mande were clearly predominant in both towns in the early twentieth century. Of the 5,122 persons living in the Canton of Almamy, consisting of Bondoukou and its dependent villages, roughly 60 percent were Islamized Mande. The percentage of Mande in the town of Bondoukou was slightly under 60 – 1,340 of 2,246. (Tauxier, *Le Noir de Bondoukou*, pp. 434–5.)

Marty estimated that 8,000 of 10,000 inhabitants in the Canton of Kong were Mande, as were virtually all residents of the town of Kong. (*L'Islam en Côte d'Ivoire*, p. 189.)

[38] "Transmission of Islamic Learning," p. 163.

To a large extent, the ultimate prominence of the Mande was based on fortunate historical circumstances. Mande colonization of the region during the early eighteenth century was quite different from the group's penetration in other areas, especially to the east of the Black Volta River. In the latter region, as Levtzion notes, the Islamized Mande were directly involved with the creation of such states as Gonja and Dagomba and were thus quickly integrated into these political systems as members of one of the component estates of the realm. Under such conditions, they were gradually assimilated and lost many of their distinctive cultural traits.[39] This was not the case, however, south and west of the Black Volta, in the Cercle de Bondoukou, and in west central Ghana, for here the Mande were not involved in the actual process of state-building but arrived as immigrant populations well after the foundation of these non-Muslim centers. They settled, for example, in the Bron state of Gyaman and in the Nafana domains of Banda as strangers, separate elements who were welcomed because of their mercantile abilities and commercial connections but were never fully incorporated into the polities. Not having contributed to the formation of the states, the Mande occupied a peripheral position within them. In time, the Mande immigrants exerted considerable influence, gaining prominent positions and rendering services to the ruling elite, yet even then they remained a group apart. But the very fact that they enjoyed special benefits and immunities, a distinct status, and a strong measure of political autonomy, proved instrumental in allowing them to preserve their religious and cultural identity. This they were able to accomplish to a degree that would have been impossible in such assimilative states as Gonja and Dagomba. Some 200 years after the fall of Begho, French travelers and administrators in the states of Gyaman and Bouna witnessed the results of this significant historical fact. They were invariably struck by the independence and prominence of the Mande. Tauxier's comments are typical of the statements made during this period:

Est-ce à dire que la situation des Dyoulas, avant l'arrivée des Français, fut celle des Koulangos ou celle des G'bins, Gouros, Nafanas, etc., sou le joug des Abrons? Nullement. Les Dyoulas, à cause de leur intelligence, de leur esprit mercantile, de leur richesse relative et de leur islamisation, avaient une situation privilégiée sous la domination abron. Les Abrons les respectaient bien plus que les autres indigènes, et, bien que fétichistes eux-mêmes, bien plus que leurs sujets fétichistes.

Il en est de même du reste dans toute l'Afrique occidentale. Quand les commerçants musulmanisés ne commandent pas un pays, ils ont une situation à part auprès des maîtres de celui-ci.[40]

[39] *Muslims and Chiefs in West Africa*, p. 13.
[40] *Le Noir de Bondoukou*, p. 264.

Although Tauxier's observations were based primarily on his research in the vital Dyula community of Bondoukou, they might well have applied to the Ligbi and Hwela of Gyaman and to those Mande groups who played a similar historical role in the adjacent states of Banda, Nsawkaw, Wenchi, and Techiman in present-day west central Ghana.

Internal factors also contributed to the ultimate position enjoyed by the Mande clans. Their commercial genius, especially their ability to control long-distance trade, tied the states of Wenchi, Nsawkaw, Gyaman, and others to the wider networks of trade that had been forged between the savannah and the Guinea Coast forest and brought to their political systems a new era of prosperity. The Mande not only formed an indispensable part of the economy of this region but provided a variety of services that were paramount in the functioning of these states. Learned Muslims offered spiritual assistance during times of stress, and they served as judicial and administrative advisors, since their ability to read and write proved highly useful to the royal courts.[41] The relationship between the Mande and non-Muslim chiefs was both unusually stable and mutually beneficial. Local leaders were acutely conscious of the need for peaceful relations with the important Muslim element, who controlled the commercial life of their states and generally supported their administrations. Although the Mande were made to recognize the ultimate authority of non-Muslim chiefs and were taxed on their market profits, no direct pressures were brought to bear to make them conform to local cultural standards. Regarded as valuable members of the societies, the Mande were accorded a high degree of independence and flourished as a semi-autonomous group under the jurisdiction of their own temporal and religious leaders.

Because of such salutary conditions, the immigrant Mande not only maintained but were constantly able to strengthen their sense of religious and cultural community. Life in the Muslim quarters of large and active markets and in their own villages was firmly guided by a religious elite headed by an Imām, and such Muslim leaders established mosques and Qur'ānic schools as they felt they were required. The success with which they pursued this goal was noted by Marty, a Frenchman who was generally unimpressed by the standards of Islamic education in French West Africa but who was clearly struck by the number and quality of religious schools

[41] The privileged position enjoyed by the Mande at the court of the Bron paramounts of Gyaman was invariably described by French writers at the turn of this century. This position continues today at the court of Kwame Adinkra, the present chief of the state. According to Adinkra, no major decision is made at the royal court at Herebo without members of the local Mande 'ulamā' being consulted. Furthermore, these Muslims participate in all state ceremonies including those devoted to the propitiation of the royal ancestors. For an excellent discussion of Muslim influence in another non-Muslim state, see Wilks, "The Position of Muslims in Metropolitan Ashanti in the Early Nineteenth Century."

in and around Bondoukou.[42] The level of Qur'ānic instruction there, and probably in other towns of the region, was impressive. A basic Islamic education was made available to all Muslims, and more advanced studies for those with the ability and desire to attain the ranks of the 'ulamā' were offered by a small group of scholars of considerable reputation.[43] Without such a well-established educational system, the Islamic community would have undergone gradual deterioration. In this area, however, the vigor demonstrated by the 'ulamā' in the field of religious education ensured the growth and development of Islam.

The impressive system of religious education and the dynamism of individual clerical leaders allowed the Mande to maintain their Islamic identity but accounted for only a limited extension of the faith. Some conversion of the Kulango, Nafana, and Bron in the Cercle de Bondoukou and west central Ghana occurred, but these successes were minimal. Proselytism was generally directed towards individuals. Those who showed an interest in adopting the religion were encouraged to attend Qur'ānic school in order to acquire the rudiments of Islamic learning, but this was not viewed as an obligation. At no time did members of the 'ulamā' in the area resort to forced conversion and jihād, for they regarded themselves as an essentially co-operative constituency in the non-Muslim states.

It seems quite likely that yet another factor, one based on doctrine, might have conditioned the non-disruptive approach of the Mande to conversion and the extension of the faith. Wilks has remarked that Mande Dyula communities in general (and the Dyula constitute the largest segment of the Mande population in the area under discussion) have tended to avoid the use of force in spreading the boundaries of Islam. According to Wilks, members of the Dyula 'ulamā' have been deeply influenced by the thoughts of Al-Ḥājjī Sālim Sūwari, a fifteenth-century Mande scholar and juris-consult of Mali, whose writings dealt with a variety of questions on Muslim law and specifically with regulations concerning the conduct of Muslims towards non-believers.

He [Al-Ḥājjī Sālim Sūwari] is also reported to have ruled on issues affecting Muslim communities in *bilād al-kufr*, pagan territory: a matter of particular concern to the far-ranging Malian traders. A full study of opinions regarded by the Dyula as based upon the legal authority of al Hājj Sālim is needed. In the absence of such, I would suggest very tentatively that two features broadly characteristic of Dyula thought may be derived from him: first, the tendency to reject *jihād*, battle, as an instrument of social and political change, and second, subscription to the ideal of withdrawal from secular political activity.[44]

[42] *L'Islam en Côte d'Ivoire*, pp. 219–20.
[43] Ibid., p. 219.
[44] "Transmission of Islamic Learning," p. 179.

How closely the Dyula, Ligbi, and Hwela adhered to such precepts, even if they derive from doctrinal sources other than the writings of Al-Ḥājjī Sālim, was dramatically demonstrated by the fact that only a very small percentage of the faithful supported the jihād waged by the Mande leader Samory Turay against the towns of Bondoukou, Banda, and Sorhobango at the end of the nineteenth century.[45] Members of the Mande 'ulamā' interviewed in 1966–7 who witnessed the destruction wrought by Samory's troops uniformly condemned his tactics while maintaining that he was a vigorous religious reformer and a fervent believer.[46] They claimed that if they had followed such a disruptive approach, they would have jeopardized their own position throughout this region. They felt that jihād produced only bloodshed and conflict and did not accomplish a true or lasting conversion to Islam.

It has been shown in the foregoing discussion that the penetration of Mande clans and the concomitant implantation and growth of Islam in the Cercle de Bondoukou and west central Ghana were achieved essentially by gradual and peaceful means. Here, as elsewhere, the Muslim immigrants, rather than uprooting or destroying the traditional societies with which they came in contact, contributed extensively and positively to their development. Their contributions can be seen even in the interactions between Muslims and local artistic traditions.

[45] Tauxier, *Le Noir de Bondoukou*, pp. 116–17.
[46] Dyula and Ligbi traditions claim that both groups supported the Bron paramount Ardjumani in his efforts to defeat Samory's troops under the direction of Sarantye-Mori, the son of Samory. Interviews at Jinini and Bondoukou, January 21 and 24, 1968.

CHAPTER 5

MUSLIM RELATIONSHIPS WITH TRADITIONAL ART IN THE CERCLE DE BONDOUKOU AND WEST CENTRAL GHANA

Having established the impact of the Islamized Mande on the Cercle de Bondoukou and west central Ghana, I shall now explore further the cultural and artistic setting within which Islam and its adherents have flourished. The region is a clearly non-Muslim environment, one in which the Mande constitute only a small segment of the total population.[1] This situation is not atypical – indeed, it is common throughout vast areas of Mande expansion.[2] Mande migrations have been characterized historically by the movement of small mobile units that have settled amidst a variety of cultures and now stand as a decided minority among their non-Muslim neighbors.

What *is* unusual about this area of Mande settlement is its ethnographic complexity. In this respect, it is very different from other regions of Mande colonization, for example, Mossiland or the Senufo country, where the Muslim Yarse and Dyula encountered relatively homogeneous non-Muslim cultures.

In the Cercle de Bondoukou and west central Ghana, the Islamized Dyula, Ligbi, and Hwela were confronted by a heterogeneous group of non-Muslim peoples. Indeed the cultural picture is so varied and dense (map 2) that one finds local populations representing three language sub-families. These include the Bron (Kwa-Akan), Dumpo (Kwa-Guang), Degha or Mo (Gur-Grusi), Nafana (Gur-Senufo), Kulango (Gur), and

---

[1] Only in Bondoukou, where the Muslim Mande population forms roughly 70 percent of the town's 7,000 persons, and in a few smaller trading towns and villages, do the Mande predominate. Elsewhere they are clearly in the minority. In the Cercle de Bondoukou and west central Ghana it can be estimated that they form no more than 15 percent of the total population.

[2] Estimates in 1957 for the areas of Bouna (Ivory Coast) and Wa (Ghana) reveal that the Muslim populations (and the Mande constitute the largest segment of these Muslim groups) of Bouna represented about 12 percent of the total and of Wa, 9 percent (Ivor Wilks, "Transmission of Islamic Learning," p. 163).

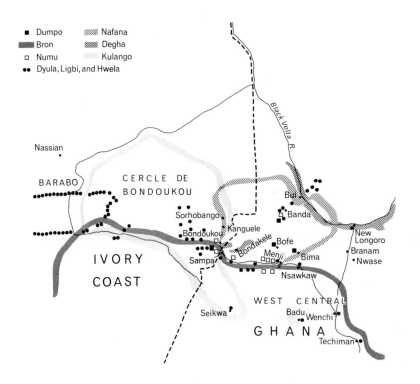

2. Distribution of cultures in the Cercle de Bondoukou and west central Ghana.

Numu (Mande-Tan).[3] Furthermore, all these peoples have been resident in the area for nearly 300 years – long enough to make this highly composite cultural setting one of some antiquity.[4]

The neighbors of the Islamized Mande within the Cercle de Bondoukou and west central Ghana include both autochthonous peoples and well-established immigrants who moved into the region prior to the eighteenth century. Those claiming to be indigenous to the area are the Dumpo, a small residual Kwa-Guang population, and the Bron, who are closely related in language and culture to the Ashanti and other Akan peoples immediately to the south and west. Both of these Kwa-speaking groups have preserved oral traditions that tend to support their claims of being the original

[3] There are other culture groups represented, but they are numerically insignificant and are recent immigrants – since about 1875. These include the Hausa, Mossi, Dagarti, Fra-fra, Gonja, Birifor, and Wala.

[4] The unusual ethnographic complexity of a small sector of the Cercle de Bondoukou and west central Ghana, the Banda district, was first noted by J. R. Goody in "The Mande and the Akan Hinterland," pp. 193–4.

75

inhabitants of the land. Dumpo traditions of origin invariably begin with an account of how they descended from the sky to their present locales, and the histories of all Bron states associate their beginnings with the emergence of their ancestors from sacred holes in the ground located on lands belonging to these states.[5] Only the Bron of the traditional state of Gyaman, centered in the important commercial town of Bondoukou, deny that they are of local origin. There the ruling lineages claim that they are the descendants of immigrants from Akwamu, an important pre-Ashanti state located in the forest region of present-day Ghana.[6] With this exception, however, the Dumpo and Bron are unanimous in their assertions that they were the first culture groups in the region.

Tales of origin are of course mythologically or poetically couched, but they must be regarded as serious claims of autochthonous standing. Indeed, their historical legitimacy is acknowledged by all neighbouring peoples who are immigrants to this area. Traditions collected among the Nafana and Degha, for example, clearly substantiate the histories of the Bron and Dumpo, for both peoples stress that they encountered these groups when they first came to settle in the region during the latter part of the seventeenth century. Furthermore, both the Dumpo and Bron control the shrines which are intimately associated with the propitiation and rejuvenation of the land, a clear index of their indigenous status and their rights to the soil.[7]

The distribution of the two indigenous cultures within the region is quite broad; this is especially true of the Bron. As Goody has noted, the Bron are located primarily south of the old trade route connecting Bondoukou and Wenchi, and the Dumpo are found north of this important artery.[8] There are, of course, exceptions to this rather neat geographical division – for example, the Bron communities of Nwase and Branam are north of the town of Wenchi – but for the most part it does describe the present distribution of these peoples. Currently the Dumpo represent only a small and scattered culture group inhabiting the villages of Bofe and Bima and the Dumpo quarter of the Nafana town of Banda. In addition, a few Dumpo families live at the Kulango village of Kanguele, six miles north of Bondoukou in the Cercle de Bondoukou, and on the Ghanaian side of the border in the Degha villages of Bondakele and Bui. The autochthonous

---

[5] Dumpo traditions of origin were collected at Bofe, a Dumpo village on the Menji–Bui road, and at the Dumpo quarter of Banda-Ahenkro, November 1966.

[6] Some confusion exists as to the origins of the Bron of Gyaman. Traditions recorded by Delafosse and Tauxier indicate that they migrated from Kwahu: Maurice Delafosse, *Vocabulaires comparatifs de plus de 60 langues ou dialectes parlés à la Côte d'Ivoire et dans les régions limitrophes*, p. 102; Louis Tauxier, *Le Noir de Bondoukou*, p. 86.

[7] Goody, "The Mande and the Akan Hinterland," p. 196, and René A. Bravmann and R. D. Mathewson, "A Note on the History and Archaeology of 'Old Bima,'" p. 136.

[8] "The Mande and the Akan Hinterland," p. 194.

Bron, on the other hand, are the largest and most prominent non-Muslim culture within the region. They are found in virtually all the southern stretches of the Cercle de Bondoukou and west central Ghana, where they inhabit their traditional states of Wenchi, Techiman, Nsawkaw, and Gyaman. As a highly centralized people with cultural and political institutions almost identical to those of other Akan peoples, the Bron have played an important role in the history of the area since the seventeenth century. Although subjected to intermittent Ashanti pressures and control, as were all peoples in this region during the eighteenth and nineteenth centuries, the Bron were not victimized by these circumstances. They proved to be highly resistant to Ashanti dominance in the northwest, and with the gradual decline of Ashanti after 1870, the Bron quickly reasserted their independence and once again achieved a predominant position in the area.[9]

Besides the indigenous Bron and Dumpo, there are other non-Muslim populations, immigrants, who have left a decided imprint on the history and cultural make-up of this region. They are the Nafana, Degha, and Kulango (three Gur cultures), and the Mande Numu, who are culturally and linguistically related to the Islamized Dyula and Ligbi.

The oldest of these immigrant cultures are the Numu, who claim to have migrated to their present location in the company of the Muslim Dyula and Ligbi. Their arrival, therefore, may be dated provisionally at the earliest period of Mande penetration in the Cercle de Bondoukou and west central Ghana – the fifteenth century. According to Numu tradition, they settled initially at Begho, where they occupied a discrete quarter of this famous market town.[10] This tradition is confirmed by oral histories of the Bron of Hani, a small village just to the southeast of the site of old Begho.[11] With the collapse of Begho in the early eighteenth century, the Numu and Muslim Mande scattered throughout this region, founding new communities that they still inhabit. At present, the Numu may be found residing in their own villages – a rather rare residence pattern for them – or in highly dispersed family units among all the cultures in this area.[12] Individual families have attached themselves to both Muslim and non-Muslim communities, where they serve as an important artisan group, fashioning the iron products essential to farming and mercantile cultures.

It was not until the end of the seventeenth century, however, that the Cercle de Bondoukou and west central Ghana experienced a significant

[9] For an excellent discussion of the Ashanti presence in this area, see Goody and Kwame Arhin, *Ashanti and the Northwest*.

[10] Numu traditions collected at Kwametintini and Brawhani, October 1966.

[11] The Bron of Hani were originally inhabitants of Begho and left the town in the company of some Numu families to settle at their present location. Interview at Hani, October 1966.

[12] The two predominantly Numu villages are Kwametintini and Brawhani, both located just to the north and west of Menji in west central Ghana.

influx of non-Islamized peoples. Then, almost simultaneously, three Gur cultures – the Nafana, Degha, and Kulango – arrived and further complicated an already dynamic ethnographic situation. The Nafana, who had left the southeastern Senufo country of Jimini after a series of succession disputes, settled to the north of Bondoukou and as far east as the Banda Hills, where they founded the small Nafana state of Banda.[13] Degha migrants, who had fled their homeland in the Sisala country of northern Ghana as a result of pressures exerted by the expansion-minded Gourounsi and Mossi, moved into the area of the bend of the Black Volta River lying immediately to the north and east of the Nafana. The majority of the Degha refugees settled along the river between the present-day towns of New Longero and Kintampo. Others moved westwards, following the course of the Black Volta and founding small communities as they went. Remnant family groups traveled as far afield as the immediate vicinity of Bondoukou, where they established a cluster of small villages.[14] From the area around Bouna in the northeastern corner of the Ivory Coast and from the adjacent Lobi country of Upper Volta came the Kulango. Driven south from Bouna by the Dagomba, they spread into the northern stretches of the Cercle de Bondoukou and were quickly incorporated into the burgeoning Bron state of Gyaman. Some Kulango families, seeking to avoid Gyaman domination, pressed southeast into the forest country south of the Bron states of Nsawkaw and Wenchi, where they created their own states of Seikwa and Badu.[15]

Thus by the end of the seventeenth century, the ethnographic composition of the Cercle de Bondoukou and west central Ghana had already been established. The Bron occupied the southern portions of the region; the Nafana, Degha, and Dumpo were firmly settled in the north; the Kulango were located along the western edge and extreme south; and the Islamized Mande and non-Muslim Numu resided at Begho and other marketing centers throughout the area. This ethnographic picture, one of great cultural heterogeneity, remained essentially unchanged during the eighteenth and nineteenth centuries and persists today.

Given this dynamic social situation, the notion of static culture units dwelling in isolation is singularly inappropriate when applied to this area (in fact, this view is almost never appropriate when applied to sub-Saharan Africa). We are dealing here not with discrete tribes living within sharply delimited borders but with a number of cultures that have interacted with each other over a period of nearly 300 years. Geographical

[13] Kwabena Ameyaw, "Tradition of Banda: Brong/Ahafo 1," p. 1. Interviews at Banda-Ahenkro, October and November 1966.
[14] Histories collected at the Degha villages of Bamboi, New Longero, Bui, Bouroumba, and Motiambo in December 1966, April 1967, January 1968.
[15] Histories recorded at the Kulango towns of Seikwa in October 1967 and Badu in March 1967.

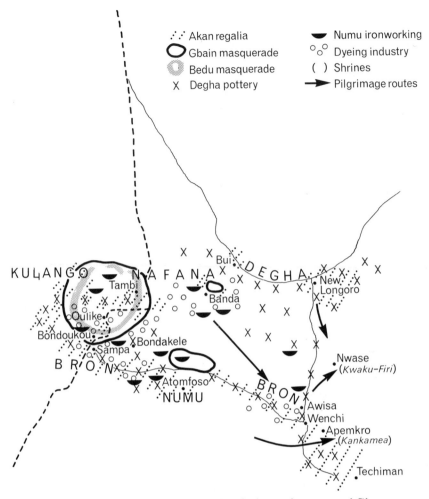

Legend:

- ∴ Akan regalia
- ⬯ Gbain masquerade
- ⬮ Bedu masquerade
- X Degha pottery
- ◗ Numu ironworking
- °₀° Dyeing industry
- ( ) Shrines
- ➤ Pilgrimage routes

KULANGO NAFANA DEGHA

Tambi Bui New Longoro

Oulike Banda

Bondoukou Bondakele

BRONG Sampa

Atomfoso

NUMU BRONG

Nwase (*Kwaku-Firi*)

Awisa
Wenchi

Apemkro
(*Kankamea*)

Techiman

3. Shared artistic traditions in the Cercle de Bondoukou and west central Ghana.

proximity, common historical experiences, avenues of trade, the mobility of specialist groups, and other factors have created a fine-spun social web embracing all peoples within the locale. Cultural interactions have been very fluid and intense; this has been the case not only among non-Muslims but has also marked the relationship of the Islamized Mande to their neighbors.

The nature of the setting, therefore, has been governed by two basic features: its ethnographic density and a very high degree of long-term cultural interaction. These twin factors have conditioned – have indeed been instrumental in fashioning – the artistic landscape of the region. They have produced an artistic environment that is essentially different from those normally described by writers concerned with the tribal arts of

Africa. For in this instance we are concerned not with an area readily encompassed by a single homogeneous tribal style but with a variety of artistic traditions that reflect the ethnographic complexity. The variety of tribal traditions has resulted in a highly dynamic artistic context characterized by the movement of art types and styles and by the mobility of artisan groups.

A survey of the arts in the Cercle de Bondoukou and west central Ghana quickly reveals the rather unusual nature of this artistic setting: for the most part artistic forms are shared by two or more groups in the region. Indeed the most important art forms are found distributed broadly throughout the area (map 3).

Numerous examples of shared art traditions occur, the sharing being based on particular historical forces and the receptivity of most peoples here to imported art types. Perhaps the most dramatic indication of this process is the very wide distribution of Akan regalia among virtually all non-Akan cultures in the region. Regalia such as blackened and white stools, *assipim* and *akonkromfi* chairs, umbrellas, the *akôfena* or state swords, various types of *kente* cloth, and armlets, anklets, bracelets, and other royal trappings occur among the Nafana, Degha, Kulango, and, in one exceptional case, among the Numu in the village of Atomfoso. Each of the recipient cultures openly acknowledges the sources of its regalia as being foreign, in most cases Ashanti. As indicated in the historical survey of the region (Chapter 4), the Ashanti presence in this area dates back to about 1725, and one of the major consequences of this control was the conscious dissemination of regalia to non-Akan peoples. Unlike other expansionary West African states, Ashanti did not attempt to control subject peoples directly; rather it tried to bring subordinate groups under the aegis of Kumasi indirectly through tributes, required attendance at state rituals, and war levies of gold and manpower. The aim was to assimilate diverse peoples culturally. To this end, gifts of regalia were awarded for services in war and continuing allegiance to the Asantehene.[16]

The acceptance of Ashanti regalia by the Nafana, Degha, and Kulango demonstrates the potential mobility of art in Black Africa. These three Gur cultures differ considerably in their social and religious make-up from the Ashanti, the Bron, and other Akan groups. Among the Degha, for instance, there are three royal families – the Pagodiatena, the Dakwadiatena, and the Techydiatena – that in succession supply an individual for the paramount stool. Regalia thus have to be acquired by all three families (plate 7).[17] This is decidedly unlike the unilineal royal descent system among the Akan.

The Nafana state of Banda also exhibits social and political features

[16] This relationship was first discussed by Goody in "The Akan and the North," pp. 22–4.
[17] Interview with the Mohene of New Longero, May 1967.

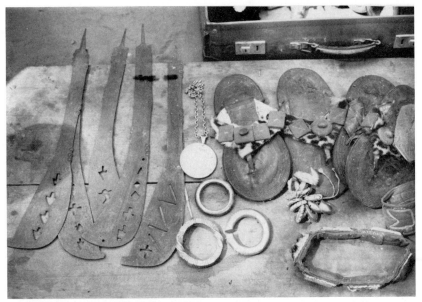

7. Degha regalia belonging to royal family Dakwadiatena. Village of Trabain.

8. Kwesi Bawgaa, head of the
Bawgaa family, pouring a
libation of gin to the four-
legged *kulogon* stool that
symbolizes the ancestral
spirits of his family. Nafana
village of Makera.

81

different from Ashanti.[18] Here two distinct royal families control the position of Mgono, the paramountcy of the state. The office of Mgono rotates regularly (except in cases of succession struggles, obvious inadequacies of claimants to the stool, or political infighting), requiring each royal family to obtain those symbols of leadership necessary to rule. In Banda only the constituted political authorities – the Mgono and his wing chiefs – may utilize regalia. Heads of families and priests of non-state cults use the typical Nafana stool, the four-legged *kulogon*, to indicate their status. The *kulogon* (plate 8) was the original royal stool; however, since the second quarter of the eighteenth century, Ashanti regalia, including the white stools, have been reserved for royalty.

For both the Degha and Nafana, differences in social structure from Ashanti – minimized somewhat by the fact that each has adopted the formal state organization of Kumasi – meant a re-interpretation of the arts of regalia before they could be logically rationalized. Such a process can be accomplished quickly and effectively, however, if the historical circumstances are right. Oral traditions collected among the Nafana and Degha indicate that their use of Akan regalia was firmly established within a generation after their initial contacts with Ashanti about 1750.

Interestingly enough, neither the Degha nor the Nafana have developed their own traditions of making the royal objects. With few exceptions (Kwabena Donkor, a Nafana, did carve some minor items such as umbrella finials and state sword handles for the Mgono of Banda), the Nafana and Degha still choose to obtain their regalia either in Ashanti or among the Bron.

In addition to regalia, shrines and cults and their associated art forms are often shared by cultures in this region. The two most widely distributed masked cults, the Gbain and the Bedu, occur among virtually all non-Muslim cultures in the Cercle de Bondoukou and west central Ghana. Indeed the Gbain is found even among the Muslim Dyula and Hwela. The movement of these two masquerades has been remarkably dynamic, although it has been tied not to political and cultural expansion but to social needs. French researchers working in the early twentieth century (Tauxier and Maurice Prouteaux) clearly indicated that the Gbain was a Muslim Mande tradition at that time, but within the last fifty years the anti-witchcraft Gbain has spread rapidly among non-Muslims, largely because of the efficacy of the masked cult.[19] In some cases, they simply adopted the Gbain as an additional protection; in others, the masquerade supplanted pre-existing cults and shrines.

---

[18] For a fuller discussion of the diffusion of Ashanti regalia in Banda, see Bravmann, "The Diffusion of Ashanti Political Art."

[19] Tauxier, *Le Noir de Bondoukou*, p. 295, note, and M. Prouteaux, "Notes sur certains rites magico-religieux de la Haute Côte d'Ivoire," p. 37.

In a very similar manner, the Bedu has come to occupy an important social-control position among the Degha, Kulango, and Nafana. The Bedu masquerade is of relatively recent origin, possibly deriving from the older masked cult of Sakara-Bounou, which was suppressed by French and British missionaries during the 1920s and 1930s. Dating from this period and inspired by the Nafana, who retain its use, the Bedu has been quickly and completely adopted by the Kulango and Degha.[20] The concerns of Bedu are many: it protects against illness and epidemic, it ensures female fertility, and it serves as a guide to social and moral conduct. Concerned with a host of societal ills, the cult has been widely accepted.

Even primarily utilitarian art forms have been diffused through the area under discussion. Degha pottery, for example, is found among all these cultures, for it is considered to be the best made and the most beautiful of all local wares. Degha women monopolize the production and distribution of pottery, and their work is thought to be so far superior to all others that it has virtually supplanted competing traditions. Many Degha pottery types are used by other cultures for ritual purposes. The three earthenware pots that make up the Bron shrine of Kodua-Asare at Offuman came from the Degha town of Bamboi about forty years ago.[21] All the large ritual washing bowls located in the sacred groves of the Gbain are of Degha manufacture. The monopoly of particular skills and the high demand for such services have combined to make the Degha potter an especially mobile artisan.

Two other artisan groups, the Numu blacksmiths and the Dyula dyers, also demonstrate the high mobility of specialists. The Numu are acknowledged to be the ironworkers par excellence in this region. They create everything from hoe blades to *yaya*, the iron anklets worn by the Gbain masquerader when he is seeking witches. Even the accessibility of imported European iron and other metal products has not diminished the importance of these artisans. Numu families inhabit virtually every town in the Cercle de Bondoukou and west central Ghana, and in every case monopolize the art of ironworking.

The dyeing industry is similarly dominated by a single culture group, the Dyula. Although these people are found primarily in the important urban marketing centers, they effectively control the business of dyeing cotton by regularly circulating among villages. Few other cultures in the area have pursued dyeing because of the decided superiority of Dyula workmanship.[22]

[20] According to Kulango, Degha, and Nafana informants, the earliest Bedu masks used were at the Nafana villages of Oulike and Tambi. That the Nafana founded the tradition seems quite plausible, since it is the Nafana at the village of Oulike who own the paramount shrine of Sakara-Bounou.   [21] Interviews at Offuman, July 1967.
[22] A vivid early description of this important activity may be found in R. Austin Freeman, *Travels and Life in Ashanti and Jaman*, pp. 223–7.

9. State swords (*akôfena*) presented to shrine of Kwaku-Firi by non-Muslim and Muslim clients of the cult. Bron village of Nwase.

10. Kankamea shrine; mud and cement. Six figures, three male and three female, serve as guardians of the spirit, which is housed in the clay bowl resting on the forked branch above altar. Bron village of Apemkro.

Many institutions in this area, shrines, cults, state rituals, and so forth, demonstrate another kind of movement: their influence is such that they inspire mobility in the large number of "strangers" who regularly travel to them. Bron shrines, like Kankamea and Kwaku-Firi, include not only a Bron clientele but non-Muslim and Muslim supplicants from throughout the area. The priest of Kwaku-Firi, for example, freely admits that many of the gifts of regalia (plate 9) given to him and the spirit of the shrine were offered by Nafana from Banda, Muslims from Bondoukou, and Degha living between Bamboi and Kintampo.[23] Some of the most ardent devotees of Kankamea (plate 10) are Kulango who have been drawn to this highly reputable protective shrine. Even important Degha political and religious figures, who have been unable to find solutions to their problems through their own shrines, travel to the small village of Apemkro where Kankamea is housed. The fact that Kankamea is an imported tradition, its homeland being in northwestern Ghana among the Lowiili, gives strangers added confidence in its powers and in the efficacy of its procedures.[24] These two shrines have not proliferated in the area, but their influence is widespread: one Nafana man has gone so far as to erect a mud shrine in his village that he says was modeled after Kankamea, although the shrines have no physical resemblance other than that both are mud structures.[25]

Artistic movement and shared traditions are obvious in any multi-tribal situation, since at least a modicum of cultural intercourse can always be expected, particularly where culture contact has existed over a considerable period of time. This is not to imply, however, that all art forms are diffused or shared, for each culture in this region has its unique traditions. The Nadrè (plate 11), for example, is a carved wooden figure of either sex that occurs exclusively among the Degha.[26] The Do masquerade, excepting one very recent case of borrowing by the Hwela of Sorhobango and its use in the past by the Dyula, is a purely Muslim Ligbi tradition.[27]

Restricted art types, such as the Do, generally have little or no relevance for neighboring peoples and thus have not exhibited the mobility of more universally applicable traditions. The Gbain, because it combats witchcraft, can move easily across tribal and religious lines, for this problem is common to all cultures; the Do tradition, on the other hand, is tied so closely to the Islamic calendar that its use by non-Muslims would be at best superfluous. Such exclusiveness may also occur when an art tradition is

[23] Interview at Nwase, November 10, 1966.
[24] Interview at Apemkro, February 22, 1967.
[25] Interview with Nôpè Kutugu, owner of the shrine of Jakari, March 6, 1967.
[26] Interviews at the Degha villages of Kandige, New Longero, Amansala, and Longero, December 9–11, 1966.
[27] The two Do masks at Sorhobango, carved by the Muslim Hwela carver Sirikye, are used only at Muslim weddings, unlike most Do masks, which are used for various Muslim holy days. Interview at Sorhobango, June 2, 1967.

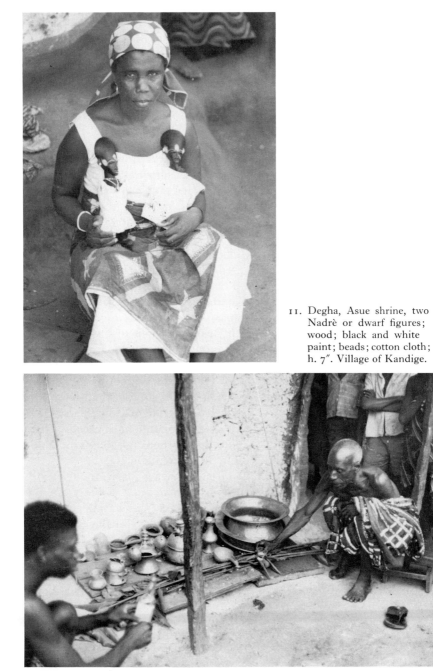

11. Degha, Asue shrine, two Nadrè or dwarf figures; wood; black and white paint; beads; cotton cloth; h. 7″. Village of Kandige.

12. Baya ceremony at Nsawkaw: annual propitiation of brass bowls and other brass items by the Kuruwaasehene of Nsawkaw.

associated with a group's historical bases. The brass bowls at Nsawkaw (plate 12), two of which are inscribed with Kufic Arabic script, are propitiated annually during the Baya ceremony by the Kuruwaasehene (the keeper of the bowls) because they are linked to the mythical origins of the Nsawkaw Bron and to the creation of their state.[28] Brass bowls are used in other Bron states as the primary receptacles for shrines, but only at Nsawkaw are they considered to be objects that validate historical origin.

We are, therefore, dealing with an area in which there are restricted as well as shared artistic traditions. All non-Muslim cultures in the Cercle de Bondoukou and west central Ghana – the Nafana, Kulango, Numu, Degha, Dumpo, and Bron – have helped create the artistic map of the region.

What has been the relationship of the Islamized Mande to this highly variegated artistic setting? Have they consciously sought to destroy and uproot local traditions found in the region? Did the Mande pressure their non-Muslim neighbors into abandoning their art forms? The available evidence plainly indicates that none of this has happened. Throughout the long period of association between the Dyula, Ligbi, and Hwela and the numerous non-Muslim peoples of this region, Islam has not had an adverse effect on local cults, rituals, and their supporting art forms. Indeed, the Mande have held a decidedly tolerant attitude towards such institutions and art traditions, and this has been true not only of the mass of believers but also of certain members of the 'ulamā'.

How could such an attitude prevail among the Mande, who are among the oldest and most heavily Islamized of West African peoples? According to the art historians, this ought to be an area devoid of all that hints at "paganism."

Although aware of their historical and religious identity and of their position as a minority, the Mande have not regarded themselves as a separate people. They do not live in marked opposition to their neighbors but cooperate with their leaders and often contribute extensively to the political and economic well-being of the states in which they reside. Muslim/non-Muslim relations in this region have been such that instances of conflict between the two groups are virtually unknown. Even today this alliance is a salutary one, and it extends to Mande living in such traditional Bron states as Gyaman and Nsawkaw and among the decentralized Degha and Kulango.

An ideal of tolerance has not only governed Mande political and social relations but has also strongly influenced attitudes towards the arts. Tolerance of representational art is found everywhere, as is evident in any village or town in which Muslims and non-Muslims reside. In such communities there are invariably shrines and cults, utilizing a variety of art forms, which continue to flourish and acquire new adherents despite the

---

[28] I witnessed the Baya ceremony at Nsawkaw on January 17, 1968.

presence of the Muslim Mande. Religious experts and practitioners are found everywhere, and they carry out their skills and activities freely and with impunity. For the large majority of Muslims, these elements, including the arts, are beyond reproach; they form a natural and fully rationalized aspect of life in this multi-tribal setting.

This is not to imply, however, that there is no opposition to such practices. Objections do exist and are generally voiced by the learned and pious, persons belonging to the religious elite. Such criticisms, however, are not expressed publicly, nor are they directed towards those in control of the rites but remain private sentiments shared by this small group of believers. Thus internalized, Muslim opposition does not represent a distinct threat to these traditions. Tensions may exist but are not made manifest. Furthermore, these feelings are only a minority opinion (indeed, not even all members of the 'ulamā' share the point of view), and they are not strong enough to disrupt the general atmosphere of tolerance and acceptance binding Muslims to non-Muslims in the region.

The vast majority of the Islamized Mande tolerate local institutions and their associated art forms, and many actively support them. Muslims throughout the area cooperate with local rulers and religious officials to help ensure the efficacy of traditional rituals and festivals. This is particularly true of such religious specialists as clerics and diviners, since these individuals are capable of rendering a wide range of services to their non-Muslim neighbors. Prayers, forms of Muslim divination, and elements of Islamic magic are readily offered by the Mande and have come to form an important part of local rituals. Non-Muslims in turn avidly seek the advice and knowledge of Muslim experts, for they are willing to adopt whatever new and additional procedures prove to be effective.

The extent to which the Muslim Mande have influenced the political, social, and religious life of various cultures in the Cercle de Bondoukou and west central Ghana is truly striking. Indeed, Islam is so prominent a feature that no society in the area has remained untouched by it. Among the Nafana of Banda, for example, the impact of the Mande is ever-present, affecting every area of traditional life. The compound of the Mgono is an especially clear example of religious syncretism, for here elements from Islam and the Nafana world are intimately brought together. Every item of regalia – white stools, *assipim* chairs, and the *akonkromfi* thrones – generally displayed publicly within the courtyard of this royal compound, has a variety of Muslim charms associated with it. Amulets (virtually all of them consisting of scraps of paper with cabalistic signs or portions from the Qur'ān written on them) are either tied under the seats or are wrapped around the legs of the royal chairs (plate 13) to protect those members of the Nafana court privileged to sit upon them. Similar charms are wedged into the cavity found in the central column of all white stools, and still

13. Non-Muslim and Qur'ānic amulets tied under seats of *akonkromfi* chair owned by the Mgono of Banda. This brass-studded chair was purchased by Kofi Dwuru at Kumasi about thirty years ago. Town of Banda-Ahenkro.

14. White stool owned by the Mgono Kofi Dwuru of Banda; wood, white chalk, brass; Qur'ānic amulets tied to central column; h. 16.5″. Town of Banda-Ahenkro.

89

others are carefully draped about this support (plate 14). In most instances both Muslim and non-Muslim talismans are attached to the objects, and protection is thereby gained from both worlds.

The use of Qur'ānic charms by the Nafana royal family is not restricted to items of regalia at the paramount chief's court. Such amulets, generally obtained from the Muslim Ligbi who reside in the wards of Sase and Kankan on the outskirts of the capital town of Banda-Ahenkro, are also found scattered throughout the Mgono's compound. All important social and ritual areas within the palace are provided with Islamic talismans as well as those made by the Nafana themselves. Suspended from the lintel of the entry to the Mgono's sleeping room are several Ligbi amulets meant to ward off evil spirits that could harm or disturb the ruler while at rest.[29] Others are attached to the rafters of his washing cubicle, for the Nafana believe that a man is especially susceptible to danger when he is stripped naked and bathing. The most important room in the compound, the Mgono's reception chamber, used for all major meetings and social occasions, is particularly well fortified with Islamic amulets. Its walls are profusely covered with talismans of every possible type manufactured by Ligbi clerics: they include the *soubalakari* or anti-witchcraft charms; the *nedoudougoulakari*, used for protection against those with evil thoughts and words; and the *neguelakari*, used to thwart a wide variety of hazards like sickness, infertility, fire, and drought. Even the room housing the paramount chief's horse requires a number of protective amulets (the horse used to be a necessary prestige animal owned by all Mgonos of Banda; this custom has not always been followed in the last two generations, although the present Mgono owns one). Indeed, these items are placed in every conceivable portion of the royal compound, for they are viewed by the Nafana in general and royals in particular as not merely desirable but absolutely necessary.

The Nafana court includes a number of other purely Muslim features. The most important cloth owned by the Mgono, for example, is openly acknowledged to be a plain white cotton wrapper with Arabic script and symbols, written with imported red, blue, and black inks, covering the entire garment (plate 15). Referred to by the Nafana as *karamoro-kioyolingo* (literally "Muslim cloth"), it is worn by the Mgono only during the most important festivals marking the Nafana ritual calendar. In its use and appearance, it is very similar to the cloth worn by the Asantehene Osei Kwame and described by Dupuis in 1819 when he witnessed a small Adae ceremony held at Kumasi:

> The courtiers were habited in full costume, as on the day of entry. The king

---

[29] Kofi Dwuru freely admitted that he has resorted to the use of Islamic talismans with greater frequency during the last ten years because of his advanced age. He stated that being physically weaker he requires a greater number of such charms to protect himself from potential dangers. Interview at Banda-Ahenkro, November 25, 1967.

himself was clothed in an under garment of blood-stained cotton; his wrists and an[k]les were adorned with fetische gold weighing many pounds. A small fillet of plaited grass, interwoven with gold wire and little consecrated amulets, encircled his temple. A large white cotton cloth which partly covered his left shoulder was studded all over with Arabic writing in various coloured inks, and of a most brilliant well formed character.[30]

For Kofi Dwuru, the current paramount chief of Banda, the *karamoro-kioyolingo* offers him maximum security, and he considers it far more valuable than the wide assortment of imported Ashanti and Bron *kente* or the locally woven Nafana cloths that also form part of his regalia. The importance of the *karamoro-kioyolingo* to Kofi Dwuru, and to Nafana royals in general, is best expressed by the fact that it is this garment which is generally worn by the paramount chief when he consults the blackened ancestral stools of the state during moments of misfortune and crisis.

Muslim prayers and various forms of Islamic divination are also a very prominent aspect of court life and ritual among the Nafana. Ligbi clerics from Kankan and Sase regularly deliver prayers for the health and well-being of the Mgono and his family. Illness in the royal family not only calls for the presence of non-Muslim specialists but also requires that the most learned *karamokos* in the state be in attendance. When Kofi Dwuru (who is now about ninety years old) was extremely ill in the fall of 1967, Ligbi clerics were constantly at his side offering prayers and *siliama-gue* (holy water), a highly effective curative consisting of special roots and herbs suspended in a blue-black liquid derived from the washing of Qur'ānic boards.[31] The well-being of the paramount is of the utmost concern to all, and important occasions, rituals or otherwise, demand that he be protected as fully as possible. No journey is undertaken by the Mgono without Ligbi diviners being consulted first and the prayers of the Sase 'ulamā' being acquired; the annual yam harvest festival calls for the participation of Ligbi clerics who pray on behalf of all members of the state, both living and dead; crucial court cases, even those dealing with purely Nafana matters, generally require the advice of Muslims; the enstoolment of the Mgono is substantiated and confirmed with the sacrifice of a goat by the Ligbi wards of Sase and Kankan.

The Islamic factor in Nafana culture is by no means limited to the royal court and the persons of the Mgono, his sub-chiefs, and his family; it can be found operating throughout the state of Banda and at all levels of society.

[30] Joseph Dupuis, *Journal of a Residence in Ashantee*, p. 142. The use of such Muslim cloths may well occur quite broadly among the Akan now. Professor Roy Sieber noted a similar robe in 1966 being worn by the chief of the stool-carvers in the Ashanti town of Mampong.

[31] *Siliama-gue* is highly regarded by non-Muslims and Muslims alike as a preventive and curative potion and is used liberally by them in rituals associated with the Gbain anti-witchcraft masquerade. See Chapter 7 for more details.

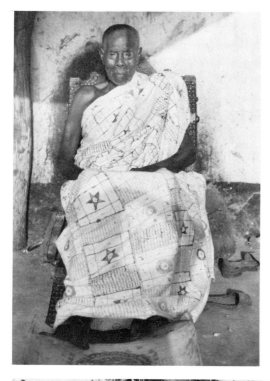

15. *Karamoro-kioyolingo* worn by the Mgono Kofi Dwuru of Banda. Cotton cloth with Qur'ānic inscriptions and cabalistic symbols; white with blue, black, red ink. Town of Banda-Ahenkro.

16. The parent shrine of Sakara-Bounou at Oulike. Altar consists of two ceramic pots and talismans.

The leading protective shrines in Banda – Senyon-Kupo and Sakara-Bounou – show clear evidence of Muslim influence. At Oulike, a small Nafana village on the Bondoukou–Tambi road and the seat of the parent shrine of Sakara-Bounou (plate 16), Qur'ānic charms are kept in close association with the altar of the cult. Two ceramic pots, distinguishable from typical Nafana utilitarian wares by the knob-like projections on their outer surface, and claimed to house the spirit of Sakara, are surrounded by talismans obtained from the Muslim Dyula at Bondoukou. They, along with an assortment of non-Muslim medicines and charms, are said to defend the spirit of the cult from witches, thieves, and misfortune in general.[32] Senyon-Kupo, a shrine recently imported from the Choruba area east of Bole in Gonja and found at Banda-Ahenkro, is protected in a similar fashion. Furthermore, the priests of both cults invariably wear *siryina*, Muslim amulets tied to leather thongs and worn as armlets, bracelets, or necklaces, which are meant to ensure physical vitality. Even far less significant shrines have adopted certain Muslim features – for example, those of Agyekuah, Jakari, and Tugu (plate 17) at Duadaso. All these shrines, consisting of mud altars and decorated with brightly painted animal or human figures modeled in relief, either have Islamic talismans embedded in them during the building process or are periodically renewed by being drenched with potions purchased from the Muslim Mande in neighboring towns and villages.[33]

Muslim Mande cooperation with and support of Nafana institutions and attendant art forms is, therefore, most intimately expressed in the relationship of the Ligbi of Sase and Kankan to the royal court of Banda. Yet it also occurs more broadly; for wherever the Dyula, Ligbi and Hwela interact with the Nafana, the impact of Islam on local ritual is a prominent feature. Most Mande within the state of Banda cooperate simply by accepting these elements of traditional life, but there are some, especially certain members of the 'ulamā', who are deeply involved in these procedures. Many of the learned and pious spend much of their time offering their advice and knowledge, and they have derived both fame and a lively income from their services. Lasane Bamba, a Ligbi *karamoko* from Sase who died in 1963 a very wealthy man, is still remembered by the Nafana for his spiritual assistance to Kofi Dwuru and Nafana royals over a period of nearly thirty years.[34] The ties between some Muslims and the Nafana are certainly deep, but this does not disqualify the former as believers. Such individuals do not represent what Marty deprecatingly described as "Marabout[s] au service des fétichistes, sans plus."[35] The Mande may contribute extensively to Nafana culture, but they are nevertheless committed to their faith.

[32] Interview at Oulike, November 23, 1966.
[33] These three shrines at Duadaso were recorded on March 6 and 7, 1967.
[34] Interviews at Sase and Banda-Ahenkro, November 26 and 27, 1967.
[35] Paul Marty, *Etudes sur l'Islam en Côte d'Ivoire*, p. 63.

17. Tugu shrine. Pythons modeled in relief protect the spirit of Tugu, as do the Muslim charms placed within altar. Ochre, white, black paint; altar h. 3′. Village of Duadaso.

18. The Ôbosom-Gyansô. The spirit of Gyansô resides in the brass bowl, which rests upon a stool and an *assipim* chair. Qur'ānic charms are placed in column of stool belonging to shrine. Bron village of Gyansoso.

94

The participation of the Mande in Nafana rituals, festivals, and court life is hardly unusual, for at least some elements of Islam have penetrated the lives of all non-Muslim peoples in the Cercle de Bondoukou and west central Ghana. All Bron states, for example, have been affected at one level or another by the Mande. In the state of Wenchi, where a sizable community of Dyula and Ligbi has been in residence since the beginning of the eighteenth century, Muslim influence is prominent. Here state rituals and more local and personal shrines demonstrate a strong interplay between "paganism" and Islam, as has been seen among the Nafana of Banda. Each of the three most important state shrines – Ôbosom-Gyansô, Drobo, and Guakuro – exhibits a number of Muslim characteristics: Qur'ānic amulets are placed in or next to brass pans housing the material manifestations of the spirits (plate 18); items of regalia are often protected and made more effective by having Muslim charms tied to them; the annual yam festival for each of the spirits is enhanced and supported by the prayers of Dyula and Ligbi clerics who are in attendance; priests of these shrines invariably consult Muslim scholars and magical experts for help during periods of stress within the state.[36] The person of the Omanhene of Wenchi is guarded both physically and spiritually by a wide assortment of amulets, Muslim prayers, and occasional sacrifices of rams and goats by the Ligbi of Wenchi town on his behalf. No state occasion is complete without the presence of the Mande, and there is hardly a shrine or religious practitioner without at least a few elements of Islam.

Similar Islamic features exist in the Bron states of Nsawkaw and Gyaman and to a smaller degree among the Degha, Kulango, Numu, and Dumpo. In Nsawkaw and Gyaman, Muslim influence is again most obvious in various state rituals and among the political and religious authorities who regulate and direct these affairs. Smaller and more loosely organized cultures – the Degha, Kulango, Numu, and Dumpo – have also incorporated aspects of Islam, but here the mix between Islam and local elements is more limited. In part this may be because Mande settlement in these areas is significantly smaller than in Banda or in the Bron states, and potential interaction between Muslims and non-Muslims is thereby reduced.[37] More important, however, is the fact that these cultures are far less complex. Political and religious hierarchies are limited in size; elaborate state occasions and rituals are either rare or non-existent; and social stratification is less pronounced. Fewer opportunities, at least on a large scale, exist for the incorporation of Islamic magic, divination, and prayers. Yet even in

[36] Kofi Abrefa Busia notes the importance of the *ôbosom* with respect to the Wenchi state in *The Position of the Chief in the Modern Political System of Ashanti*, pp. 31–2.

[37] The economic and urban orientation of the Muslim Mande is obvious in the Cercle de Bondoukou and west central Ghana, where they are found predominantly in towns like Wenchi, Nsawkaw, Banda-Ahenkro, Sampa, and Bondoukou.

19. Male and female figures,
Digèla shrine; wood and
chalk; male h. 11″;
female h. 14.5″. Numu
village of Brawhani.

20. Nkunsa shrine, wooden figures. Bron village of Awisa.

96

these societies, Muslim practices have been adopted. Personal shrines everywhere, even those of little repute, contain at least some Islamic elements. The priest of Digèla, a Numu shrine at the village of Brawhani, for example, rubs Qur'ānic amulets against two carved figures (plate 19) that serve as the messengers of the spirit so that they may transmit the messages more lucidly.[38] Dumpo and Degha earthpriests pour libations of Mande holy water on earthshrines to ensure the continuing fertility of the soil. A Kulango village chief will travel considerable distances to obtain the services of a cleric who may well bring him good health. Muslim influence within these cultures is less extensive and certainly less dramatic, but that it does exist cannot be denied.

The relationship of the Mande to local life often goes beyond tolerance or even intimate forms of support. It is quite common to find the Mande participating in many of the shrines and rituals encountered throughout the area; participation may range from membership or affiliation to service as leaders and counselors. Mande throughout the Cercle de Bondoukou and west central Ghana can be found at shrines, seeking the comfort of local anti-witchcraft cults, or attempting to resolve, through the agency of non-Muslim specialists, certain problems that could not be dealt with or eradicated by Islamic methods. In the Bron town of Awisa six miles north of Wenchi, Dyula and Ligbi women are frequent clients of Nkunsa (plate 20), a small but powerful shrine devoted to the problems surrounding female fertility.[39] The priest of Yarapi, a Degha cult located at the remote village of Kandige and acknowledged to be a powerful deterrent to witchcraft, includes among his devotees Mande Muslims from as far away as Bondoukou and Sorhobango, some fifty miles to the west.[40] Ill and infirm Muslim elders are anxious to partake in the Bedu masquerade (a tradition found among the Nafana, Kulango, and Degha) so that they may be touched by the masked dancers and perhaps regain their health. The two Biè carved figures (plate 21) in the Nafana village of Kabre, known for their abilities to help those who have suffered misfortune in business, farming, and trading, are frequently consulted by Dyula, Ligbi, and Hwela traders.[41] State festivals among the Bron are attended by many Muslims, not only because they consider themselves members of their polities and thus feel obliged to participate, but also because the non-Muslim prayers and procedures that renew the life of the state and its citizenry for the coming year are felt to be effective for all.

The large majority of Muslims who participate in these institutions do so simply as members or occasional supplicants, but there are some who

[38] Interview at Brawhani, October 24, 1966.
[39] Interview with Kwesi Yeboah, priest of the Nkunsa shrine at Awisa, September 21, 1966.
[40] Interview with Kojo Yilu, priest of Yarapi at Kandige, January 9, 1968.
[41] Interview with Siè Langboô, owner of Biè figures, at Kabre, October 17, 1966.

97

21. Biè shrine, wooden figures; left h. 16″, right h. 23″. Nafana village of Kabre.

are much more intimately involved and who have gained prominent positions in the organizations. At Apemkro, a small Bron village on the road east from Wenchi to Offuman, the important protective shrine of Kankamea is headed by a Bron, Kwesi Donkor. His chief advisor is a Muslim Ligbi, however – Sadja Bamba, a native of Wenchi but now a resident of Apemkro – whom he consults regularly about problems confronting the clients of Kankamea. Sadja inherited his position from his father, Bukhari Bamba, one of the men instrumental in bringing Kankamea to Apemkro in the late 1930s, a time of severe economic stress throughout the region after repeated failures of the cocoa crop. The Bron of Apemkro claim that it was Bukhari who convinced the Odekuro (chief) of the village that only a new and very powerful spirit could cope with such a problem, and it was he, along with two non-Muslim elders, who traveled to Birifu in northwestern Ghana in order to purchase an offshoot of the parent shrine located there. The imported shrine was said to have worked almost immediately; its fame spread throughout the Bron states of Wenchi and Offuman; and Bukhari was made the principal advisor to the first priest of Kankamea. When he died about ten years ago, his son Sadja assumed his important role.[42]

There are yet other instances of the Mande having gained important roles in cults and shrines. The Gbain cult, an anti-witchcraft masking tradition, has been adopted by all non-Muslim groups in this region within the last thirty years. For the most part, they have sought out and obtained the cult on their own initiative, but where Muslims have instigated such procedures on behalf of their neighbors, they have generally assumed positions of responsibility and control. This clearly occurred in the Degha village of Zaghala, where Osmane Wattara, a Dyula, serves as one of the two Gbain-tigui, or heads of the Gbain. It was he and Mengye Duah, a Degha, who originally acquired, from Sorhobango in 1956, the Gbain, its paraphernalia, and the various magical medicines necessary for its operation.[43] Essentially the same sequence of events resulted in Muslims holding high positions in Gbain cults elsewhere: among the Numu of Brawhani and Kwametintini and at the Kulango village of Yerekaye. A few Muslims with the special skills necessary for the continuing operation of some cults have also come to enjoy a particularly high status within them. Adama Dudumaye, a Muslim Hwela from Bourouponko and the most accomplished Gbain dancer in the Cercle de Bondoukou, serves as the major consultant to Degha priests of Senyon-Kupo at Bouroumba and Bondakele. His knowledge of anti-witchcraft procedures is extensive, and he is constantly called

---

[42] Interview with Yaw Amanqua (Odekuro of Apemkro), Kwesi Donkor, and Sadja Bamba, February 28, 1967. The cost of acquiring the shrine of Kankamea about thirty years ago was equal to about £70 Ghanaian – i.e. £56 or $140 today. This sum included the cost of two cows, two sheep, two goats, ten guinea fowl, fifteen large pots of pito (millet beer), and food and lodging for the two artisans who came to Apemkro to erect the original shrine for the village.   [43] Interview at Zaghala, December 15, 1967.

upon by these priests to help and advise them. Overall, only a limited number of Mande have attained such positions of status, but the few instances that do exist unquestionably reveal how deeply some Muslims have become involved in the life of the region.

The evidence available concerning the relationships of the Mande with thier neighbors in the Cercle de Bondoukou and west central Ghana therefore contradicts the long-held assumptions that Islam is necessarily antithetical to traditional life. In this particular area, the Mande have not only come to accept the world about them but have participated in it in a highly constructive and intimate manner. Just how peacefully the Mande have managed to interact with these cultures is confirmed by my being unable to record a single instance of Mande Muslims having destroyed traditional art forms. Where traditions have been forced underground or uprooted, the pressures came from the colonial regimes or Christian missionaries, not Muslims. This happened, for example, to the Sakara-Bounou, a powerful anti-witchcraft masked cult at the turn of this century; it was forced into hiding during the 1920s and 1930s. Bron elders at Odumase, on the outskirts of Sunyani in Ghana, and the Nafana at Oulike, north of Bondoukou, still recall the burning of their Sakara masks by Baptist missionaries forty to fifty years ago.[44] (Their descriptions of these masks, two at Odumase and three at Oulike, are very similar to Freeman's description of the Sakara-Bounou masks that he encountered in this area in the late 1880s.[45]) They claim that the cult continued to function secretly during the period of suppression but that Sakara masks were no longer carved; in fact, no masks have been used since Sakara came out of hiding in the 1940s. The only acts of Muslim intolerance and destruction of the arts reported were those ascribed to Samory's troops, who destroyed countless shrines in the Cercle de Bondoukou during the invasion of this area at the end of the nineteenth century. Significantly, however, locals maintained that the Dyula, Ligbi, and Hwela were not involved in these campaigns and that they were solidly opposed to Samory's goals and tactics – confirming the statements of these peoples.

Tolerance has characterized Mande thinking with respect to non-Muslims, and this basic attitude has allowed them to interact peacefully with their neighbors and their cults, shrines, festivals, and associated art forms. In the remaining chapters I shall describe in detail three of these cults, all utilizing masks – the Bedu, Gbain, and Do – with regard to Muslim involvement in them.

[44] Interviews at Oulike, December 21, 1967, and Odumase, July 24, 1967. The Kulango of Seikwa asserted that their Sakara-Bounou masks were destroyed in the mid-1920s by the District Commissioner. Memory of the songs associated with the Sakara remains, and three elderly Seikwa women – Abena Ntô, Afua Agyewa, and Ama Tawiah – were able to sing several of them. Interview at Seikwa, January 16, 1968.
[45] Freeman, *Travels and Life in Ashanti and Jaman*, pp. 148–55.

CHAPTER 6

THE BEDU MASKING TRADITION

Of all traditional art forms, according to writers who decry Islam as a force of destruction, it is the mask that to Muslims must be the most obvious and noxious symbol of the "pagan" world. Masks are generally the largest items physically and are among the most public of art forms, and their cults may involve the participation of virtually everyone in a given community. They are unquestionably the most dramatic expression of "paganism." Yet in the Cercle de Bondoukou and west central Ghana, there is always some Mande involvement in the three masking traditions found there (map 4).

The involvement of the Mande in the Bedu, Gbain, and Do masking associations exemplifies well the varied relationships that can exist between Muslims and figurative art traditions. The Bedu is clearly a non-Muslim tradition and does not exist among the Dyula, Ligbi, and Hwela. Yet despite its clearcut orientation, the Mande have openly tolerated and accepted this masquerade. The Gbain is found among both Muslims (the Dyula and Hwela) and non-Muslims. Although its present distribution is more concentrated among non-Muslims in the region, it is definitely Muslim in inspiration: indeed, it is a tradition that is acknowledged and documented by locals as having been adopted from their Muslim Mande neighbors. The Do masquerade is the fullest expression of a purely Muslim masking tradition. Its distribution is quite limited. It occurs only among the Muslim Ligbi, except that two Do masks are owned by the Hwela of Sorhobango. It is intimately tied to Islamic holy days and Muslim functionaries; in fact, it is so completely involved with Muslim life that its utility outside this context is inconceivable.

Let us consider the Bedu tradition in some detail before dealing with the masquerades tied more closely to Muslim practices. Historical data for the Bedu are decidedly limited because this important and popular masquerade (restricted to the Cercle de Bondoukou) is of relatively recent origin. My research into the histories of Bedu masks associated with the Nafana, Kulango, and Degha indicated that the tradition is no older than two generations. This probability is strengthened by the fact that in no village had the Bedu masks been replaced more than one time.

4. Present distribution of the Bedu, Gbain, and Do masquerades in the Cercle de Bondoukou and west central Ghana.

Oral traditions collected about the Bedu and the still-prominent Sakara-Bounou cult reveal an important link between the two. At Oulike, the seat of Sakara in the Cercle de Bondoukou, village elders claimed that the cult originally included two large plank-like masks. This claim is supported by evidence from Delafosse, who visited the village of Ourigûé (Oulike) in April 1902 and noted a mud relief of a mask on the exterior wall of the "Sakara-bounou" hut.[1] His reproductive sketch is of a large face mask with a disc-like superstructure (plate 22), seemingly very similar to the masks described by the elders of Oulike in November of 1967. The old Sakara masks at Oulike were destroyed about fifty years ago by the first French Catholic missionaries in the area.[2] French religious and colonial officials regarded this anti-witchcraft cult as a ruthless organization that exploited naive villagers. The same attitude existed among the British, and Sakara

[1] Maurice Delafosse, *Les Frontières de la Côte d'Ivoire, de la Côte d'Or et du Soudan*, pp. 119–20.
[2] Interviews at Oulike, November 23, 1966; December 21, 1967; January 5, 1968.

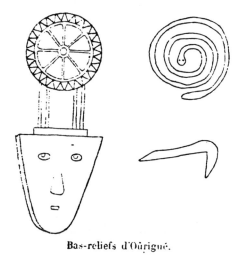

Bas-reliefs d'Ourigué.

22. Mud relief of a mask on the wall of the "Sakara-bounou" hut.

cults in adjacent areas of the Gold Coast were also suppressed.[3] The extent of Sakara at the turn of the twentieth century seems to have included much of the region under discussion here, and it is likely that all Sakara cults suffered similar fates. R. Austin Freeman, who encountered "Sakrobundi" at the Bron town of Odumase and at the Nafana village of Duadaso in 1889, emphasized the importance of the cult in the Gold Coast at that time.[4] Within thirty to forty years after his visit, however, all Sakara-Bounou masks had been destroyed and the cult had gone underground.

The elders at Oulike suggested that the principal shrine of Sakara was kept in hiding for a period of about ten years, not being brought out again until around 1930, at which time masks were no longer associated with the cult.[5] It was at about the same time, according to Oulike elders, that the first Bedu masks appeared in the area.[6] Although Sakara continued to deal with witchcraft, it did so without the use of masks, and this seems to have made it less abhorrent to French officials. The Bedu employed masks but dealt with "positive" issues – human fertility, prevention of epidemics, and internal social control – and was thus apparently tolerable to the colonial administrators. These administrators either did not notice or conveniently ignored the striking visual similarity of the new Bedu masks to the old Sakara-Bounou ones.[7]

To my knowledge, only two examples of Sakara-Bounou masks exist.

[3] Interview at Duadaso, March 6 and 7, 1967; at Seikwa, January 16, 1968.
[4] *Travels and Life in Ashanti and Jaman*, pp. 148–9.
[5] Interview at Oulike, December 21, 1967.   [6] Interview at Oulike, January 5, 1968.
[7] In their overall appearance, these two mask types are very close indeed. This is particularly true of the male Bedu mask, which is occasionally carved with two graceful horns above the plank-like face. Differences in details do exist but are minor.

23. "Sakrobundi mask from Jaman";
wood; ochre, black, white paint;
h. 58".

24. "Sakrobundi" mask: wood; ochre,
black, white paint; h. 59".

One is in the British Museum and is labeled "Sakrobundi mask from Jaman" (plate 23).[8] It was collected by Captain (Sir) Cecil Armitage, who was in the colonial service in the Gold Coast at the end of the nineteenth century.[9] The second mask is in Celia Barclay's collection in Waltham Abbey, England, and was also collected by Armitage (plate 24). The two pieces are very similar in both total form and detail. Both are large flat ovoid masks with two curved horns forming a superstructure. In both instances the flat face portion of the masks is covered with raised geometric motifs. The British Museum example has a bold triangular pattern covering its surface, whereas the Barclay mask has a combination of triangular and square designs. The central portion of both pieces is filled by an abbreviated human face, the eyeholes being the openings through which the

[8] Leon Underwood, *Masks of West Africa*, p. 48, plate 26.
[9] W. B. Fagg, *African Sculpture*, p. 112. Fagg attributes this example to the Nafana, probably on the basis of evidence obtained from "Sieber and his followers," but this attribution lacks any real evidence. The Nafana village of Oulike did serve as the seat of Sakara, but the tradition was and is found among numerous peoples in this area – the Bron, Degha, and Kulango as well as the Nafana.

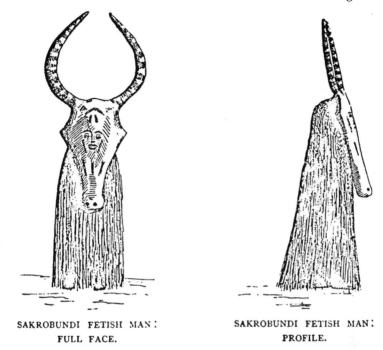

SAKROBUNDI FETISH MAN :
FULL FACE.

SAKROBUNDI FETISH MAN :
PROFILE.

25. "Sakrobundi Fetish Man" at Odumase.

26. Masked dancers at Bondoukou.

masked dancer would have seen. At the bottom of each mask is a rudimentary projection which the dancer would have gripped to stabilize the large, unwieldy mask while performing. Even the painted surfaces of these masks are identical, both incorporating red, black, and natural ochre colors.

The only major difference between the two masks is that the British Museum example has a carved wooden loop on the inside of the superstructure, which serves as a graceful reiteration of the more prominent horns. Minor differences occur in carved details. The edge of the British Museum example has a curled motif at the sides of the mask, possibly indicating ears. The small face in the center of the flat plank has a tri-lobed hairdo, and two small triangular projections flank the rectangular area connecting the horns to the body of the mask. The Barclay mask lacks the curled motif and has no hairdo, but there are four triangular projections attaching the horns to the rest of the mask. These masks recall both the drawing made by Freeman at Odumase in 1889 of a Sakara mask worn by a priest (plate 25) and the Delafosse sketch done at Ourigûé in 1902 (plate 22).[10]

The earliest documented Bedu mask can be found in the work *Côte d'Ivoire* by Clotilde Chivas-Baron, who visited the Ivory Coast in the mid-1930s. While at Bondoukou she witnessed a masquerade that included two large plank-like masks. Her rather impressionistic description names neither the occasion nor the masks that appeared but does reveal that the atmosphere was joyful, that it was a non-Muslim tradition, and that Muslims witnessed the ritual.[11] Fortunately, she did photograph the two masked dancers (plate 26); the masks that they are carrying, plus their full-length raffia gowns, clearly indicate that she was observing a Bedu performance. The appearance of women in her photograph confirms the public nature of this masked display, a feature of the Bedu everywhere. That the masks are Bedu is obvious from their configuration. They are large flat oval masks with bold geometric areas of paint on the surface. One mask is surmounted by horns (male?) and the other by three laterally joined x's (female?). Three round projections in the center of the mask faces, representing the eyes and mouth, have been punched through so that the dancers can see. The unusual superstructure of one of these masks does not disqualify it as a Bedu but is simply a difference in detail.

This early photograph is an especially valuable document because the masks depicted are virtually identical to the two Nafana Bedu masks of Bondoukou (plate 27) that I recorded in 1966. Although the two masks were kept in Degawiile, a small Nafana village three miles to the south, they belonged to the Nafana of Bondoukou. The masks were kept at Degawiile because the old Bedu shrine in Bondoukou had been destroyed by fire in

[10] Freeman, *Travels and Life in Ashanti and Jaman*, p. 155; Delafosse, *Les Frontières de la Côte d'Ivoire*, p. 120.   [11] pp. 180–1, photograph opposite p. 180.

27. Bedu masqueraders and masks;
wood; ochre, black, white
polychrome; male mask (left) h.
58″, female mask h. 52″. Nafana
village of Degawiile.

28. Bedu mask, female (?); wood;
ochre and white paint; h. 61″.

1962 and the people felt that the replacement masks would be safer in the small farming village. They were carved shortly after their predecessors had been destroyed, and they are very like those photographed by Chivas-Baron. The rather unusual (female?) Bedu – the one with three x's – is paralleled closely by the new female Bedu and, in fact, is the only example of such a superstructure found in any village currently using the masks. The horned mask, a typical example of the male Bedu, is also reminiscent of the Chivas-Baron example. The Nafana of Degawiile stated that the recent pair is the second set of Bedu that they have owned, and it is therefore entirely possible that Chivas-Baron observed and photographed the original pair of Bondoukou Bedu.[12]

Chivas-Baron has left us the only documented example of early Bedu masks in or out of context. All other examples (in private collections and museums and in my field data) have come to light during the past ten years. The late entry of the Bedu into European collections is doubtless a result of the recent origin of the tradition and not, as Fagg surmised, because the masks have been produced for tourist consumption.[13]

The corpus of museum and privately owned Bedu masks is limited. Their quality ranges from excellent examples equivalent to those I saw in the field to ones that may have been carved for the tourist trade. Two Bedu owned by the Locksley/Shea Gallery in Minneapolis, Minn. appear to be examples of relatively recent manufacture.[14] One of the masks shows few traces of use, being too crisply carved and the paint being totally intact. The second mask (plate 28) reveals some wear, but the carving and the painted surface are not carefully finished. Because of these features, it is probable that these two masks were not intended for ritual use.

The collected Bedu fall into two classes: those with a superstructure consisting of a large disc with a hole in the center and cut-out portions flanking it, and those with a superstructure of horns. This difference, according to informants in the field, indicates the sex of the mask, those with the disc generally being referred to as female and those with the horns, male. Informants were not, however, consistent with respect to this distinction, for in a few cases the horned examples were said to be female. All but one of the collected Bedu masks have two parallel vertical posts connecting the face of the mask to the superstructure.

[12] Interview at Degawiile, November 2, 1966.
[13] Fagg suggested to me in a personal communication in January 1966 that these were quite probably "tourist" pieces. In later conversations after my return from the field (February 1968, April 1968), he continued to maintain this, as is apparent in his recent comments on this mask type (see his *African Sculpture*, p. 112). In all fairness to Fagg, some examples of the Bedu have been created for the art markets in Europe and the United States. While in the field, I saw several pieces being carved for these markets. But the majority of these masks in Western collections appear to be legitimate.
[14] Acquired by the gallery in the autumn of 1969. Personal communication from Gordon Locksley, November 1969.

29. Bedu mask, female (?); wood; ochre,
white, blue-black paint; h. 98".

30. Bedu mask, female (?); wood; ochre,
white, blue-black paint.

Beyond the overall similarities, there are a number of variations within
the type. The Bedu noted in the Furman Gallery (New York City) catalogue *Masterworks of Primitive Art* is slightly over eight feet tall (plate
29).[15] (Few of the Bedu masks seen in the field approached this height.
Most of the works were four to five feet in height,[16] the exceptions being
the recently carved female masks at Kanguele and Sorhobango and the
older female Bedu at Yerekaye.) The face portion of the mask is a very
narrow triangle with the eyes and mouth cut out in a square fashion. The
painted motifs on the surmounting disc consist of three large circles below
a half moon. All of these features are unusual. A Bedu probably in the
collection of the National Museum in Abidjan, Ivory Coast, and cited by
Bohumil Holas in *Masques ivoiriens*, is decidedly peculiar (plate 30).[17] This

[15] Aaron Furman Gallery (New York City), *Masterworks of Primitive Art*, plate 33.
[16] Drid Williams states in her article "The Dance of the Bedu Moon" that the female
Bedu that she saw in the field measured ten to eleven feet in height and the male
examples ranged from seven to eight feet. Both measurements must be an exaggeration
unless she was measuring from the ground to the top of the masks while they were in use.
[17] p. 90. Holas does not give the locations of the figures he reproduces. I assume it is a
piece from the National Museum at Abidjan because Holas generally documents his
works with pieces from the collection there, where he is director.

31. Bedu mask, female (?); wood; ochre, white, blue-black paint; h. 71.5".

32. Bedu mask, male (?); wood and tin; ochre, white, blue-black paint; h. 62".

example is not a monoxyle carving but consists of seven pieces of wood joined: four pieces making up the disc superstructure, two the posts, and one the face. I have encountered no other examples treated in such a manner. The shape of the face is an isosceles trapezoid, a feature that also is unparalleled. The painted surface of the surmounting disc is covered by fifteen large dots; this is again unique.

Other Bedu in Western collections are much more typical, differences occurring in rather minor details. The mask in the Antwerp Ethnographic Museum (plate 31) is very close to many of the female Bedu recorded in the Cercle de Bondoukou.[18] The face portion has three clearly defined holes in its center, and the edge of the surmounting disc is notched all around. The four curvilinear cuts in the disc are also a common stylistic component of female Bedu. The example in the Paul Tishman collection in Los Angeles and another Bedu probably in the National Museum in Abidjan are again quite typical except that the posts connecting the superstructures to the faces of these two masks are bent.[19] A male Bedu owned by John and

[18] Adr. Claerhout, *Arts d'Afrique, d'Océanie, d'Amérique*, plate 21.
[19] Roy Sieber and Arnold Rubin, *Sculpture of Black Africa: The Paul Tishman Collection*, p. 50; Holas, *Masques Ivoiriens*, p. 28.

Dominique de Menil (plate 32) is unusual in that tin has been applied to the horns and to the area connecting them to the face.[20] The two narrow metal strips at the base of the horns were probably applied to prevent further cracks from developing in that area. Whether the larger square piece of tin, inscribed with the word "kerosene," has a functional purpose or is a whimsical addition is not known. Another male Bedu, in a private collection in Milan and reproduced by Franco Monti in *African Masks*, is typical in every respect except the bold polychromy on the face.[21]

The data accompanying the examples of Bedu masks currently in museums and private collections are often confusing. Inadequate documentation of collected objects of African art has always been a problem, but it reaches its nadir where the Bedu tradition is concerned. Some of the inaccuracies presented are undoubtedly due to honest mistakes and to assumptions based on insufficient evidence, but it is equally true that others represent fictions created by amiable dealers (both African and European) eager to satisfy collectors.

Monti refers to the Milan Bedu in the following manner:

Sakrobundi mask . . . Grumshi (Gyaman); northern region, Ghana . . . This mask represents Sakrobundi, the spirit of the forest, adorned with antelope horns. It is thought that this gigantic mask was used by the Ashanti people in a war ritual . . .[22]

It is impossible to know where this information originated, but most of it is misleading and inaccurate. The reference "Sakrobundi" is understandable, for the mask does relate stylistically to those noted by Freeman and Delafosse, which were the only sources dealing with "Sakrobundi" available to Monti (the Bedu tradition was totally undocumented until the current fieldwork[23]). However, the attribution to the "Grumshi" (presumably the Grunshi or Gourounsi) is without proper foundation. It is apparently based on Freeman's rather vague conjecture regarding the origins of "Sakrobundi" in Gyaman: "It appeared, however, that the worship of Sakrobundi had been introduced into Jaman from the north – possibly from Gruinsi, Moshi, or Dagomba – in comparatively recent times."[24] My own research into Sakara-Bounou did not reveal any northern or Grunshi origins for this tradition. This conclusion is based on data I obtained from priests and members of Sakara-Bounou in the Cercle de Bondoukou and on responses to inquiries further north in both Gonja and the region around Wa. Monti further confuses the picture by relating the

[20] Museum of Primitive Art, *The John and Domenique de Menil Collection*, p. 46.
[21] p. 74. [22] p. 72.
[23] Drid Williams's article on the Bedu masquerade profited considerably from data provided me.
[24] *Travels and Life in Ashanti and Jaman*, p. 148. Freeman did not travel farther north than Bondoukou.

Grunshi to Gyaman, and Gyaman to northern Ghana. Some of the Grunshi do live in northern Ghana, but for the most part they inhabit the southern stretches of Upper Volta. In addition, a numerically insignificant Grunshi population, mostly farm laborers, has very recently migrated to the town of Bondoukou in the Ivory Coast, but they are not involved in the Bedu. Gyaman is the Twi name for the Bron state established in the late seventeenth century around the town of Bondoukou, but since Monti places Gyaman in northern Ghana, it is most improbable that he is aware of this immaterial relationship between the Bondoukou area and the Grunshi. Monti's references to the Ashanti are equally without foundation. Freeman states plainly that he did not encounter Sakrobundi in Ashanti.[25] Furthermore, there is no evidence that the Ashanti have ever used masks of any kind or that Sakrobundi has been used in a war ritual by anyone or referred to as a "spirit of the forest."

Claerhout, who also incorrectly attributes a Bedu (the mask at Antwerp) to the Grunshi of Ghana, is far more circumspect: "Ce genre de masques n'est connu que depuis quelques années. L'origine n'est pas encore déterminée avec certitude et leurs fonctions ne sont que présumées."[26]

The previously described mask in the Furman Gallery catalogue is referred to as a "Mask of the Sun" from Ghana.[27] Masks associated with the worship of the sun do not exist in Ghana or in the Ivory Coast. In fact, there is no evidence to date for their existence anywhere in Black Africa. It is impossible to know who concocted this attribution.

Despite the contradictory and often fallacious data associated with collected examples of these masks, they are all clearly Bedu. The value of these examples lies in the fact that they do give us a good indication of stylistic nuances within a specific type: in this case, one that is both recent in origin and quite limited in its geographical distribution – i.e., within the Cercle de Bondoukou from the town of Bondoukou itself to the regions immediately to the north and west of it. In 1967–8, Bedu masks were found in the Degha village of Motiambo, the Nafana villages of Degawiile (the masks owned by the Bondoukou Nafana) and Tambi, and among the Kulango at Kanguele, Sorhobango, Debango, Bozangui, and Yerekaye. Villages that had had the Bedu prior to this period but whose masks had been stolen or destroyed by natural forces included Oulike (Nafana), Bouroumba (Degha), and Kyende (Kulango). Members of these three villages indicated that they wished to replace the missing Bedu but that the expense involved prohibited them from doing so at the time. Where the tradition was found the masquerade included two masks, one male and one female, except in the towns of Bozangui, Yerekaye, and Debango, where only female Bedu existed.

---

[25] Ibid. [26] *Arts d'Afrique*, plate 21.
[27] *Masterworks of Primitive Art*, plate 33.

The importance of the Bedu, according to Kulango, Nafana, and Degha informants, lies in its ability to handle a variety of social and cultural problems. The death of an important elder in any of the villages that own the masks requires the appearance of the Bedu dancers, since the protective character of the ceremony is especially needed at such a time. Other than these occasions, the activity of the Bedu is confined to the month-long festival of Zaurau, which coincides approximately with the latter part of November and most of December. During this time the other concerns of the masquerade become evident. One of these concerns is human fertility, and women who have had difficulty conceiving and young girls who wish for many children hope that the masked dancers will touch them during their performances. The masks are also thought to hold a definite curative potential, especially for children. Mothers strap sick children to their backs and dance about the masqueraders so that the Bedu may speak to and touch the youngsters. In addition, the Bedu seems to have a general apotropaic value, being able to avert every misfortune from agricultural disaster to a decimating epidemic: the activities of the Bedu during Zaurau are believed to prevent the recurrence of any problem that has arisen during the preceding year. The nightly masquerade also provides a cathartic experience for the entire community. Coming at the close of the harvesting season, the festival is a time of relaxation, exuberance, even abandon. The Kulango term for this period, "Bèlèhodo," meaning "you may be beaten without repercussion," aptly describes the social attitudes prevailing during Zaurau.

The preparations for the Bedu month are few but are meticulously carried out. The masks must be repaired, since the soft wood of the silk cotton tree decays quickly. Then they are washed and repainted. The *nyungu* (home), a small hut on the outskirts of the village or a room within the compound of the family that owns the Bedu masks, is swept and washed. The *sokoro* (raffia costumes) and the *biinzani* (raffia bangles worn by the masqueraders) are aired and mended. Members of the families that control the Bedu must rehearse and review the songs and dance steps that are a necessary feature of the masquerade. When the month of the festival arrives, the dancers perform every evening. As night falls, villagers leave their compounds to gather at the central clearing that is found in all villages. Soon the masked dancers, led by one or two male attendants, enter from one of the major footpaths leading to the village. The masquerader impersonating the female moves slowly and gracefully, imitating the walk of a woman, the mask swaying gently. The male masquerader follows the female in order to protect her, moving brusquely and unpredictably, and shaking a fly-whisk to clear the path of children and other curious onlookers who have crowded around in anticipation of the performance.

Arriving at the clearing, the masqueraders greet the assembled villagers

113

and then visit a number of compounds in order to bless the inhabitants, especially the sick. Those so honored offer money to the Bedu dancers. Both masqueraders speak in high-pitched voices, bestowing their blessings in an esoteric language. Owners of the Bedu claim that the languages are archaic forms of Kulango, Nafana, and Degha that are no longer understood by the villagers but have been retained for purposes of the masquerade. The tour of the village by the masks requires about an hour; with the completion of this part of the ritual, they return to the central clearing.

From this point on, the Bedu ceremony is carried out within the clearing. Accompanied by drummers, the masqueraders lead the villagers in songs and dances, the festivities lasting well into the night and sometimes until daybreak. The songs touch on all facets of local life. They may lampoon chiefs and elders, a quarrelsome mother, a witch, or an irresponsible youth. Many songs ridicule, in blunt and explicit terms, deviant sexual behaviour or male and female sex organs, typifying the social license permitted during Zaurau. Throughout the night, the revelry and mockery are enjoyed in an atmosphere of camaraderie, for the villagers make the most of these opportunities to bypass traditional taboos. Yet they know they will be accountable for their behavior once the Bedu month is over, and they are aware of the serious purpose underlying the appearance of the Bedu dancers. It is difficult ever to forget completely the myriad dangers that constantly face man and the necessity to attempt to avert these dangers by whatever means promise success.

Although the Bedu is always controlled by non-Muslims, the Muslim Mande in these villages, and elsewhere, are affected by the tradition.[28] At Sorhobango (a town composed of two large quarters, one Muslim Hwela and the other Kulango), the Bedu masquerade is witnessed by all and is performed for the benefit of both religious groups. In December 1966 I viewed a performance of the Bedu that began with the masked dancers walking in a stately manner to the compound of *Karamoko* Sora, a cleric who had been gravely ill for the preceding few days. He was greeted and symbolically embraced by the masked dancers, and the grass-thatched roof to his house was touched by the Bedu. The masks then visited the compound of the Sa, the secular head of the Hwela, to greet him. Later in the evening, when the masqueraders were performing in the large clearing situated between the Hwela and Kulango sectors of the town, virtually all Hwela clerics, including the Imām, were present. Hwela Muslims interviewed on the spot were quick to acknowledge that this Kulango tradition was an important safeguard for the entire community of Sorhobango. Some

---

[28] Some Muslim participation occurs wherever the Mande inhabit or live in close proximity to non-Muslim villages utilizing this masquerade. Many of them simply observe the festivities, but others join in the dances and songs and want to be touched by the masked dancers.

33. Bedu mask, female; wood; ochre, blue, white paint; h. 81″. Carved by Sirikye. Village of Ycrekaye, 1967.

34. Bedu mask, female; wood; ochre, white, blue paint; h. 67″. Village of Bozangui, 1967.

35. Bedu mask, female; wood; ochre, white, blue paint; h. 63″. Village of Debango, 1967.

36. Bedu masks, male and female; wood; ochre, white, blue paint; male (left) h. 66″,
female h. 81″. Carved by Sirikye. Village of Sorhobango, 1967.

young Muslim boys attending the elementary Qur'ānic school in the village
poked fun at the proceedings, and some shouted deprecating comments such
as *diankôôn* (long-head), but they were reprimanded by Muslim elders
standing near them. Absolutely no hostility was demonstrated by Muslims;
indeed, they generally exhibited a good deal of respect for the Bedu, and
many were convinced of its essentially positive qualities.

Muslim involvement with Bedu may at times be much deeper than I have
already noted. Of the various Bedu masks currently in use in the Cercle de
Bondoukou, an overwhelming majority were carved by the Muslim Hwela
artist Sirikye.[29] Examples of his work which have been carved during the
last fifteen years can be found at Kanguele, where both the male and female
masks are of his hand; at the Kulango villages of Yerekaye and Bozangui
(plates 33 and 34, both female masks); at Debango (plate 35, female); and
at Sorhobango (plate 36, male and female pair). All of these Bedu are clearly

[29] Although born at Sorhobango and a resident of that town, during the time of my fieldwork Sirikye was living in the village of Oawe, where he was being treated by a Kulango
herbalist for a variety of ills including a badly broken ankle. In his early forties, he has
been carving for nearly twenty years and is acknowledged by both Muslims and non-
Muslims as the most prolific and talented carver in the Cercle de Bondoukou. As a
Muslim who attended Qur'ānic school at Sorhobango and Accra for two years, he is a
perfect example of the pragmatic believer who is involved in the faith but is unwilling
to ignore the world about him.

37. Bedu masks, male and female; wood; ochre, white, blue paint; male (right) h. 73″, female h. 81″. Carved by Sirikye. Village of Kanguele, 1966.

recognizable as Sirikye's work, for the female masks have the very obvious notched motif around the surmounting disc, which is one of his trademarks. The male mask at Sorhobango has a small half-moon design paralleling the sweep of the horns, a Sirikye trait; the male example at Kanguele (plate 37) is unusual in that it also has the notched design around the disc. Not only has Sirikye carved most of the Bedu masks in use, but villagers who desire the Bedu claim that they will seek him out and commission him to carve the masks.[30]

The very positive orientation of the Bedu has prompted many Muslims, even members of the 'ulamā', to cooperate with the tradition. The large and joyous meal served on the final evening of the month-long Bedu ceremony is attended by Muslims. Muslim women, in fact, help to prepare food for this feast. *Karamokos* occasionally offer a short prayer on behalf of the Bedu before it is retired to the *nyungu*. Such prayers are meant to safeguard the Bedu while it rests.

Muslim involvement in the Bedu masquerade is easily understood. Those interviewed claim that its public nature, its lack of esoteric ritual,

[30] The elders at Oulike, Kammala, and Bouroumba said that they will ask Sirikye to carve their masks, for his prices are fair – he asks approximately 10,000 West African francs (£20 or $50) for a pair – and his workmanship is undeniably the finest. There are carvers who charge less for these masks, but their work is inferior.

and its concerns for the health and prosperity of all mean that the tradition should be neither decried nor ignored. The Imām of Bondoukou regards Muslim attendance and participation with some disfavor, since strictly speaking the Bedu falls outside the purview of Islam. He realizes, however, that the concerns of Bedu are those of all men, and thus he accepts the fact that Muslims are involved in this tradition.

CHAPTER 7

THE GBAIN MASKING TRADITION

Defenders of the axiom that Islam is inimical to traditional art might well excuse the participation of the Mande in the Bedu masquerade on the same grounds as the Muslim participants themselves do. Yet even if we accept such excuses for Muslim tolerance of the Bedu, we cannot where the Gbain is concerned, for this anti-witchcraft masking tradition is far more intimately tied to the Muslim world, and its concern is one usually associated with "paganism."

Witchcraft is an important problem for the various cultures in the Cercle de Bondoukou and west central Ghana, as it is for so many African societies. A witch, generally speaking, is an anti-social person. The anti-social behavior may be overt or merely the holding of negative thoughts about another person. Such actions and attitudes must be controlled, since they are potentially disruptive to the society. Where the Gbain cult is found, it is responsible for providing this control. Whenever an accusation of witchcraft is made within a community, the Gbain acts to resolve the problem. If the cult members know who is at fault (that is, if the accusation is against a particular individual), their ritual functions as a police action that orders the witch to appear before the elders of the cult the morning following the masquerade. Even when the community is free of specific accusations, the Gbain performs on a regular weekly basis to discourage the operation of witches.

The early writings of the French administrators Louis Tauxier and Maurice Prouteaux prove invaluable in the reconstruction of a recent chronology for the Gbain. Prouteaux, a French officer in the Cercle de Bondoukou in 1915–16, described in considerable detail a Gbon (or Gbaons) ritual enacted by the Muslim Ligbi of Bouna in 1914. Prouteaux equated the Ligbi Gbon with similar masked rituals he had seen during his many years in the Ivory Coast:

On retrouve les mêmes masques, les mêmes rites, les mêmes confréries chez les peuplades les plus diverses: M. Delafosse en a signalé et j'en ai vu moi-même chez les Séné des districts de Boundiali et de Korhogo, je les ai retrouvés chez les Dioulas de Kong [the famous Muslim Dyula center of learning], chez ceux, d'origine différente, de Bondoukou et villages environnants (notamment Sorhobango et Bondo [also heavily Islamized communities]) . . .[1]

[1] "Notes sur certains rites," p. 37.

119

At Bouna, the Gbon mask was owned and maintained by the Ligbi, and this mask had a specific name, "Sourado."[2] My own inquiries revealed no individual names for Gbain masks nor any Ligbi group in which the cult existed. However, oral traditions collected among the Ligbi at both Bouna and Bondo-Dyoula indicated that there had indeed been Gbain cults in both of these towns but that they had stopped functioning about a generation ago.[3]

The details recorded by Prouteaux regarding the Gbon at Bouna indicate that this tradition was strikingly similar to the Gbain that I found in the Cercle de Bondoukou. Like the Gbain cult observed in 1966–7, the primary function of the Gbon at Bouna was as a deterrent against witchcraft. Secondarily it performed at the funerals of members of the cult. Although it was controlled by the Ligbi, the influence of the Gbon ranged far beyond this segment of the population.

Des hommes de tous les autres quartiers, tant musulmans que non musulmans, Dioulas que Koulangos, font partie de sa confrérie, et elle étend ses promenades dans tout le village. Aussi, lorsque resonne son tambour, Bouna tout entier se fait silencieux et désert.[4]

This all-inclusive membership was also a feature of the Gbain cult observed in 1966–7.

Prouteaux's descriptive details of the actual performance of the rite at Bouna are almost identical to the current operations of the Gbain. The Gbon carrier came out late at night preceded by drummers and dancers, younger members of the cult who performed in front of the mosque while waiting for the arrival of the masked dancer. The women and very young children in the town, not merely those in the Ligbi quarter, remained in their compounds, for if they witnessed the Gbon, barrenness or death would most certainly await them. According to Prouteaux, it was almost eleven at night before the masked dancer made his appearance. His entrance was accompanied by the sounds of drumming, blowing on a cow's horn, flailing (no longer a part of the Gbain ceremony), and striking an iron gong and by low-pitched songs sung by the young males in the cult. The Gbon carrier was dressed in a full-length raffia costume to keep his identity secret, and he capered about the open square in front of the mosque. His dance was a highly athletic display including prodigious leaps, crouching and kneeling movements, and rapid turns, and it lasted for nearly an hour. Having finished his performance, the Gbon carrier, accompanied by a member of the cult, went through the town in search of witches.[5]

---

[2] Ibid., p. 38.
[3] Interviews at Bondo-Dyoula, June 7, 1967, and Bouna, August 10, 1967. The cults had fallen into abeyance because of pressures from the 'ulamā'. *Karamokos* at both Bondo-Dyoula and Bouna stated that considerable controversy and animosity resulted from this pressure and that there was still a fair amount of interest in the Gbain at both towns.
[4] Prouteaux, "Notes sur certains rites," p. 39.   [5] Ibid., pp. 47–8.

In addition, Prouteaux recorded some of the extraordinary powers attributed to the Gbon by members of the cult. The Gbon was capable of supernatural feats, for the masked dancer could sit upon a pile of glowing coals and extinguish them without harming the Gbon or its raffia costume. Any carrier of the Gbon was able to leap onto the roofs of houses, even into the tallest branches of a tree, in order to secure a better vantage point for the pursuit of witches. Sourado could carry hot coals in its mouth without burning itself. The power of the Gbon was so great that one of the leading Muslims in the town cautioned Prouteaux to wash himself with a prescribed medicinal liquid before viewing the performance.

Mais je sentis que l'un de mes compagnons, un musulman, et des plus notables du quartier, était très préoccupé. A mesure que l'arrivée du Sourado devenait imminente, il donnait des signes d'une réelle anxiété. A la fin, n'y tenant plus, il me fit un discours assez embarrassé, dont le fond était à peu près que la vue du Sourado est dangereuse pour les non initiés, et que, s'il m'arrivait un accident le soir en rentrant ou le lendemain, il se ferait des reproches de m'avoir amené ici. Aussi me supplia-t-il de me soumettre à une légère formalité qui devait écarter toute crainte de la colère de l'esprit ... Le sonneur de clochette m'apporta une calebasse d'eau, qui, la nuit, paraissait pure, et y trempant la main je me mouillai légèrement le front et le visage. Cette ablution fut considérée comme suffisante, mais dans la pratique ordinaire, elle a lieu dans une case ou l'un des initiés répand lui-même l'eau lustrale sur le néophyte.[6]

Thus protected, Prouteaux could withstand the powers of the Gbon and would not be harmed either by his proximity to the masquerader or by the fire emitted from the mouth of Sourado while it sought its prey.

As with the Gbain, only initiated male members of the Gbon could witness and participate in the ritual. At Bouna the only exception to this rule was that class of old women who were past menopause and who therefore did not represent a threat to the mask. Prouteaux states that these women occupied an important functional role in the society, for at Bouna the Gbon had to obtain permission from one of them before the masked dancer could enter the town to perform its duties. If permission was not granted, the Gbon had no recourse but to appear at another time. This feature was not restricted to the Gbon cult at Bouna, for Prouteaux states that

Cette intrusion des femmes dans les confréries n'est pas particulière aux Ligbis de Bouna. Il paraît qu'à Bondo, village musulman des environs de Bondoukou, à Bondo où le Gbon, disent les indigènes, "est le plus fort de tous," ce sont des femmes qui préparent et entretiennent les vêtements et tous les accessoires.[7]

In a few villages in 1966–7 old women were allowed to witness the rites of the Gbain. At no time, however, did these women serve as caretakers,

---

[6] Ibid., pp. 43–4.   [7] Ibid., p. 51.

nor were they actually involved in the functioning of the cult in the way noted by Prouteaux for the Gbon at Bouna and Bondo.

Prouteaux does not describe the style of the Bouna Gbon mask in any detail, but he does state that it was reminiscent of other horizontal masks, carved in the form of bush cows, which he had seen near Bondoukou, at the Muslim Mande center of Kong, and in the Senufo country around Korhogo. All Gbain masks seen in the field in 1966–7 conformed to the basic horizontal bush-cow style. The Ligbi Gbon was capable of breathing fire, which enabled the masked dancer to combat the power of witches, and this is still a critical feature of the Gbain. The annual festival of purification for Sourado and the cult members at Bouna occurred at precisely the same time that Gbain masks are cleansed today – on the nights of the ninth and tenth days of Dyombende (the Muslim festival of Asura), which occurs during the first month of the Islamic year, Muharram.[8] Thus in virtually all respects the Ligbi Gbon recorded by Prouteaux at Bouna in 1914 is identical to the Gbain cult noted by me in 1966–7 in west central Ghana and the northeastern Ivory Coast. Prouteaux's findings can thus be considered the earliest recorded evidence for this masking tradition.

Tauxier adds an important dimension to our knowledge of this cult, for he notes its rather limited distribution shortly after Prouteaux's observations, namely 1918–20. According to him, this masked society, although no longer existing at Bondoukou itself, could still be found in certain Muslim villages and towns throughout the countryside. The tradition was functioning at Bouna, Bondo-Dyoula, and, in greater density, in the regions of Barabo and Nassian. (Unfortunately, he does not specify the places in Barabo and Nassian in which the Gbain flourished.) He also cites the important Muslim Hwela towns of Damisa (Namasa) in the Gold Coast and Sorhobango, just north of Bondoukou, as major centers of the Gbon or Gbain tradition.[9] The cult is active and flourishing today in all the Muslim communities enumerated by Tauxier except Bouna and Bondo-Dyoula.

A particularly important aspect of Tauxier's list of towns and villages having Gbain cults is the absence of non-Muslim communities. The impression gained from his writings is that this masking tradition was limited to, and in the control of, the Muslim Dyula, Ligbi, and Hwela in the period around 1920. Locals could participate in the rites of the Muslim-dominated Gbain and could even become members of importance in the society, as was observed by Prouteaux, but they did not seem to have their own organized Gbain cults. This was certainly not the case in 1966–7, for the tradition at that time occurred in numerous Kulango, Degha, Nafana, and Numu villages, where in all cases the Gbain was owned and controlled

---

[8] Ibid., p. 52.
[9] Tauxier, *Le Noir de Bondoukou*, p. 295, note.

38. Gbain mask; wood, feathers, cord,
    cloth; l. 26″.

39. Gbain mask; wood, clay, cord, cloth;
    l. 29″. Carved by Sinna. Numu
    village of Brawhani, 1966.

40. Gbain mask; wood, cord, cloth,
    feathers; l. 26″. Kulango village
    of Sagabile, 1966.

123

41. Gbain mask; wood; l. 31".

by the non-Muslims. Thus between 1920 and the time of my fieldwork, the Gbain must have spread rapidly beyond its Muslim strongholds to these groups, a hypothesis substantiated by the traditions of origin collected for this masked cult at several non-Muslim villages in the region.[10] These traditions clearly point to the important roles played by such Mande centers as Sorhobango, Bondo-Dyoula, and others in the dissemination of this anti-witchcraft cult.

There are, to my knowledge, no old examples of the Gbain in either museums or private collections. Indeed, I know of only three examples of this mask type out of context, and these specimens were acquired quite recently. One (plate 38) is owned by the Harry Franklin Gallery in Los Angeles and was purchased in 1967.[11] No documentation accompanied the piece when it was obtained, but it conforms fully to Gbain masks that I recorded in the field. In its style the mask approximates a Gbain used at the Numu village of Brawhani (plate 39) and is reminiscent of the Kulango Gbain at Sagabile (plate 40). The Franklin piece is carved in the form of a bush cow with powerfully conceived yet gracefully curved horns. The secondary motif on the mask is two small four-legged animals which pro-

[10] The oldest examples of communities borrowing the Gbain from Muslim Mande peoples come from the Numu (Mande) village of Brawhani in the Banda district of western Brong-Ahafo, and the Kulango center of Sagabile in the Cercle de Bondoukou. The former credit the towns of Nassian and Sorhobango as the sources for their two masks, and the latter credit Bondo-Dyoula. Interviews at Sagabile, June 6, 1967, and Brawhani, November 10, 1967.

[11] This Gbain mask recently appeared in print in H. M. Cole, *African Arts of Transformation*, p. 46.

ject from the sides of the helmet. The mask is worn horizontally, as are all Gbain, with the dancer looking out of the maw. Feathers and talismans attached to the snout of the mask, and a patina consisting of eggshells, mud, traces of blood (animal, undoubtedly), and palm wine, are typically Gbain. The authenticity of this piece cannot be questioned, given the inclusion of all these features.

The second collected Gbain example (plate 41) was acquired by the Locksley/Shea Gallery in 1969.[12] Although a rather recently carved piece still showing the traces of adze marks and having almost no ritual patination on the surface, it is nonetheless an important object. The mask is probably the work of Sirikye, the prominent Muslim Hwela responsible for so many of the Bedu masks in the Cercle de Bondoukou and also the most important carver of the Gbain. The Lockley/Shea piece is strikingly similar to the Gbain mask carved by Sirikye for the Kulango village of Oawe in about 1961 (plate 42). Like the Oawe work, it has a double head and two sets of horns with a small figure of a guinea fowl perched on top of them, but it is not as competently carved as the traditional example. It is nevertheless a good specimen of the Gbain masks that Sirikye has begun to carve, in addition to his traditional works, for the tourist trade.[13]

The Gbain mask that I collected at Bouroupônkô in the Cercle de Bondoukou in 1968, now in the collection of Professor Roy Sieber, was carved by the Muslim Hwela Adama Dudumaye from Debango (plate 43). This is a very recent piece, having been carved in 1961, yet it is still an important document of the mask type. It was used over a period of seven years as a "training mask" by Adama, who would take this Gbain to non-Muslim villages in order to demonstrate how the masquerade operated. Adama is considered to be one of the most knowledgeable Muslims in matters concerning the Gbain. He is well versed in the intimacies of its powers, the songs necessary for its ritual performance, the dance steps performed by the carrier of the mask, and even the well-kept secrets of how the mask breathes fire.[14] This particular mask was not an advertising piece only but on occasion was used by Adama when a non-Gbain-using village needed the services of the mask. The single face of this mask is

[12] Personal communication from Gordon Locksley, November 1969.
[13] Sirikye has no qualms about carving for both markets. Objects that he carves for the Abidjan market require little thought, and no ritual preparations are required except for pouring libations to the tree. Traders who commission these works place few demands on his skills, but they do urge him to produce quickly, for the masks are highly desired items. Gbain masks carved for local use, however, are far more difficult to produce, for consumers are knowledgeable and expect the masks to be both effective and skillfully carved.
[14] Adama claimed that he had learned the secrets associated with breathing fire in 1957 from a Senufo priest at Korhogo and a Hausa *karamoko*, Abu Bakari of Kano. Breathing fire is done simply by placing glowing cinders in a small perforated clay cup, which is glued inside the maw of the mask; the dancer blows against the cup and sparks are emitted. Interview at Bondoukou, December 11, 1968.

42. Gbain mask; wood, cord, cloth; l. 34″. Carved by Sirikye. Kulango village of Oawe, 1966.

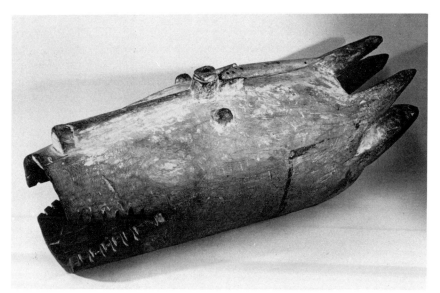

43. Gbain mask; wood and chalk; l. 27″. Carved by Adama Dudumaye of Debango, 1968.

44. Gbain mask; wood, cord, skull; l. 26″. Nafana village of Bouroupônkô, 1967.

45. Gbain mask; wood and chalk, traces of ochre paint; l. 22″. Photographed in Gbain shrine at Sorhobango, 1966.

treated in a tubular manner, having little sculptural definition on the surface. It relates stylistically to the Gbain mask in use at the Nafana village of Bouroupônkô (plate 44) except for the fact that the latter is double-faced, has a pair of carved cow's horns attached to the top of the head, and has a small skull tied to the horns.[15] The heads of this mask are tubular, very much like the head of the Sieber example.

Although today the Gbain is found among both the Dyula and the Hwela, it also flourishes amidst such non-Muslim populations as the Kulango, Degha, Numu, and Nafana. There are indications beyond the weight of historical evidence already cited that the Gbain was originally a Muslim Mande tradition. The data from Tauxier and Prouteaux indicate that the cult existed only among the Mande in the Cercle de Bondoukou and the Cercle de Bouna in the early twentieth century. The Gbain cults I encountered among non-Muslims in 1966–7 were acknowledged as having been imported from Muslim communities over a period of the last thirty to forty years. A good deal of prestige is attached to the Islamic center from which the tradition has been acquired.[16]

The distribution of the Gbain mask in 1966–7 clearly reveals the paramount position played by the Muslim Mande with respect to this cult. I found the Gbain in only three Mande communities: the Hwela sector of Sorhobango (plate 45); the Dyula village of Sandhuei (plate 46); and the predominantly Hwela village of Namasa (plate 47), where it is owned by the Nafana but is heavily dependent on the Hwela population. These three centers, however, have had an inordinate influence on the distribution and use of the Gbain, for virtually every non-Muslim village utilizing this masquerade has derived its tradition from one of these towns. The Degha of Zaghala, who currently own two Gbain masks, and the Kulango of Sagabile and Yerekaye, who each have one functioning mask, say they obtained their cults at Sorhobango. The Numu of Brawhani and Kwametintini and the Kulango of Oawe also regard the Sorhobango Hwela as the source of their Gbain traditions. The Nafana of Bouroupônkô acquired theirs from Namasa. I was told that Sandhuei was an important source for the Gbain in Barabo some twenty years ago but that the tradition in this area, except at Sandhuei itself, has now died.[17]

---

[15] The use of a skull on the Bouroupônkô Gbain is exceptional. It is noteworthy that despite repeated inquiry, the Nafana would not indicate the kind of skull that was used on the mask; and this fact, plus the skull's size and the type of skeletal structure, suggests that it might well be that of a human child.

[16] A strong sense of "pride of place" was noticeable for Gbain cults deriving from the Hwela town of Sorhobango and the Ligbi center of Bondo-Dyoula. When a village acquires a Gbain from a Muslim community, a ritual link is formed. Muslim services are both sought and offered in order to maintain the new shrine.

[17] The Gbain did exist in the Dyula villages of Delaware, Lalo, and Bandakani Soukoura some ten to fifteen years ago, but the tradition was stopped by a variety of pressures. At Bandakani Soukoura, the 'ulamā' burned the mask, and at Lalo and Delaware the

46. Gbain mask; wood, netting, cloth, raffia; l. 23.5″. Dyula village of Sandhuei.

47. Gbain mask; wood; l. 33″. Photographed in Gbain ritual precinct at Hwela village of Namasa, 1966.

The Islamized Mande, generally the Dyula and Hwela, are not only the sources for Gbain cults but also remain prominent in the operation of the cults once they are disseminated. Turuga Bamba, a Ligbi from Bondo-Dyoula, where the tradition did exist about thirty years ago, still produces amulets for the Gbain mask at Sagabile.[18] Adama Dudumaye, a Hwela, is consulted about the Gbain by the Degha at Zaghala and the Nafana of Bouroupônkô. Clerics from Sorhobango must attend the annual purification ceremony of the masks on *san ielema seri* (see pp. 136–43) in all non-Muslim villages where the Gbain was inspired by their tradition. This kind of ritual link with Muslims exists wherever non-Muslims have adopted the Gbain.

In many instances the Gbain masks currently utilized by locals have even been carved by Muslims. The Hwela carver Sirikye is responsible for the masks at Oawe and Zaghala (plate 48) and for the original mask (not now functioning) at Sagabile (plate 49). The Gbain at Yerekaye (plate 50) is said to have been carved by a Hwela from Sorhobango named Saidu Garagye, who died in the early 1960s. Saidu Dudumaye, the brother of Adama, carved the Gbain at Bouroupônkô. Even non-Muslims who have carved Gbain masks for their own villages, like Kwadwo Gbyogoma from Kwametintini (plate 51) and Kawbena Sinna from Brawhani (plate 39), both Numu, have done so under the tutelage of Muslim carvers.

The organization and workings of the Gbain also point to the Muslim orientation of the cult. The major festival of purification for the Gbain mask, a crucial annual undertaking among both Muslims and non-Muslims, occurs on the important Islamic holy day of Asura. This is the new year ceremony coinciding with the tenth day of the first month of the Muslim calendar, Muharram. Members of the Mande family refer to this month as Dyombende or Dyomande and to the tenth day itself as *san ielema seri*. Muslims believe that it was on the tenth day of Dyombende that the great flood receded and Noah's ark grounded safely, allowing for the continued propagation of human and animal life. Important local events, some based on historical fact, others of a less precise nature, are also claimed to have taken place during this month and particularly on *san ielema seri*.[19] Furthermore, Mande informants regarded Dyombende as a most auspicious period for the practicing of both positive and negative magic. Subara (witchcraft) was said to be rampant at this time, and thus all possible precautions,

masks simply rotted away and were not replaced. There are Dyula in all three communities, however, who are hoping that the masquerade will be reinstated. Interviews at Delaware, Lalo, and Bandakani Soukoura, November 29 and 30, 1966.

[18] See note 3.

[19] Samory's destruction of Kong in 1897 and his ultimate capitulation to the French in 1898 were both described as having occurred on *san ielema seri*. Informants at Bondo-Dyoula claimed that it was on *san ielema seri* that Al-Ḥājjī Moro Bamba led their retreat from Begho.

48. Gbain masks; wood, clay, cord; left l. 20.75″, right l. 19″. Carved by Sirikye. Degha village of Zaghala, 1966.

49. Gbain mask; wood; l. 24″. Carved by Sirikye. Remnants of original Gbain mask at Kulango village of Sagabile, 1966.

50. Gbain mask; wood, cord, cloth,
clay paint; l. 32.5″. Carved by
Saidu Garagye of Sorhobango.
Kulango village of Yerekaye, 1966.

51. Gbain mask; wood, feathers, cloth, clay; l. 27″. Carved by Kwado Gbyogoma of
Kwametintini. Numu village of Kwametintini, 1966.

including the propitiation of the witch-seeking Gbain on the morning of *san ielema seri*, are taken.

That the purification of Gbain masks should in fact occur during Dyombende and specifically on the tenth day is understandable only in terms of the total meaning and emphasis of this Islamic festival. According to the Hwela of Sorhobango and the Dyula of Sandhuei, the month of Dyombende is the most magical time of the entire Muslim year. Plants and animals generally esteemed for their prophylactic and curative qualities are said to be especially efficacious at the time of the new year. Women spend the first ten days of Dyombende collecting a wide variety of roots, leaves, and herbs, some to be sold at local markets as medicines and others destined for the making of incense that will serve as protection against sterility, witchcraft, and bodily ills. Medicines and prophylactics concocted during Dyombende are considered to be so powerful that their effects will last throughout the year.[20] At Namasa, a small and commercially insignificant Hwela-Nafana village on the Wenchi–Bondoukou road, market activity based on the selling of *sebe* (amulets) is particularly intense during the first week of Dyombende. Larger commercial centers like Bondoukou and Wenchi, dominated by Mande and Hausa traders, experience similar economic booms at this time.[21]

The magical nature of this month has far deeper ramifications, however. For many Dyula and Hwela, the month of Dyombende is filled with portent for the entire year, and it is considered necessary for men to conduct themselves in a most laudable manner.[22] Religious leaders call upon the faithful to be tolerant, charitable, and observant of the five pillars of the faith, and schoolmasters likewise exhort their young students to study and follow the dictates of the Qur'ān. Members of the 'ulamā' claim that a person's actions during Dyombende will determine his pattern of behavior for the coming year and are thus harshly critical of socially deviant conduct. Parents impress upon their children the need to behave properly and to heed the advice of their elders at this time. Familial and connubial harmony are greatly desired during Dyombende, and every effort is made to alleviate problems within the household. Dyula traders who spend much of the year away from home attempt to return during this month in order to ensure familial stability. Dyombende is thus a period when optimal social cohesion is necessary within the Islamic community; all activities are directed towards this end.

This entire set of positive social attitudes and injunctions is predicated on, and indeed serves as a counterpoise to, the belief that Dyombende is

[20] This attitude also applies to the medicines collected for the Gbain itself and used throughout the year to ensure that the mask will remain effective.

[21] Interviews at Wenchi, April 16 and 17, 1967; Bondoukou, April 18 and 19, 1967; and Namasa, April 20–2, 1967.

[22] Interview at Wenchi, April 16, 1967.

the month most favored by witches, negative spirits, and practitioners of evil in general. According to the Imām of Bondoukou, anti-social characters are also aware of the efficacy of Dyombende and attempt to practice their nefarious deeds at this time in the hopes of ensuring success throughout the year.[23] For *Karamoko* Yakuba of Namasa, a highly respected cleric, the first nine days of Dyombende are fraught with danger, for witches can be heard roaming the village nightly in search of victims.[24] Learned Muslims claim that the best possible defense against marauding witches is a diligent reading of the Qur'ān during this month. Knowledge of the Qur'ān alone, however, cannot sustain one completely through such periods of stress, and it is therefore advisable for the faithful to fast at the very least on the ninth day of the month, when evil lurks everywhere, and as often as possible in addition during the first ten days of Dyombende. The learned, as well as Muslims with little or almost no instruction in the faith, will resort to yet other means of insuring themselves against potential dangers. At the Ligbi center of Bondo-Dyoula and the Hwela-Nafana village of Namasa, large cooking fires are rekindled late in the evening of the ninth day so that people may prepare themselves for bed in safety. After all members of the family have retired to their sleeping rooms, one of the old women of the compound will extinguish the fire and then light as many small kerosene lamps as are available. These will be placed at the entryway to each of the sleeping chambers and allowed to burn through the night as a final precautionary measure.

The most widely accepted and used prophylactic agents against the evils so rife at Dyombende, among both the 'ulamā' and the mass of believers, are amulets or talismans. Belief in the power of amulets is generally very strong among the Islamized Mande, who refer to them as *sebe, sewe,* or *fila.* This belief is manifested most strongly during Dyombende. Clerics, who hold a virtual monopoly on the making of amulets, claim that those fabricated at other times of the year simply will not curb the appetites of witches at Dyombende, and they stress the need for people to buy *sebe* that are made during this month. Some, for example *Karamoko* Yakuba, even feel that only those talismans which are produced on the eve of *san ielema seri* will guarantee an individual against the dangers of witchcraft.[25] All amulets fashioned during the first month, whether they be sewn in a leather case, enclosed in a cloth pouch, or simply wrapped in spun cotton or various leaves, will include samples of various roots and leaves that have been collected during the first nine nights of Dyombende. A typical *soubalakari* – an amulet designed specifically to ward off witches and soul-eaters – consists of a leather case containing a piece of fabric or cardboard inside which is placed

---

[23] Interview with Imām Al-Ḥājjī Muḥammad Timitay of Bondoukou, June 12, 1967.
[24] Interview at Namasa, April 20, 1967.
[25] Ibid.

a small scrap of paper inscribed with verses from the Qur'ān, Arabic characters, or symbolic markings. *Soubalakari* made during Dyombende will also include small amounts of pulverized medicines (the roots and leaves), which are sprinkled on the paper.[26] Such amulets are worn during Dyombende as pendants, attached to leather or raffia armlets, bracelets, or anklets, or are placed in the pockets of robes or tucked into the folds of cloth wrappers. In some instances, several talismans – either of the same prophylactic nature or of different types to ward off a variety of evils – are grouped together in order to ensure greater protection. Talismans are carried on the human body and are kept in various spots in compounds; they may be suspended from the lintels or doorposts leading to bedrooms or eating areas, placed near a washing stone or above an enclosed and roofed washing cubicle, or tied to furniture.[27]

Other uses for *sebe* occur at Dyombende: the Ligbi of Bungazi (Ghana) are said to tie amulets to the branches of trees flanking the well-traveled paths leading from the village to streams used as sources for drinking water, to the communal toilets, and to numerous farms.[28] At Sorhobango, Namasa, and Bondo it has been noted that some Dyula, Ligbi, and Hwela tie *sebe* to the hair of their sheep and goats in order to safeguard the animals from negative spirits. Acknowledging Dyombende as a time fraught with danger, Muslims in the Cercle de Bondoukou and west central Ghana will use amulets in every conceivable fashion to protect not only themselves but also their livelihoods and their possessions.

Two themes clearly dominate the period of Dyombende and the festival of *san ielema seri*. One is based on the positive qualities ascribed to this magical first month of the Muslim year, a period when man's conduct is said to influence his actions and behavior until the following new year's ceremony. Feasting, joyous songs, dancing, displays of worldly wealth, and the acquisition of medicines are all necessary parts of this facet of Dyombende. Inextricably woven with the positive is the more sinister side of Dyombende. The optimism associated with the arrival of the new year is tempered by awareness of the potential dangers that exist – witchcraft, illness, family strife, crop failure, business reverses, and death. Various precautionary rites and acts aid man in his struggle against the forces that could easily bring sorrow and ruin to himself, his family, and his relatives. Included in such preventive rituals during Dyombende, in Muslim and non-Muslim locales where the Gbain cult operates, is the annual propitiation and purification ceremony devoted to this anti-witchcraft mask. This ceremony, as will be seen, is dominated by the same concerns and aspira-

[26] Of the various types of Mande talismans available, it is the *soubalakari* that is most often attached to the mask itself.

[27] Interviews at Wenchi, April 16, 1967, and Namasa, April 20–2, 1967.

[28] Interview at Bungazi, April 27, 1967.

tions that mark all other rites practiced by the Islamized Mande during this month.

The operation of the Gbain masked cult normally falls outside the cycle of Islamic festivals and usually functions in Muslim and non-Muslim communities on a weekly basis. The weekly pattern is not invariable, however, for if a village is plagued by witchcraft, the masked cult will perform nightly if necessary to resolve the problems that have arisen.[29] Its appearance may in fact coincide with a Muslim holy day, but this is not planned. During Dyombende, however, and particularly on *san ielema seri*, this masking tradition becomes intimately tied to the Muslim calendar and to Islamic procedures, for cult owners and members agree that this time of the year is crucial for the Gbain. *San ielema seri* is the new year's ceremony for the mask and its cult and is felt to be the occasion when the powers of the Gbain are renewed and fortified so that it will effectively counter witches not only during Dyombende but throughout the coming year. The rituals surrounding this masking tradition are judiciously performed among Muslims, and the rituals practiced by non-Muslims are patterned, albeit somewhat loosely, on the methods adopted from the Islamized Mande.[30]

The Gbain is cared for during Dyombende in much the same way that the individual Muslim cares for himself. In virtually all communities in which the Gbain flourishes, the first nine days of Dyombende are devoted to caring for the mask and the ritual precinct in which it is kept.[31] Cult members are required to offer their services daily, each member helping to refurbish the small hut of the Gbain. This is called the Gbain-Lou and is always located on the outskirts of a village or town, removed from the normal traffic patterns of the inhabitants (plate 52). The Gbain-Lou must be swept clean, for it is believed that the negative spirits rampant at this time will invade the sacred area in numbers, thereby annoying the spirit of the mask. The uprights, the roof beams, the elevated platform on which the mask is kept, and the grass roof are all sprinkled with a solution of water and medicinal leaves and then fumigated in order to further protect the Gbain. Younger boys who are members of the cult spend their time clearing the area about the Gbain-Lou by removing weeds and fallen branches and by smoothing the ground leading from the entryway of the precinct to the hut. The most important tasks, of course, concern the mask itself, for the

[29] At the Numu village of Brawhani I was told that the Gbain mask paraded nightly for nearly two weeks during an outbreak of measles in 1964.

[30] Non-Muslim performances of the Dyombende rites associated with the Gbain will vary depending on the ritual connection that exists with the Muslim centers from which the Gbain were obtained. More recently adopted cults, which are not yet well established and thus are highly dependent on Muslim ritual experts, adhere more closely to Muslim Mande standards.

[31] I was able to observe the eighth, ninth, and tenth days at Namasa (April 20–2, 1967). Many of the descriptive data that follow are based on observations during these three days and on subsequent interviews.

52. Gbain mask carried in the Gbain-Lou at Numu village of Brawhani, 1967.

Gbain must be carefully washed, fumigated, and, if necessary, mended and repainted. These responsibilities fall to the head of the cult, the Dyotigui (spirit head), and the Dyologo (carrier of the mask), who perform their duties at night, secreting themselves even from the other members of the cult.[32] All measures to strengthen the Gbain are viewed as precautions against the malevolent nature of witches; they are collectively referred to as Dyombende Filakabara (protective medicines of Dyombende).

The preparations for the Gbain ceremony that have taken place on the first nine days of Dyombende reach a climax on the eve of *san ielema seri*. The sequence of events on this evening at Namasa may be viewed as broadly characteristic of those of all groups utilizing Gbain masks. At sunset, all families – whether Muslim Hwela or Nafana and Bron – assemble within their compounds to enjoy a lavish supper consisting of yams, cassava, corn, beans, guinea fowl, chicken, and the meat of either a sheep or a goat. For the Hwela, the generosity displayed by the head of a family on this evening is very important, since Allāh will look favorably upon a generous man throughout the year to come. After the meal, a mosque service is held to mark the beginnings of *san ielema seri* and to ask protection against the evil spirits that will be especially powerful throughout this night. With the

---

[32] Although I was not permitted to watch these specialized activities, the Dyotigui, Yaw Kra, described them to me. Interview at Namasa, April 22, 1967.

completion of their prayers, some of the Hwela Muslims join their fellow cult members at the Gbain-Lou in order to carry out final preparations.

It is now almost nine o'clock, and in the village protective fires are being lit in virtually every compound. At the Gbain-Lou, the Dyotigui (in this case, Yaw Kra, a non-Muslim Nafana) lights a fire in front of the small hut. According to Yaw Kra, fire can repulse witches by the heat and light it emits and thus is used in the sacred grove as an additional precautionary measure.[33] Plants and leaves are now collected by a select group of Gbain members, all of whom are considered to have at least a fair degree of knowledge of medicines and prophylactics, and each individual will spend nearly an hour in the surrounding bush searching for the necessary items. As I mentioned previously, the first eight nights were also devoted to acquiring these items, but Gbain cult members claim that the most efficacious medicines are derived from materials collected on the eve of *san ielema seri*. It is on this magical night that elements of the natural world are infused with their greatest power and vitality.[34] Within a couple of hours the harvest of plants, leaves, and roots is accomplished, and the cult members return to the ritual grove.

The preparation of certain medicines, directed by the Dyotigui, now begins and lasts well into the night. Some of the ingredients are taken to Muslim herbalists, who are not necessarily members of the cult but whose services are needed to obtain additional safeguards for *san ielema seri*. Other portions are given to *karamokos*, who will use these products to make a variety of *sebe* that will be presented to and attached to the Gbain mask during the purification festival to be held the following morning.

The early morning hours of *san ielema seri* at Namasa are filled with activity. Before daybreak women and children leave the village to fetch water from the Nimpeni, a small river southwest of the village. Everyone bathes on this morning, preferably with water from the Nimpeni rather than with water drawn from the wells at Namasa, since flowing water is believed to have special healing qualities on this auspicious day. The elderly and infirm, who will benefit the most from bathing, await the return of the women while assembling the various herbs they have gathered during the first nine days of Dyombende, which will be mixed with their bath water. After washing, people dress in their finest garments; anyone who

[33] The use of fire as an agent against evil forces is widespread, being found among Muslim groups throughout West Africa. See J. Spencer Trimingham, *Islam in West Africa*, p. 77.

[34] Early in this century, Prouteaux noted that medicines for the Gbon at Bouna were collected by the Muslim Ligbi on this night: "Les plantes qui servent à préparer les drogues rituelles doivent être naturellement cueillies dans la nuit de 9 au 10 diomandé . . . Chacun sait . . . que c'est la nuit magique par excellence, au point qu'une personne n'a, cette nuit-là, qu'à sortir dans la brousse et à couper un rameau de n'importe quel arbuste pour que les onguents et les boissons préparés avec ces feuilles prises au hasard la guérissent certainement." "Notes sur certains rites," p. 52.

has been able to afford a new cloth, gown, or sandals will parade them today.[35] Protective talismans made for *san ielema seri* are placed on one's body or tied to one's clothing.

On the outskirts of Namasa, the Dyotigui and various cult members are busily preparing the sacred precinct for the annual purification ceremony. The mask, raffia costume, and such other accoutrements of the Gbain as cows' horns, iron gongs, armlets, and anklets have all been sprinkled with water brought from the Nimpeni by the wife of the Dyotigui. This is yet another procedure regarded as a necessary precaution against lurking witches and other evil. Two very large clay pots imported from the Degha pottery center of Bondakele are lined with leaves and filled with the potions that were prepared by non-Muslim herbalists during the night (plate 53). The liquids provided by Muslims are considered to be especially potent, since the pulverized leaves and roots have been combined with *siliama gue* ("Muslim water"), obtained by washing Islamic writing boards or slates (*walaga*). The most powerful liquids are said to be from boards with verses from the Qur'ān written on them; these verses when washed off are immediately bottled lest the mixture lose its magical properties.[36] Interestingly enough, Gbain members indicated that the strength of the Muslim holy water is directly dependent on the degree of learning attained by the Muslim who prepared it. The Muslim and "pagan" solutions mixed in the two bowls are now taken by the Dyotigui, who sprinkles the liquid on the washing stones next to the bowls, around the perimeter of the ritual clearing, on the Gbain-Lou, and on the Gbain mask itself, which is fully wrapped in raffia and placed on the ground in front of the hut in which it is normally housed. Finally, both the Dyotigui and Dyologo rinse out their mouths and wash their bodies from the same bowl of water used to anoint the Gbain (plate 54).

By mid-morning the members of the cult are notified that all is ready for the start of the purification ceremony, and they assemble at the grove. Many of the adult males of Namasa, both Muslim and non-Muslim, and their sons belong to the cult, and the precinct is quickly filled. Strangers from other villages and towns will also attend if they are initiates of the cult (two Bron elders from Gaoso, some seventy-five miles to the south, were present on this occasion).[37] Salutations are exchanged, respects are paid to the

[35] "Conspicuous consumption" on this day is not disapproved of but is instead considered to be an act that will encourage good fortune during the coming year.

[36] For discussions of the magical qualities associated with Islamic script by non-Muslim peoples of northern Ghana, see J. R. Goody, "Restricted Literacy in Northern Ghana," pp. 204–6.

[37] Three elderly and infirm Degha men from Kabre, a small Nafana-Degha village on the Sampa–Jinini track, were present to seek medicines from the Gbain. All three had sought medical attention at the Methodist Hospital in Wenchi and from local herbalists and as cult members had decided to attend the Dyombende ritual in order to bathe in the magical waters used at the ceremony.

53. Degha clay containers, diameter 2.0′ to 2.5′, holding medicinal herbs and potions used by members of Gbain cult at *san ielema seri*. Hwela village of Namasa, 1967.

54. The Dyotigui Yaw Kra washing himself at festival of *san ielema seri*. Hwela village of Namasa, 1967.

Dyotigui and Dyologo, and each man in turn will greet the Gbain, which is wrapped in a raffia costume and laid out on the ground in the center of the clearing (plate 55). Food prepared throughout the morning by women of the Dyotigui's compound is brought to the site by young boys who are members of the cult and placed next to the raffia mound containing the Gbain mask. The Dyotigui welcomes all those present, offers a libation of *siliama gue* to the spirits of the Gbain and its predecessors, and sprinkles the pile of raffia and the ground surrounding it with the holy water. Elders of the cult then surround the Dyotigui, for the Gbain should not be seen on this day, and he proceeds to tie Qur'ānic charms fashioned the previous night to the forehead and muzzle of the mask. Following this, the Dyotigui gives a short discourse on the evils of witchcraft, the powers and merits of the Gbain, and the importance of *san ielema seri* as that period when the Gbain is revitalized for yet another year. This brings to a close the more formal aspects of the purification rite.

Having completed this part of the ceremony, the Dyotigui takes the remainder of the *siliama gue* to the washing stones and anoints them and the ground upon which they are placed. Undressing completely, he washes himself with the medicinal liquid from the two large pots, being especially careful to cleanse all orifices, these being the areas of the body believed to be most susceptible to harm from witches. Every member of the cult follows his lead, the entire procedure requiring several hours. When the Dyotigui has finished bathing he returns to the side of the Gbain, where a large portion of the meal prepared for this occasion awaits him, and he offers the first morsels of food to the mask (plate 56). Musicians belonging to the cult, who have been tuning their drums, now begin to play and sing familiar songs in honor of the Gbain. The ritual bathing, feasting, singing, and dancing associated with the Gbain highlight the remainder of the cere-mony in the grove. The affair lasts until early afternoon and is marked by gaiety and camaraderie.

Yet even during this most ebullient segment of the Gbain ritual, there are precautions taken to safeguard those assembled, and most of them are clearly Islamic in orientation. Not only are the mask, ritual accoutrements, and cult members protected by the medicinal potions that accompany the purification ceremony, but a measure of safety is also gained by the very food consumed on this day. The meal, prepared by the women in the Dyotigui's compound under the supervision of his wife, is referred to as the Dyombende *doumou* (feast) and must follow a precise ritual recipe com-bining a variety of meats that have been boiled and stewed with peppers in water obtained from the Nimpeni early that morning. Beef, fowl, and the meat of goat and sheep are included because these animals are highly regarded for their virtuous qualities. An even more important reason for their inclusion is that these are the foods that the Gbain enjoys and from

55. Gbain mask wrapped in raffia and in center of the Gbain-Lou. Hwela village of Namasa, 1967.

56. Gbain mask being fed at *san ielema seri*. Hwela village of Namasa, 1967.

142

which it derives its strength. Furthermore, the generosity displayed by the cult towards the Gbain at *san ielema seri* is said to be an indication of the manner in which the Gbain will be treated throughout the year. Especially necessary in the preparation of this meal is the addition of pieces of smoked meat (generally that of the goat and sheep and, if possible, of the ram) from animals sacrificed by Muslim cult members on the great feast *dongi-ma* or Lanndi Kabiru, which occurred thirty days earlier (on the tenth day of the last month of the previous year). Muslims belonging to the cult stress that this procedure is absolutely essential if the Gbain is to maintain its power, and they claim in addition that such meat is also eaten by the faithful when they feast on the eve of *san ielema seri*, because the blessings and goodness of *dongi-ma* (the festival considered by both the 'ulamā' and the average believer to symbolize the old year) are thereby transferred to and grafted onto the new year. Thus, when the Gbain receives the first morsels of this feast, which are placed by the Dyotigui on top of the raffia costume enclosing the mask, it is incumbent on the cult head to offer pieces of the smoked meats donated by the Muslims for this purificatory ceremony.[38]

A further safeguard resorted to by Gbain members during the ritual of *san ielema seri* is the lighting of various small fires near the washing stones, around the Gbain-Lou, and at several spots fringing the Gbain precinct. These are considered to be crucial, for fire (*tah*) is felt to be a most effective agent against witches and evil. This is based on the belief that witches breathe fire and that it is their ability to do so that allows them to plague mankind. Man can thwart witches by using fire that he himself creates to neutralize one of the most powerful aspects of these malevolent beings.[39] It is felt that on this morning witches are especially attracted to the sacred precinct (enticed by the food, the merriment, and the songs) and must be repulsed by both the heat and light shed by these small bonfires. Some individuals stay particularly close to the fires, and others leap over them; both acts are considered to be additional safety measures against evil. Sā Ismayilla, the secular head of the Muslim Hwela community of Namasa and not a member of the Gbain cult, regarded these procedures as simply an extension of the precautionary torchlight parades staged by Muslim children on the eve of *san ielema seri*.[40] According to the Sā, such practices are intended to protect the participants as well as to cleanse and strengthen him.

The cult songs (*dongyiri*) sung on this occasion are selected with a mind to further protecting the cult and its individual members. Although there is nothing specifically Islamic about these songs, they are Mande Dyula in origin. Among the Kulango, Nafana, and Degha who have adopted the

[38] Interview with *Karamoko* Yakuba and Sā Ismayilla of Namasa, April 22, 1967.
[39] The ability of the Gbain to breathe fire is critical if the cult is to operate successfully.
[40] Torchlight parades occur infrequently nowadays, greater emphasis being placed on other precautionary measures.

Gbain, most of the songs associated with the cult are sung in Dyula and are acknowledged as having been borrowed from these Muslims along with the cult itself. Songs are sung at all ritual appearances of the Gbain, but only at *san ielema seri* is the entire repertory known by a cult group attempted. This is done to entertain the Gbain, to publicize its strength and abilities to uproot witchcraft, and to warn evil spirits that might attempt to do harm at this time. At Namasa, participants in the cult claimed that it was desirable to create a new song in honor of the Gbain on this day, for this would reconfirm the love of the members for the Gbain and would also aid in frightening away any witches who were present at the festivities. Such a song was created in Dyula by Yaw Kra, the Nafana cult head, and introduced at the very beginning of the drumming and singing in the grove. The number consists of a lead portion sung by the drummers, the Dyotigui, and the Dyologo and a response handled by all the other cult members – a musical pattern typical of Gbain songs:

Sieleko sene magnole, ara korata kafre.
(Whoever says that this stone is not heavy, pick it up and see.)

According to Yaw Kra, the song was inspired by the fact that many individuals felt that the Gbain was particularly vulnerable to witchcraft on this day, since even though it was covered with its raffia costume it was being publicly displayed. His intentions, therefore, were to convey in song that even in this state the Gbain was a dangerous spirit, not an inert stone incapable of action. The song was directed towards all spirits tempted to evil action, daring such creatures to test the powers of the stone (the Gbain), which lay in the grove exposed to all.

A wide variety of songs are performed touching on the manifold aspects of witchcraft. In many the witch is described as a destructive animal, as in this example:

Eyia gyara bekumgu dobesu.
(There are lions of the bush and of the compound.)

The lion of the savanna survives on the meat of other wild animals, but the witch can satisfy its appetite only with the flesh of human beings, who reside in the compounds. Some songs speak of the disasters that may result if the forces of witchcraft are not curtailed:

Kamele saya dutigi.
(Deaths of young men, fallen town.)

Any town or village in which the young are dying has been attacked by witches and will gradually become the haunt of these evil forces. Other songs warn man against the devious character and nature of the witch:

Oh subara musu yereko mymuoye kojungu bakonono.
(Oh laughing witch woman whose inner being is evil.)

One can never recognize a witch from its external behavior, for its façade will hide the evil intentions that lie within. Witchcraft is said to be housed in the heart and mind, and therefore a witch may laugh while actually scheming to do harm. Thus even the most joyful and exuberant aspect of *san ielema seri* is tinged with the fear that pervades the entire festival, reminding man of his precarious situation and of the seriousness of witchcraft.

I have focussed a good deal of attention on the annual purification festival associated with the Gbain in order to demonstrate the strong Islamic content of the tradition. A similar degree of Islamic influence can be seen in the weekly performances of the Gbain, which serve quite literally as insurance against the machinations of witches. Even at the weekly level, a typical masquerade includes the ritual washing of the Gbain carrier (Dyologo) with a variety of potions, including *siliama gue*. This is to ensure against any danger befalling the Dyologo and to strengthen him while he searches for witches. The Gbain mask itself is also anointed with these potions, and it invariably has Qur'ānic charms tied to it. No Gbain performance can take place without these Muslim elements, which are viewed by all as essential precautions. The songs and drum patterns accompanying the masked dance are virtually all derived from the Dyula and Hwela, and even the fire-breathing feature of the mask is acknowledged to be Mande in origin. In communities where the Gbain is controlled by non-Muslims, it is common to find Muslims in attendance at performances. So strong are the Gbain's ties to Islam that cult leaders are loath to talk about the masking tradition without a Muslim expert at hand.

Wherever the Gbain is controlled by non-Muslims, they acknowledge that without Muslim expertise the tradition would soon die and that this would be disastrous for the community, since the cult so effectively combats the problems of witchcraft. It is no doubt the effectiveness of the Gbain that accounts for the extensive involvement of Muslims in the masquerade and even for the Muslim origin of the tradition. That Muslims developed a method of combatting witches should not be surprising, since witchcraft plagues all societies in West Africa, whether Muslim or "pagan." Seen in this light, Muslim participation in the Gbain masquerade is quite natural and is acceptable even to those Muslims who are not involved themselves.

Objections to Muslim participation in this masking tradition come only from the most learned members of the faith, such as Al-Ḥājjī Muḥammad Timitay, the Imām of Bondoukou, a widely respected Islamic scholar. The Imām has visited such Gbain centers as Sorhobango and Sandhuei in an attempt to discourage the faithful from participating in the masquerade.[41] As a defender of orthodox theology, he strongly disapproves of relying on

[41] Interview at Bondoukou, April 18 and 19, 1967.

any power other than faith in Allāh for protection against evil. Yet his disapproval is confined to occasional attempts at persuading his followers to give up the cult. With the pragmatism that has characterized Islam throughout its history in West Africa, he acknowledges that abolishing the Gbain would be disastrous for the communities that have the tradition, since it affords proven protection against one of man's gravest dangers.

CHAPTER 8

THE DO MASKING TRADITION

It would be convenient, no doubt, to hypothesize that the Imām of Bondoukou objects to the Gbain because it violates Islam's proscriptions on figurative art. Attractive though such a hypothesis might be, however, it is simply not true. In repeated interviews the Imām's objections to the Gbain were limited to the non-Muslim nature of the masquerade. As a learned Muslim he recognized the tradition as unorthodox, whatever its trappings and apparent origins. But as an African he also recognized the need of his followers to be protected from witches and only regretted that they found it necessary to seek help other than Allāh's. Even without the comments of the Imām himself, such a hypothesis would falter when yet another masquerade, the Do, is considered, for here we are faced with a tradition that is exclusively Muslim. Displays of the Do masquerade are often accorded Muslim secular and religious leaders, and the Imām, as spiritual head of all Muslims in the Cercle de Bondoukou and west central Ghana, is frequently honored by performances of the Do when visiting towns and villages within his domain. This he considers entirely fitting, since a tradition confined to Muslims would be the sort of display most respectful of a Muslim leader.[1]

There is no precise record of the origins of the Do tradition – no way to reconstruct the way that a so-called "pagan" art form, the mask, came to be integrated in a practice so thoroughly Muslim that non-Muslim neighbors of the Mande see no value in acquiring the masquerade or participating in it. The earliest evidence of the Do comes from the records of R. Austin Freeman, a member of the 1888 British boundary expedition to Bondoukou that was seeking to contain French territorial ambitions east and north of that town. A photograph of a Do mask, though not labeled as such, first appeared in Freeman's *Travels and Life in Ashanti and Jaman*, published in 1898; he cites it as a "Sakrobundi mask of polished black wood, from Jimini."[2] According to his own account, Freeman never visited Jimini, which lies about one hundred miles west-northwest of Bondoukou; indeed, no British colonial official ever traveled farther west than Bon-

---

[1] The Imām considers the mask a symbol of "paganism," but he never mentioned its being an example of "figurative art."

[2] p. 152.

57. "Sakrobundi mask of polished black wood from Jimini" collected and designated by R. Austin Freeman.

doukou, for the French jealously guarded their territorial claims beyond this important border town. The attribution is, at best, second hand, but this does not minimize its importance as the earliest recorded example of a Do-type mask.

Stylistically, the Freeman piece conforms to numerous Do masks I encountered in the Cercle de Bondoukou and west central Ghana in 1966–7. The Freeman example (plate 57) is a small face mask (15¾″ high) composed of a human face and an elaborate, but stylized, headdress.[3] Its overall features are reminiscent of the well-known Senufo Kpelie masks, but there are major differences in detail. The face is far more naturalistically treated than are those of the Kpelie tradition. A proliferation of details about the face – generally found on the Kpelie in the form of "legs," horizontal motifs jutting out from the areas of the ears and cheeks, or open-work projections flanking the sides of the head – are missing in the Freeman mask. Features such as the ears, eyes, nose, and mouth hew much more closely to a naturalistic norm, and the raised scarification patterns are not as sharply defined as in Kpelie examples.[4] Incised decora-

3 W. B. Fagg and Margaret Plass, *African Sculpture*, p. 150.
4 Freeman (p. 428) remarks on the similarities between facial scarification on Jimini males and those markings appearing on this mask: "Among the tribal marks of this kind I may mention those carried by the natives of the Jimini district to the northwest of Bontuku, which consisted of a small circular tubercle about the size of a sixpence above each eyebrow, and an elongated projection on the cheek, below each eye. These are very well shown on the wooden Sakrobundi mask from Jimini . . ."

148

tion on the face of the Do mask consists of a triple scarification pattern worked from the corners of the lips to the cheeks. Although one encounters examples of Kpelie masks with the same motif, it is neither as consistent nor as prominent a design element as in the Freeman piece or examples of Do masks that I recorded in the field. The importance of this particular scarification pattern with respect to Do masks, according to numerous informants, is its representation, in a restricted fashion, of the scarification marks commonly found on adult Mande males.[5]

There is, however, a basic problem in designating the Freeman piece as the earliest recorded Do mask, since Freeman himself refers to this example as a "Sakrobundi" mask. The disagreement is obviously in need of some clarification. Freeman writes at some length of "the great inland fetish, Sakrobundi or Sakrobudi,"[6] and goes on to describe in detail a masked performance of this cult, which he witnessed in the Bron town of Odumase in the Gold Coast some fifty miles southeast of Bondoukou. Freeman was particularly impressed by the masked dancer, who was the priest of the cult and who capered about directing the singing and dancing of the cult members who accompanied his display.

The centre of the circle was, however, occupied by the most remarkable figure of the group, the principal fetish man . . . He was enveloped from head to foot in a covering of the soft fibre of which the kilts were made, and to the front of this was attached a huge wooden mask in the semblance of an antelope's head surmounted by a pair of curved horns. The mask was painted red and white, the horns being decorated with alternate rings of these colours to represent the annular projections which appear on the horns of the animal. On the forehead a grotesque face was painted, and above this there were two holes for the fetishman to look through.[7]

From Freeman's description and the drawings that accompany his text, it seems clear that this example of a "Sakrobundi" mask was of a totally different character from the piece he labels as being from Jimini and also

---

[5] This Mande scarification pattern was first noted among another southeastern Mande group, the Gbanya of Gonja, by Maurice Delafosse in *Les Frontières de la Côte d'Ivoire, de la Côte d'Or et du Soudan*, p. 128.

[6] Fragmentary evidence for the existence of a "Sakrobundi" cult in this region at the end of the nineteenth century can be found not only in Freeman's *Travels and Life in Ashanti and Jaman* (pp. 148–55), but also in the writings of Delafosse, *Les Frontières de la Côte d'Ivoire* (pp. 119–20), and Louis Tauxier, *Le Noir de Bondoukou* (p. 184). Unfortunately the data conflict, and it is hard to obtain a clear picture from these sources. However, I did collect traditions pertaining to this cult, which is still functioning in an anti-witchcraft capacity in certain Kulango and Nafana villages. Masks were not associated with Sakara in 1966–7, but the cult head at Oulike (Cercle de Bondoukou), where the paramount shrine is located, claimed that masks had been used in the past. He described these masks as large, flat, and brightly painted pieces like the "Sakrobundi" examples Freeman saw and recorded in context at Odumase and Diadaso but totally unlike this small Jimini piece. Interview at Oulike, April 29, 1967.

[7] *Travels and Life in Ashanti and Jaman*, pp. 151–2.

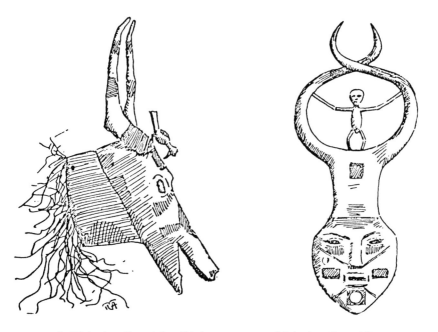

58. "Sakrobundi mask" at Diadaso.   59. "Sakrobundi mask" at Diadaso.

refers to as "Sakrobundi." According to his drawings, the "Sakrobundi" mask seen at Odumase was a very large face mask (plate 25, p. 105) nearly the size of the priest; indeed, Freeman describes it as a "huge wooden mask."

Drawings of two other examples of Sakrobundi masks that he found in the Nafana town of Diadaso (O.S. Duadaso), also located in the Gold Coast but only nine miles east of Bondoukou, are again very different in style from the "Jimini" piece. One is clearly a horizontal mask (plate 58), which he claims represents an antelope's head, and the other (plate 59) relates in general to the Odumase example in that it is also a large face mask with "a more or less grotesque human face surmounted by the characteristic horns."[8] The Sakrobundi mask from Odumase and the two that Freeman sighted at Diadaso were noted within a definite context. This was

[8] As mentioned in Chapter 6, masks associated with the Sakrobundi cult were ruthlessly destroyed by both Christian missionaries and French and British colonial officials. Freeman's data, plus the oral traditions I collected at the Sakrobundi shrines of Odumase and Oulike, indicate that they were generally tall plank-like masks such as that described by Freeman at Odumase and one of the examples at Duadaso. Elders of the cult indicated, however, that there were also horizontal masks associated with Sakrobundi, such as the second one Freeman described at Duadaso. The large plank-like masks were to inspire the later Bedu tradition, but apparently the horizontal examples associated with Sakrobundi were not revived.

not true, however, of the elegantly carved and rather small face mask that he apparently collected at Bondoukou, a mask acquired out of context, probably from a trader, and labeled a "Sakrobundi mask from Jimini."

The great stylistic differences between the three certain Sakrobundi examples on the one hand and the much smaller "Jimini" specimen on the other were expressed by Freeman himself:

In all cases the incurved horns seem to be a characteristic feature in the masks, for even in the specimen from Jimini . . . which was much more highly finished and artistically executed than any other that I saw, and was a perfectly recognizable representation of a native of Jimini, the ornamental appendage above the face will be seen to be a conventionalization of the horns similar to that in the second Diadaso mask, but carried further . . .[9]

From the evidence presented by Freeman, it seems certain that the small face mask "from Jimini," now in the British Museum, was not part of the Sakrobundi tradition. The Sakrobundi cult was the only masking tradition that Freeman witnessed and recorded, and it seems reasonable to assume that he assigned the "Jimini" mask to the only masking cult with which he was familiar.

A further problem concerning this piece is its point of origin. Freeman states that it was from Jimini, which, as I have mentioned, is an area of the Ivory Coast lying about one hundred miles west of the region under consideration. Like the Cercle de Bondoukou, this sector is heavily influenced by Mande groups, and thus Freeman's attribution of origin might well be correct. Indeed, my own research revealed (unfortunately too late for the information to be verified) that as recently as 1963 the Ligbi of Bungazi and Menji (both in Ghana) acquired some of their Do masks at Satama Sokoura, an important Mande community in Jimini.[10] It seems quite plausible, then, that the Freeman Do mask came from this region.

The issue of the origin of this mask is confused considerably by William Fagg in a recent publication in which he states that the piece was collected by Freeman "near Jimini just inside Ghana."[11] One can only assume that Fagg is referring to the small village of Jinini, which is just to the east of the Ivory Coast border in Ghana and about eleven miles north-northeast of Bondoukou. Jinini is a very mixed center consisting of a small Nafana

[9] *Travels and Life in Ashanti and Jaman*, pp. 151–2.
[10] Ligbi elders in both villages claimed that the Jimini town of Satama Sokoura was an important center for the carving of Do masks. Satama is an ethnographically mixed community with a dominant Mande element and including southern Senufo or Jimini families. Masks were said to be carved by both the Mande and Senufo at Satama, although the Ligbi purchased their Do from their Muslim Mande brethren. Interviews at Menji, January 14, 1968, and Bungazi, December 28, 1967.
[11] Fagg and Plass, *African Sculpture*, p. 150.

quarter and a heavy concentration of Mande Dyula and Ligbi.[12] However, given the scope of Freeman's reference ("a perfectly recognizable representation of a native of Jimini") it seems much more likely that the piece originated from the general area of Jimini in the Ivory Coast than from the specific village of Jinini in Ghana.

Besides the Freeman piece, there are several other masks collected at the turn of the century that conform closely in style to Do types. Sir Cecil Armitage, a captain in the colonial service in the Gold Coast between 1893 and 1920, acquired a sizable collection of Africana during this period. In his collection there are two masks (depicted in Leon Underwood's *Masks of West Africa* and incorrectly attributed to the Baule) that are almost identical to two of the Do masks I recorded at the Ligbi town of Bondo-Dyoula (Ivory Coast).[13]

One of these pieces is a small face mask not unlike the example collected by Freeman. The mask (plate 60; Underwood, plate 24) consists of a human face with rather naturalistic features and the scarification marks at the corners of the mouth that are common to Do face masks. Instead of the crescent motif on the Freeman piece, two horns issue from the top of the forehead; these are treated in a straightforward manner and represent animal horns. The mask noted at Bondo-Dyoula, so very close to this piece in type and style, was referred to by the Ligbi as a bush cow or *siginkura-ayna*.[14]

The other mask (plate 61; Underwood, plate 25) collected by Armitage is a type worn on the diagonal over the forehead. This mask is unusual for a Do because it is not, strictly speaking, a face mask and because it represents a wart hog. The head is treated summarily, with the design emphasis being placed on the smooth outline of the head, the elongated snout, and the two very prominent tusks. Incised linear motifs on the surface of the mask are totally lacking, these being replaced by four rounded knob-like projections, two on either side of the forehead and two carved just to the outside of the eyes. I encountered only one Do mask (plate 62) of this type in the field, also at Bondo-Dyoula, where it was called *leu* (wart hog).[15] In virtually

[12] It was revealed at Jinini that Do masks had in fact been used in the past but that the tradition was not revived after Samory's son, Sarankye Mori, pillaged Jinini in 1895 on his way to Bondoukou. Interview at Jinini, January 21, 1968.

[13] The bulk of the Armitage collection is now owned by Dr and Mrs Gordon Barclay of Waltham Abbey, England. Mrs (Celia) Barclay inherited this collection from her father, Maurice Cockin, who had purchased these pieces directly from Armitage. Almost no data were obtained, and Underwood attributed these two masks (his plates 24, 25) to the Baule simply on the basis of style.

[14] Interview at Bondo-Dyoula, January 4, 1968.

[15] Another example of a Do wart hog mask was photographed by Roy Sieber at Bungazi in the state of Banda in 1964. This specimen was far more crudely conceived than either the Armitage example or the *leu* mask I noted at Bondo-Dyoula. When I first recorded the Do masks at Bungazi in February 1967, the *leu* was no longer in existence, having been stolen the year before.

60. "Baule" mask from Ghana; wood; h. 10". 61. "Baule" wart hog mask; wood; h. 11".

62. *Leu* or wart hog mask used
in Do masquerade; wood;
white, ochre, blue paint;
h. 16". Ligbi village of
Bondo-Dyoula, 1967.

63. Do mask; wood; h. 14.75". **153**

64. Do mask; wood; h. 16".

65. Do mask; wood; h. 11.75".

every respect, the piece I photographed in 1967 is identical to the Armitage example. The only discrepancies, these minimal, are that the mask at Bondo-Dyoula is about four inches longer, is carved in a slightly more attenuated fashion, and had traces of clay paint remaining from its last public appearance. Otherwise the similarities are haunting and indicate that both pieces are undoubtedly out of the Do tradition.

Further examples may be cited. At the Cambridge University Museum of Archaeology and Ethnology there are two masks (plates 63, 64) that clearly fall into the Do category. These two examples were collected, according to the date in the acquisitions register, in about 1890 by R. C. H. Jenkinson of the Life Guards (presumably while he was serving in the Gold Coast) and donated to the museum in 1923.[16] Except for small variations in the treatment of the headdresses (both are surmounted by leaf-like designs) these face masks are true to the Do type.[17] In addition,

[16] Cambridge University Museum of Archaeology and Ethnology catalogue nos. Z.15182-A (16" h.) and Z.15182 ($14\frac{3}{4}$" h.).

[17] The surfaces of these two masks lack the degree of patination found in the Freeman and Armitage pieces, yet both seem to be legitimate examples. Sweat marks appear on the insides of the masks, and faint traces of clay paints are still evident around the mouths and eyes. In any case, Jenkinson collected these examples well before such items were conceived of as tourist bait.

three masks in the Rautenstrauch-Joest-Museum für Volkerkunde in Cologne are distinctly of the Do tradition. These were purchased by the museum in 1905 from W. O. Oldman, a London dealer and collector of ethnographic art, who described these masks in his sale catalogue as coming from the Gold Coast hinterland.[18] All three masks conform fully in style to Do masks seen in the field, but one is unusual in that its headdress consists of looped horns (plate 65).

These eight early examples of Do masks deriving from the period of initial European contact with the northeastern Ivory Coast and west central Ghana (and there are probably others) establish a historical dimension for this Islamized Mande masking tradition. It is rare and fortunate to have such extensive documentation for art forms made of perishable materials.

Additional historical confirmation for the Do tradition may be found in early French ethnographies on the Ivory Coast. F. J. Clozel, a colonial officer who was elected governor of the Ivory Coast in 1903, included in his work *Dix ans à la Côte d'Ivoire* a photograph of "masked dancers at Bondoukou."[19] The masks being worn, although difficult to discern because of the poor quality of this early photograph, are recognizable as those of the Do cult. Even the costumes, composed of a raffia skirt, locally woven trousers and shirts, and cloth capes tied to the back of the face masks and allowed to drape over the upper torso, are identical to the attire worn at the present time by Do dancers. (These capes traditionally were of locally woven cotton cloth but today are imported Dutch and Manchester cotton prints.) Unfortunately, no data accompany this photograph, but we can assume from the style of the masks and the costumes depicted that the scene is one of Do dancers at the predominantly Muslim town of Bondoukou.

Some fifteen years later, Louis Tauxier, who was in the Cercle de Bondoukou from September 1918 until August 1920, described in *Le Noir de Bondoukou* what must have been a Do masked ritual. According to Tauxier, the Dyula of Bondoukou celebrated the conclusion of Ramadhan with public and festive masked dances every evening for seven days after the breaking of the fast. For Tauxier, this was an obvious case of the retention of certain "pagan" characteristics within a heavily Islamized environment. He observed that, unlike the animal masks common to so many cultures of the Sudan, these were in the form of human faces.

Mais à Bondoukou, chez les Dyoulas de nos jours, on a . . . des masques à figure humaine, à double figure, plus ou moins fantaisistes et qu'on procure, il me semble, à Koumassie, chez les commerçants européens.[20]

---

[18] Rautenstrauch-Joest-Museum für Volkerkunde, Cologne, catalogue nos. 15092, 15093, 15094. Cited by Oldman in his February 1905 catalogue (no. 23) as nos. 7209, 7210, 7211.   [19] p. 193.

[20] p. 295, note. Tauxier's assumption that these masks were obtained by the Dyula from European merchants in Kumasi is highly imaginative but hardly probable.

Although Tauxier neither described the masks in any detail nor gave their names, it is apparent that he was referring to Do masks. This assumption is in part based on the functional context that he described for the masks. They were intimately tied to the feast days following Ramadhan, a feature I noted for the Do tradition in 1966–7. Furthermore, a photograph that follows his description of the rite clearly reveals two Do dancers. This photograph, however, presents a number of problems. It was taken not by Tauxier but by the French administrator Maurice Prouteaux when he was in the Cercle de Bondoukou in 1915–16.[21] In addition, the caption beneath the photograph is exceedingly vague: "masked dancers at Bondoukou." Although the plate logically follows Tauxier's statement of the masked dance, he does not refer to the photograph in his text. Can the reader assume – for this appears to have been Tauxier's intention – that the plate is in fact of a Dyula masquerade occurring after the festival of Ramadhan?

Even if the photograph does not illustrate the ritual described by Tauxier, it is an important document. A careful look at the masks and costumes being worn by the dancers in Bondoukou reveals that they are typically Do. Furthermore, women and children appear in the scene, indicating the highly public nature of this spectacle, a feature of Do performances today. The men in the crowd behind the masked dancers are dressed in typical Muslim festival attire – long, flowing white cotton gowns and caps – possibly identifying the religious affiliation of the audience.[22] This possibility becomes a likelihood when considered in the context of the houses shown in the photograph, which are typically Mande-Sudanese in style. They are all flat-roofed, and some of them have buttresses, pylons to either side of the doorway, pinnacles, and geometric open-work designs gracing the upper walls – all features characteristic of Mande architecture not only at Bondoukou but throughout the vast areas of Mande expansion.[23] What can safely be deduced from the photograph is that we have here a masked dance, almost certainly a performance of the Do, occurring in one of the Muslim Mande quarters of Bondoukou. Whether this is a photograph of the masked ritual conducted by the Dyula after the close of Ramadhan, as described by Tauxier, is a question that cannot be answered.

Particularly interesting in Tauxier's account are his comments that these masks were used by the Mande Dyula of Bondoukou, for in 1966–7 I found Do masks only among the Ligbi. The sole exception to this was among the

[21] Ibid., p. ix and plate 22.
[22] As Goody has pointed out (p. 62 above), Muslim attire alone is insufficient evidence on which to base religious identification.
[23] J. Spencer Trimingham, *Islam in West Africa*, p. 196. For an account of Mande architecture in Bondoukou at the turn of the century, see Freeman, *Travels and Life in Ashanti and Jaman*, pp. 214–18.

Hwela of Sorhobango, where two such masks had been introduced recently by the Ligbi of Bondo-Dyoula. Additional evidence that the Dyula once used Do-like face masks comes from Prouteaux's pre-1920 description and photograph of a masked dance held by the Dyula of Kong.[24] Although Kong lies outside the area under consideration – about 175 miles northwest of Bondoukou – the historical connections between the Islamized Dyula of the two towns are intimate. A great many of the Dyula in both centers trace their histories back to Begho, and commercial and religious ties between Kong and Bondoukou appear to have been strong.

The masked dance that Prouteaux recorded among the Kong Dyula had many features in common with the Do performance at Bondoukou described by Tauxier. Both occurred during the period after Ramadhan and lasted for seven days, although the one at Kong did not begin until the eighth or ninth day after the end of the fast.[25] Another parallel is the completely public nature of the dances, for women and children were not only present but actually participated in the ritual. Like the Do masquerades I witnessed in 1966–7, the Kong festival took place in a clearing in front of the Friday mosque (Jamiu) late in the afternoons, except on the first day, when the ritual occurred at night.[26] Prouteaux and Tauxier both described the carnival atmosphere associated with the appearance of the dancers; the seven days were filled with joy, pleasure, relaxation, and relief from the month-long fast.

There are, however, a number of discrepancies between Prouteaux's account of the Kong masquerade, the Do rite described by Tauxier, and the Do rites I saw. The festival and masquerade at Kong were referred to by Prouteaux as "Lo," which according to Bochet is the Malinke term used by the Mande living in Senufo country to refer to the major secret society of the non-Muslim Senufo. The Senufo themselves call this society "Por."[27] But the Senufo Lo or Por is a very different type of association from the Do, as it is a multi-functional, esoteric, male-dominated social-control cult concerned with initiations, burials, agricultural fertility, and so forth.[28] The Dyula masquerade at Kong shared none of these features, except possibly the appearance of the mask at the funerals of chiefs (a feature of the Do) – which Prouteaux suggests but does not confirm.

Prouteaux's description and a plate of two of the masks (plate 66) used at the post-Ramadhan ceremony at Kong indicate that these face masks were much closer in style to the Kpelie used by the Senufo within their Lo society than to Do masks. Typical Kpelie pendants or "legs" projected

---

[24] Maurice Prouteaux, "Divertissements de Kong," pp. 605–50. The plate of masked dancers appears opposite p. 632.   [25] Ibid., p. 624.   [26] Ibid., pp. 625–6.

[27] Gilbert Bochet, "Les Masques Sénoufo: de la forme à la signification," p. 672.

[28] For descriptions of the functions of the Lo or Por society among the Senufo, see Bohumil Holas, *Les Sénoufo (y compris les Minianka)*, pp. 143–52, and Robert John Goldwater, *Senufo Sculpture from West Africa*, pp. 9–12.

66. Do masqueraders at Kong.

67. Do bush cow mask; wood; h. 13".

from the cheeks of the masks, facial features were more sharply delineated and incised geometric designs filled the facial area of the masks. Yet in the striking combination of earth reds, blues, and whites, and in the attempt to beautify them by carefully draping gold and silver chains about the horns and faces, these Kong masks do resemble Do masks. Thus it is only in name, and in the sculptural similarities between these masks and the Kpelie, that the Kong Lo masquerade and the Senufo tradition had any commonality. Functionally and contextually the masks recorded by Prouteaux definitely fall within the Do pattern and point to a possible geographical extension of the Do as practised by the Mande Dyula in the early part of this century.

Various examples of Do masks have come to light in museums and private collections in recent years, and some of them are quite close to the early examples already noted. A very fine Do bush-cow type (plate 67), which the Ligbi refer to as *siginkuru-ayna*, is in the collection of Katherine White Reswick. As Fagg has remarked, it is almost identical to the piece collected by Armitage at the turn of this century and owned by Celia Barclay. Fagg goes so far as to suggest that it is "almost certainly by the same carver."[29] The Reswick piece is about three inches larger, lacks the

[29] Fagg, *African Tribal Images: The Katherine White Reswick Collection*, plate 17.

68. Do *leu* mask; wood; labeled "Senufo Warthog mask."

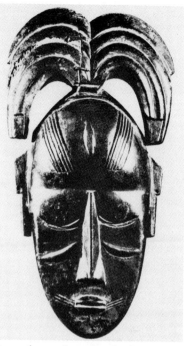

69. Do mask; wood; traces of paint; h. 14";
labeled "Face mask (kpélié?)."

four vertical marks above each eye, and has three instead of two scarification marks at either side of the mouth, unpierced ears, and a more graceful flaring motif between the hairline and the horns. With these exceptions in minor detail, the two masks are alike in every way and could be, as Fagg suggests, the work of the same carver.

Another important example of a Do type is a mask (plate 68) belonging to Ladislas Segy.[30] Although labeled "Senufo Warthog mask," this piece is clearly another example of the Do *leu*.[31] Like the *leu* mask I documented at Bondo-Dyoula and that in the Barclay collection, this work is not a face mask but one worn at an oblique angle over the forehead. It conforms fully to the *leu* type in that it is a rather naturalistic depiction of the wart hog, with two graceful tusks extending from the sides of the snout. Only in stylistic details does it vary from the two other examples. The four large bosses appearing on the Bondo-Dyoula and Barclay pieces are dramatically reduced on the Segy mask. The tusks are placed at the sides of the snout rather than being carved as a continuous motif emanating from it. Further-

[30] Ladislas Segy, *African Sculpture*, plate 43.
[31] It is hard to imagine a Senufo attribution for this piece, since it is typologically and stylistically far removed from Senufo carving.

159

more, the Segy example has a second set of tusks carved on the lower portion of the snout. The *leu* is a particularly important Do mask type, for it is considered to be the leader in the masquerade.

A third example (plate 69), in the private collection of Mr and Mrs Samuel Rubin, conforms closely to the Do mask collected by Freeman at Bondoukou in 1889.[32] Although the coiffure-superstructure is quite different, the face portions of the masks parallel each other. Both humanoid faces are treated quite naturalistically, careful attention having been lavished on carving the eyes, nose, slightly protruding lips, and raised scarification marks at either side of the nose. Oblique striations on the forehead enclose a raised almond-shaped motif, and three scarification marks resembling cat's whiskers are at either side of the mouth. Even the slightly bulging forehead and the highly polished deep brown patination are identical. The Rubin example has a hairdo instead of a headdress, but the semi-circular forms show distinct parallels. Three small raised dots, two above the eye-slits and one on the almond motif (possibly metal tacks), in the Freeman example do not appear on the Rubin mask.

Other Do masks exist out of context. A work in the Museum of Primitive Art in New York City (plate 70), acquired in 1960, resembles several pieces seen in the field.[33] Two masks also sculpturally fall within the Do classification but are unique in that they are overlain with strips of metal.[34] A piece in the Paul Tishman collection (plate 71), labeled by Goldwater as a mask from the southeastern Senufo region, bears less resemblance to Do masks encountered in the field but may well represent a type no longer in use.[35] The rather generalized naturalistic treatment of the face is very like the Do, as is the handling of facial detail and of the hair, which is arranged atop the head in the manner of a segmented bun.

Given the recent examples from museums and private collections as well as the data from the nineteenth century, the Do tradition is of some historical standing. The tradition was still alive in 1966–7 (the period of my fieldwork) but was found only among the Ligbi and Hwela. The Dyula of Bondoukou claim that the tradition fell into abeyance some forty years ago as a result of pressure from Imām Kunande Timitay, a rigorously orthodox leader. I found the Do among the Ligbi at Bouna and the Hwela of Sorhobango (towns 125 miles apart); at Bondo-Dyoula, a predominantly Muslim Ligbi town northwest of Bondoukou; and at Bungazi, a Nafana and Muslim Ligbi village in the Banda region of west central Ghana. The Ligbi-dominated community of Menji, some fifteen miles to the east of Bondoukou, and the Ligbi quarter of Wenchi also had the Do, but they

---

[32] Goldwater, *Senufo Sculpture*, plate 34.
[33] Ibid., plate 35.
[34] Ibid., plates 37, 38.
[35] Ibid., plate 36.

70. Do mask; wood; h. 15.75″; labeled "Face mask (kpélié?)."

71. Do mask; wood; traces of paint; h. 14″; labeled "Face mask (kpélié?)."

were not in operation during the period of my fieldwork. The Wenchi masks were accidentally burned in a dry-season fire in 1963, and the Menji Do were stolen in late 1965. Neither set of masks had been replaced by the time I departed from the field.[36]

The distribution thus appears to be quite limited. In actuality, however, it is much greater, for communities that do not own Do masks often borrow them. This occurred, for example, at both Sase and Kankan, the two Ligbi wards of the town of Banda, where Do masks from Bungazi were used at wedding feasts. The Ligbi at Banda-Nkwanta, an important town some fifteen miles north-northeast of Banda, also frequently borrowed the Do masks from Bungazi. Indeed, any community wishing to use these masks may call on Ligbi who own them. In such cases a substantial fee must be

[36] The elders in the Ligbi centers at Wenchi and Menji were generally in favor of acquiring new masks, but little initiative had been taken by members of the 'ulamā'. Several reasons were given for these delays: the masks would have to be purchased in the Ivory Coast, for there were no longer any Do carvers on the Ghana side of the border; carvers who had been contacted and who were still practising their craft were charging very high prices – 3,000 to 5,000 West African francs per mask; and a few members felt that Do masks were not worth the expense, as they were simply festive additions and not essential to the efficacy of Muslim holy days. Interviews at the Ligbi quarter in Wenchi, October 17, 1966, and at Menji, November 7, 1966.

72. Do masks and masqueraders; wood; blue, ochre, white paint; cloth costumes; left h. 12.5″, right h. 15.25″. Ligbi quarter of Bouna, 1967.

73. Do mask; wood; ochre, blue, white paint; cloth; h. 11.5″. Hwela quarter of Sorhobango, 1966.

74. Do mask; wood; ochre, white, blue, black paint; cloth; h. 14″. Hwela quarter of Sorhobango, 1967.

75. Do masks; wood; ochre, white, blue, black paint. Left to right: bush cow, 10″; noble or Muslim elder, 12″; wart hog, 16″; hornbill, 8″; noble or Muslim elder, 12″. Ligbi village of Bondo-Dyoula, 1967.

76. Do masks; wood; ochre, white, blue, black paint. Left to right: thrush, 11″; bush cow, 11″; hornbill, 9.5″; sheep, 7.5″; maiden's husband, 12″. Ligbi village of Bondo-Dyoula, 1967.

77. *Mbong* (baboon) masks; wood; black, white, ochre paint; cloth. Nafana/Ligbi village of Bungazi, 1967.

78. Do masks; wood; ochre, white, black paint. Left: sheep, 10.5″; right: bush cow, 12.25″. Nafana/Ligbi village of Bungazi, 1967.

79. Do masks; wood; ochre, white, blue, black paint. Left: thrush, 13.25″; right: Gonja woman, 9.75″. Nafana/Ligbi village of Bungazi, 1967.

paid. The charge may be as much as £10 Ghanaian (£3.40 or $8.50) for a single evening's performance, but this is considered to be a reasonable demand.

In the four towns where the Do existed in 1966–7, the number of masks varied considerably. At both Bouna (plate 72) and Sorhobango (plates 73, 74) there were only two masks, these being *kyemve* (beautiful maidens). At Bondo-Dyoula there were ten masks in use: the *leu* (wart hog), two *hôringyo*(noble person or Muslim elder), one *saragigi* (sheep), two *yangaleya* (hornbill), one *kokogyinaka* (thrush), two *siginkuru-ayna* (bush cow), and the *fendyoana* (maiden's husband, plates 75, 76). In the Nafana-Ligbi village of Bungazi there were six Do: two *mbong* (baboon), a *siginkuru-ayna*, a *gbanyamuso* (beautiful Gonja woman), a *saragigi*, and a *kokogyinaka* (plates 77, 78, 79). Interestingly enough, only three years prior to my field-work, Roy Sieber recorded twelve Do face masks at Bungazi. My inquiries in 1967 revealed that five of the masks had been stolen and a sixth had deteriorated to the point where it was no longer usable.[37] The number of Do masks owned by a Muslim town is not important in any ritual sense, but it is a sign of prestige and an index of the wealth of the community. The Ligbi of Bouna and the Hwela of Sorhobango both claimed that they were seeking to increase their number of Do masks but had not done so because of the expense.[38]

The appearance of Do masks follows a rather set formula. Do dancers are led to each performance hidden behind a large cotton cloth so that they cannot be seen until the ritual officially begins. Masks must appear in pairs, and the pairing process has significance, the types that are juxtaposed being either identical in configuration or related in subject matter, importance, or intent. At Bondo-Dyoula, for example, the face mask *siginkuru-ayna* (bush cow), will appear with the mask of *hôringyo* (the Muslim elder), for the former is regarded as an important sacrificial animal and the latter as the cornerstone of the Muslim faith. The pairing of masks may change, however, for during the post-Ramadhan Do masquerade at Bondo-Dyoula in 1967 the two *hôringyo* masks performed together (plate 80). The *leu*, although representing an animal unclean to Muslims, is highly regarded for its strength and beauty and begins the ceremony alone at Bondo-Dyoula, since this is considered a good foundation on which to base the ritual. The *yangaleya* (hornbill), appreciated for its positive qualities, ends the ceremony in a solo performance in hopes that the affirmative essence of the bird's influence will prevail.

In all instances the masks I found were owned and maintained by members of the 'ulamā'. They may be kept in the compound of the Sā (the temporal head of the Muslim Ligbi community), as at Bungazi, or

[37] Interview at Bungazi, April 27, 1967.
[38] Interviews at Sorhobango, June 2, 1967, and Bouna, August 15, 1967.

80. Do *hôringyo* masks and masqueraders; wood; ochre, white, blue, black paint; cloth and raffia; left h. 12″, right h. 12″. Post-Ramadhan ceremony, Ligbi village of Bondo-Dyoula, 1967.

they may be in the possession of the Imām, as at Bondo-Dyoula. The masks are inherited by successive Sās, Imāms, or learned *karamokos*. These keepers of the Do are accorded a special honorific, Do-tigui ("chief of the Do"), but are referred to as such only during the ritual appearances of the cult. The involvement of the 'ulamā' with this masking tradition is noteworthy, since it is a reflection of the totally Muslim orientation of the Do.

This Muslim orientation is also immediately apparent in the calendar of Islamic holy days to which the appearances of the cult are tied. Wherever I recorded the Do, I was told that the masks performed during the most important public Islamic festivals. In particular, the Do were brought out during the week after Ramadhan, a period anxiously awaited by even the pious, for the month-long fast is a most difficult time. The Ligbi refer to this festival as *mingare tulu* (Dyula), literally "the feast of the month of drinking." The end of the fast, signaled by the new moon, introduces a period of gaiety and relief; on that night guns are fired to announce the close of the arduous month.[39] On the following morning, the new month is officially ushered in by the Imām, who delivers prayers exalting the name and deeds of Allāh. An equally important act on this morning, occurring

[39] *Mingare tulu* was celebrated at Bondo-Dyoula from January 12 until January 18, 1967.

167

before the public prayer, is the giving of alms by all household heads to the poor, sick, and infirm and to the religious leaders of the community. It is through this act of charity, the Ligbi claim, that Ramadhan is totally expelled from the community until the following year. For many Ligbi, however, it is the appearance of the Do masks later that evening, and on the six subsequent afternoons, that ultimately and dramatically symbolizes the breaking of the fast.

The Do performance at the end of Ramadhan involves all members of the Ligbi community. For two days prior to the event, the masks and costumes are carefully prepared, and necessary repairs are made. The masks are generally repainted, since the earth pigments wear off quickly. The entire mask face is covered first with a black pigment (*koro*, obtained from the *dyurufi* tree leaf, which is burned and its ashes mixed with palm oil). Red clay (*bõon*) and an indigo pigment either locally produced from the *garadèko* (indigo plant) or an imported German dye will be used to decorate the masks. To complete the palette, the Ligbi use white clay (*guè*), henna, and a powder obtained by pulverizing the kola nut (*oro*). These pigments are applied to various parts of the mask, especially the raised scarification marks on either side of the mouth, the beauty marks on the forehead and cheeks, and the eyes, eyebrows, and headdress. Henna is applied to the mouth, paralleling the use of henna by Ligbi men and women for prophylactic purposes. Painting a Do mask not only protects the surface but also beautifies it. Such an activity is described by the Ligbi as *fehima* ("to make beautiful and protected").

The first performance begins shortly after the dinner hour. Everyone in the community except the drummers and masked dancers will congregate in front of the Friday mosque, where they sit according to rank. Members of the 'ulamā' sit together close to where the drummers will be. Everyone is dressed in his finest clothes, and the women are bedecked with jewels. Shortly after the majority of the villagers have arrived, the drummers enter and begin tuning their drums. These generally include one or two *loonga* (pressure drums), two *pintima* (small single-membrane drums adopted from the Bron), and a large lead drum (*sadjo*). A *yambara* (calabash rattle) is played by one of the elderly women, who will direct the singing. After the drums have been tuned the masqueraders are introduced by a chant: "*fenoyina tarhamasi amasie ba*" ("something extraordinary is coming"). Out of nowhere leaps a masked figure, the *nèfyèdou* ("he who frightens children"), dressed in a bright yellow raffia skirt, gloves, bangles, a woven shirt, and a woven sack mask. Brandishing a whip, he clears the dancers' circle of children who have crowded in too close. He orders the crowd to quiet down while he takes advantage of his prestigious position by making passes at young girls in the audience. When the crowd is quiet, the *nèfyèdou* goes to the edge of the circle and calls out to the *leu*, the first of the Do dancers. The *leu* performs a solo dance, which has a unique song and drum pattern to accompany it. He is followed by a pair of dancers, who likewise have a specific dance and accompaniment. Other pairs of dancers perform in turn, all displaying remarkable technical ability. The athletic young men dance so vigorously that sometimes they must stop to rest and be fanned by attendants. The entire performance may last as long as three hours.

The performances on subsequent afternoons throughout the week follow the same pattern. The cumulative effect of the rituals is to liberate the community from the long period of self-denial that marks the observance of Ramadhan.

Do performances at the close of another solemn period serve similarly to mark the return to a normal routine. During the first nine days of the last month of the Islamic year (Dhu'l Ḥijjā), preparations are made for *īd al-qabir*, a sacrificial feast held on the tenth day. The feast day is called Lanndi Kabiru by the 'ulamā', and *dongi-ma* ("day of singing") by the rest of the Muslim Ligbi community. The essence of the holy day is purification, which demands a period of physical and psychological preparation. The nine days preceding *dongi-ma* are consequently devoted to prayer, almsgiving, and the observance of certain prophylactic measures. Ligbi men are forbidden to shave their heads and cut their nails, and they are obliged to smear small amounts of henna on the palms of their hands in order to avert the dangerous jinn that are believed to be rampant at this time. Women cover themselves with henna even more lavishly and use it to tint their hair. Almsgiving is considered especially praiseworthy on these days, and clerics also recommend that the community pray every night before the great feast. The more pious Ligbi will travel to the outskirts of Bondo-Toumourai to visit the grave of Al-Ḥājjī Moro Bamba, in order to acquire a measure of holiness through their physical association with his remains.[40] Some will fast on the ninth day from sunrise until sunset, for local clerics claim that Allāh will forgive those who fast on this last day for their evils during the previous year.

Sacrificial animals must be ritually purified and prepared the night before *dongi-ma*. Generally a sheep or goat will be offered by the head of a household, although it is incumbent on the Imām to sacrifice a ram.[41] Henna is

---

[40] Al-Ḥājjī Moro Bamba was acknowledged by the Ligbi of the Cercle de Bondoukou as their most important religious and historical figure. He was said to be the religious leader of the Bamba at Begho just prior to the demise of the town and to have led an important segment of Ligbi from Begho to Banda and then westward into the Ivory Coast, where they settled the present twin towns of Bondo-Dyoula and Bondo-Toumourai. His importance is reflected in the numerous Ligbi pilgrims who came to pray annually at his grave.

[41] Although I was not present in any Ligbi village during the festival of *dongi-ma*, March 23–5, 1967, I was able to obtain a detailed account of the ceremony from the Ligbi 'ulamā' at Bungazi, December 27, 1967.

usually applied to the throat of the animal, but some prefer to mark their animals on the forehead or on the front legs; like human beings, the animal is thus protected from evil spirits and made ceremonially clean. Food is withheld from the sacrificial animal on the ninth night, it being considered efficacious for it to fast symbolically.[42] It is only immediately prior to the actual sacrifice on the following morning that the animal is given some mashed yam and water.

The morning of the tenth day is dominated by a public prayer led by the Imām, who gives thanks to Allāh for having given all members of his community life and health. Allāh and Muḥammad are praised for their works, beneficence, and power, and then a short discourse on the meaning of sacrifice is given for the benefit of all assembled, especially for the children and others who have had little instruction in the faith. The Imām then sacrifices a ram on behalf of the entire community, cutting the throat of the animal and allowing some of the blood to drip on the ground. This ends the public prayer and everyone returns home. Each family head must now make a like offering in the hopes of dispelling the evils that plagued his household during the year. That night portions of the sacrificed animal are shared by all members of the family, and it is after this meal that the Do dancers perform for the benefit of the community. The public appearance of the Do on this evening brings to an end the series of purificatory rites attached to this solemn period of the Muslim year.

There are yet other occasions requiring the appearance of the Do. At Bondo-Dyoula I was told that the Do may come out on the tenth day of Dyombende. This occurs only during particularly unfortunate years, those with a large number of deaths, uncontrollable diseases, and so forth.[43] Marriage ceremonies, restricted among the Ligbi and other Mande peoples to two major dates during the year (three weeks after Ramadhan and at the end of Dhu'l Ḥijjā), may also be an opportunity for the Do to appear. This depends on the wealth of the bridegroom, who has already invested heavily in his bride. It is only the rare young man who can afford the added expense and concurrent prestige of hiring Do dancers to perform at his wedding.

In all Ligbi villages and towns where the Do occurred, they were said to appear at the funeral rites of all members of the 'ulamā'; this is optional for other Muslims, male and female, but non-Muslims in the community are never accorded such a privilege. The cult generally performs on the

---

[42] The practice of applying henna to sacrificial animals is no longer strictly followed at Bungazi, for many feel that as long as animals are not fed they will be ritually clean. Interview at Bungazi, December 27, 1967. A similar attitude was expressed at Bondo-Dyoula, January 4, 1968.

[43] At Bungazi the most recent appearance of the Do mask during Dyombende was in 1964, when it was brought out because of the political crises gripping the country. According to the Bungazi Ligbi, things had deteriorated so badly under Nkrumah that life had been particularly difficult that year. Interview at Bungazi, December 28, 1967. (I do not know whether the mask has reappeared since my departure from the field.)

third day after the burial, the procedure of the burial hewing closely to Islamic requirements and including such features as the washing and dressing of the corpse, the orientation of the body towards Mecca, the marking of the grave with stones, and so forth.[44] The third day is considered an especially proper day for the appearance of the Do, for this is when the spirit departs from the body of the deceased. At this time the surviving members of the family must offer a large but simple meal, consisting of fried corn, mashed yam, and meat, to all friends and relatives. If a family elects not to have the Do perform, the cult may be asked to attend a similar commemorative feast on either the seventh day or the twelfth day after the burial. On such occasions the masked dancers lead all assembled women in song to help alleviate the painful experience of death. Like the prayers intoned during the washing and dressing of the corpse, the Do masquerade is considered to be especially effective at keeping evil spirits away from the physical remains of the deceased. A similar measure of protection is said to be derived by the surviving family members, who in their bereaved state are particularly susceptible to the evil machinations of the jinn.[45]

The Do masking tradition also occupies a quasi-political role, for it can appear at important political gatherings. Do songs have even been composed for specific political occasions. When K. A. Busia, the opposition leader during the Nkrumah regime, visited Menji in 1964 he was greeted by Do masqueraders who performed a song created in his honor:

> *Kambelebalu lakaribaga adoma farinyafo akambili-bayara Busia.*
> (Fame can be achieved by doing something well, for look and
> see what has been achieved by Busia.)[46]

Even a national political tragedy may be commemorated in this manner. After the 1967 assassination of General Kotoka, a highly popular member of the military National Liberation Council that supplanted the ousted Nkrumah regime, a funeral dirge was composed in his honor by the Do cult at Bungazi:

> *Sunguru arana Kotoka-kyie aranafere.*
> (Kotoka did well; let the whole nation gather and praise him.)[47]

Once the national day of mourning had passed, this particular dirge was incorporated into the general body of Do funeral songs, with the stipulation that it be sung only to honor the deaths of important males of the town.

The multiplicity of roles enjoyed by the Do, both within the Islamic festival cycle and at more secularized Muslim levels, is remarkable. It must

---

[44] Burial procedures among the Ligbi follow those in general use among West African Muslims. For an overall view, see Trimingham, *Islam in West Africa*, pp. 178–84.

[45] Interview at Menji, January 14, 1968.

[46] Recorded at Menji, January 14, 1968.

[47] Recorded at Bungazi, January 17, 1968.

be stressed that in every instance the Do is tied only to Ligbi communities and to the needs of this heavily Islamized population. Given its totally Islamic nature, it is not surprising to find that the Do has remained an exclusively Muslim Mande tradition. "Pagan" groups in the Cercle de Bondoukou and west central Ghana, who are prone to assimilate various aspects of Muslim Mande culture, claim that the Do holds little meaning or utility for them. Among the Kulango, the Do is regarded as *membo ninngo,* literally "an amusing dance," and is considered to be a purely Muslim affair.[48]

[48] Cultural borrowing is a highly pragmatic phenomenon even when involving art forms. Thus, although the Do has remained a Muslim Ligbi tradition, the exact opposite is true for the Gbain cult, which has been readily adopted by "pagans" in the area around Bondoukou.

CONCLUSION

The fallacy of the axiom that Islam and "pagan" art traditions are necessarily incompatible should be obvious from the foregoing evidence. In the Cercle de Bondoukou and west central Ghana we find a variety of ways in which Muslims can positively relate to non-Muslim cultures and their traditional art. The most striking examples are found in the Bedu, Gbain, and Do masquerades. Although only peripherally associated with the Bedu, since it is a tradition controlled by non-Muslims, the Mande cooperate and participate in this masking ceremony. The Gbain and Do, however, are obviously Muslim Mande masquerades. Of the two, the Do is most closely bound to Islam. Even when operating at more secularized levels, as in the case of weddings and funerals, the Do must follow Muslim practices and procedures and is never used in a non-Muslim context. Not only is its distribution restricted to the Islamized Ligbi (the only exception being the Muslim Hwela of Sorhobango), but the ownership and custody of Do masks is invariably vested in the 'ulamā'. Thus the tradition is tied to the very core of the Muslim community.

The Muslim content of the Gbain anti-witchcraft tradition is also strong, indeed dominant, and pervades the most vital aspects of the cult. The regular ritual appearances of the Gbain are not aligned with the Islamic calendar, but the most important act performed on behalf of the Gbain – its purification and rejuvenation – must coincide with *san ielema seri*, the most magical day celebrated by all Muslim Mande. To ignore this day, even for non-Muslims utilizing the Gbain, would condemn the mask and the cult to impotence during the coming year and thereby deprive the community of its major safeguard against witchcraft. In addition, the basic techniques used to enhance the power of the Gbain are plainly Muslim in origin. The efficacy of a Gbain is directly related to the number of Qur'ānic amulets that are tied to the mask, and it is also essential that it be constantly washed with *siliama gue* and fed remnants of the meat derived from the sacrifices offered by the faithful at *dongi-ma*.

Whereas the Do is viewed by nearly all Muslims as a positive addition to the community and as a tradition that is not in conflict with the precepts of the Qur'ān, no such unanimity of opinion exists regarding the Gbain. Deep divisions occur among both the majority of the faithful and the 'ulamā' as to the legitimacy and necessity of the Gbain, and the response to the cult ranges from total acceptance to utter rejection. Despite such controversy, the tradition persists and is found in its most vital form among the Islamized Mande; offshoots of the cult among neighboring peoples are considered to be far less effective than their Muslim counterparts. Both the Do and Gbain continue to function within a Muslim framework because they perform roles necessary to the Islamic community and to individual believers.

The involvement of Muslims with "pagan" practices is by no means unique to these cults. The Muslim Mande participate in numerous aspects of local life. They are present at all major state festivals, and often elements of Islamic magic are associated with the wide range of art forms used on such occasions. The Muslim Ligbi of Wenchi, for example, attend the enstoolment of the Wenchihene and offer public prayers for the future well-being of the paramount and for the blackened ancestral stools of the state. Muslim clerics serve as important advisors to traditional political functionaries. At Banda, major court cases require the presence of Muslim Ligbi clerics, and the Bron king at Herebo insists that all important state decisions be deliberated with noted Mande Dyula elders.

Mande involvement in non-Muslim religious practices is everywhere evident. Some Muslims are merely supplicants at shrines, where problems that cannot be alleviated by Islamic procedures are brought to local practitioners in the hope that such difficulties may be resolved by them. In other instances, the Mande may simply seek additional safeguards against everyday problems. Where the Mande avail themselves of both Islamic and "pagan" techniques, they do not feel their behavior implies spiritual ambiguity or a weakening of faith. Rather it represents the pragmatism with which Muslims in this region regard the world.

It is obvious that Islam in West Africa is not an extension of the faith in its pristine form but is rather a highly flexible and syncretic phenomenon. Indeed, its long history and success in West Africa would have been impossible if Islam were wantonly destructive of traditional life. In fact, the particular suitability of Islam to the demands of culture contact lies in doctrinal sympathy to many aspects of local tradition (witchcraft, the use of magic, and divination). In practice Islam is far more pragmatic than Western religions when confronting the tribal world. It seems that Western writers have imputed to Islam much of the arrogance and intolerance displayed by their own culture towards traditional African life. Contacts between Muslims and non-Muslims have been characterized by a high degree of interchange and reciprocity. Muslims in general are willing to accept certain aspects of "paganism," and vice versa. This is true not only of the mass of believers but also of members of the religious elite, who realize that Islam can survive as a faith and continue to expand its influence only so long as it is willing to react flexibly to the non-Muslim world.

It is important to reiterate that what occurs in the Cercle de Bondoukou

82. "Dioula" masquerader in a cloth costume.

81. "Dioula" masked ceremony in the region of Korhogo.

and west central Ghana between Muslims and their neighbors is not exceptional. This has been demonstrated by the fragmentary evidence for the existence of masking traditions in other heavily Islamized regions such as Nupe, Bobo-Dioulasso, and Gonja. Yet other evidence exists. Two provocative photographs in Holas's recently published *Masques ivoiriens* indicate that such a tradition may well exist among the Mande Dyula in the Cercle de Korhogo (plates 81, 82). In the same work, Holas cites a bush cow mask (plate 83) attributed to the heavily Islamized region of Odienné in the northwestern Ivory Coast. My own field evidence suggests that Mande Muslims at Kong and in the southern Senufo country of Jimini also may utilize masks, for they have been responsible for certain examples of the Do used by the Ligbi in Bungazi and Bondo-Dyoula. Further afield, Germaine Dieterlen has observed that the Muslim Bozo in the confluence area of the Niger and Bani rivers utilize both figurative and masking traditions. The Islamized Mande Dafing or Marka of San in Mali apparently use Bambara-like masks, whereas other Dafing clans located in northwestern Upper Volta seem to be responsible for yet another mask type, highly reminiscent of Bobo masks but conceived in a more humanoid fashion.

These examples obviously suggest areas where Islam and tribal art traditions co-exist, and these areas are in need of further research. Every

83. Bush cow mask from the Islamized region of Odienné, northwestern Ivory Coast.

instance of Muslim/non-Muslim interaction is unique and requires individual and thorough investigation. Only in this way will a fair documentation of the effects of Islam on the arts be accomplished. Scholars can no longer ignore those areas of Africa in which Islam exists, for they can no longer assume that these areas will be devoid of indigenous art.

BIBLIOGRAPHY

A. Books

Allen, Christopher, and Johnson, R. W. (eds.). *African Perspectives*. Cambridge: University Press, 1970.

Al-Qayrawānī, Ibn Abī Zayd. *See* Qayrawānī, Ibn Abī Zayd al.

Anderson, J. N. D. *Islamic Law in Africa*. London: Her Majesty's Stationery Office, 1954.

Arnold, Thomas W. *Painting in Islam*. New York: Dover Publications, 1965.

Arnold, Thomas W., and Guillaume, A. (eds.). *The Legacy of Islam*. Oxford: Clarendon Press, 1931.

Arthur, John. *Brong-Ahafo Handbook*. Accra: Graphic Press, n.d.

Bascom, William Russell. *African Arts: An Exhibition at the Robert H. Lowie Museum of Anthropology*. Berkeley, Cal.: Robert H. Lowie Museum, 1967.

Binger, Louis-Gustave. *Du Niger au Golfe de Guinée*. 2 vols. Paris: Hachette, 1892.
Esclavage, Islamisme et Christianisme. Paris: Société d'éditions scientifiques, 1891.

Bousquet, Georges H. *L'Islam maghrebin*. Algiers: La Maison des Livres, 1941.
Précis de droit musulman. 2 vols. Algiers: La Maison des livres, 1950–54.

Bowdich, T. E. *A Mission from Cape Coast Castle to Ashantee*. London: John Murray, 1819.

Braimah, J. A., and Goody, J. R. *Salaga: The struggle for Power*. London: Longmans, 1967.

Busia, Kofi Abrefa. *The Position of the Chief in the Modern Political System of Ashanti*. London: Oxford University Press, 1951.

Caillie, René. *Travels through Central Africa*. 2 vols. Reprinted from the 1830 edition. London: Cass, 1968.

Casa da Mosto. *Voyages in Western Africa*. Trans. and ed. G. R. Crone. Hakluyt Series II, no. 80. London: Hakluyt Society, 1937.

Chivas-Baron, Clotilde. *Côte d'Ivoire*. Paris: Emile Larose, 1939.

Claerhout, Adr. *Arts d'Afrique, d'Océanie, d'Amérique*. Antwerp: Musée d'Ethnographie, 1966.

Claridge, W. Walton. *A History of the Gold Coast and Ashanti*. 2 vols. London: John Murray, 1915.

Clozel, F. J. *Dix ans à la Côte d'Ivoire*. Paris: Augustin Challamel, 1906.

Clozel, F. J., and Villamur, Roger. *Coutumes indigènes de la Côte d'Ivoire*. Paris: Augustin Challamel, 1902.

Cole, H. M. *African Arts of Transformation*. Santa Barbara: University of California at Santa Barbara, 1970.

Cragg, Kenneth. *Counsels in Contemporary Islam*. Edinburgh: University Press, 1965.

Curtin, Philip D. (ed.). *Africa Remembered: Narratives by West Africans from the Era of the Slave Trade.* Madison: University of Wisconsin Press, 1967.

Delafosse, Maurice. *Vocabulaires comparatifs de plus de 60 langues ou dialectes parlés à la Côte d'Ivoire et dans les régions limitrophes.* Paris: E. Leroux, 1904.

Les Frontières de la Côte d'Ivoire, de la Côte d'Or et du Soudan. Paris: Masson et Cie, 1908.

Le Peuple Siéna ou Sénoufo. Paris: P. Geuthner, 1908–9.

Haut-Sénégal – Niger. 3 vols. Paris: Emile Larose, 1912.

Delange, Jacqueline. *Arts et peuples de l'Afrique noire.* Paris: Gallimard, 1967.

Dupuis, Joseph. *Journal of a Residence in Ashantee.* London: Henry Colburn, 1824.

Elisofon, Eliot, and Fagg, W[illiam] B[uller]. *The Sculpture of Africa.* New York: Praeger, 1958.

Fagg, W[illiam] B[uller]. *The Art of Western Africa: Tribal Masks and Sculptures.* London: Collins (with UNESCO), 1967.

African Tribal Images: The Katherine White Reswick Collection. Cleveland: Cleveland Museum of Art, 1968.

African Sculpture. Washington, D.C.: International Exhibitions Foundation, 1970.

Fagg, W[illiam] B[uller], and Plass, Margaret. *African Sculpture: An Anthology.* London: Studio Vista, 1964.

Faris [Farès], Nabih A. (ed.). *The Arab Heritage.* Princeton, N.J.: Princeton University Press, 1944.

Freeman, R[ichard] Austin. *Travels and Life in Ashanti and Jaman.* Reprinted from the 1897 edition. London: Cass, 1967.

Frobenius, Leo. *The Voice of Africa.* 2 vols. Reprinted from the 1913 edition. New York: Benjamin Blom, 1968.

Gardi, René. *African Crafts and Craftsmen.* Trans. Sigrid MacRae. New York: Van Nostrand Reinhold, 1969.

Gaston, Joseph. *Côte d'Ivoire.* Paris: Artheime Fayard, 1944.

Gaudefroy-Demombynes, Maurice. *Muslim Institutions.* Trans. John P. MacGregor. London: Allen and Unwin, 1950.

Geertz, Clifford. *Islam Observed: Religious Development in Morocco and Indonesia.* New Haven: Yale University Press, 1968.

Goldwater, Robert John. *Senufo Sculpture from West Africa.* Greenwich, Conn.: New York Graphic Society, 1964.

Goody, J. R. (ed.). *Literacy in Traditional Societies.* Cambridge: University Press, 1968.

Goody, J. R., and Arhin, Kwame. *Ashanti and the Northwest.* Supplement No. 1 of *Research Review.* Legon: Institute of African Studies, 1965.

Greenberg, Joseph Harold. *The Influence of Islam on a Sudanese Religion.* New York: J. J. Augustin, 1947.

Languages of Africa. Bloomington: Indiana University, 1963.

Guillaume, M. A. *The Traditions of Islam.* Oxford: Clarendon Press, 1924.

Henry, Joseph. *L'Ame d'un peuple africain: les Bambara.* Bibliothèque Anthropos, vol. 1, no. 1. Münster: Aschendorffschen Buchhandlung, 1910.

Holas, Bohumil. *Les Sénoufo (y compris les Minianka).* Paris: Presses Universitaires de France, 1957.

Bibliography

Holas, Bohumil. *Cultures matérielles de la Côte d'Ivoire.* Paris: Presses Universitaires de France, 1960.
Changements sociaux en Côte d'Ivoire. Paris: Presses Universitaires de France, 1961.
Arts traditionnels de la Côte d'Ivoire. Abidjan: Ceda, 1967.
Masques ivoiriens. Paris: Geuthner, 1969.
Ibn Battuta. *Voyages.* Arabic text with French translation by C. Defrémery and B. R. Sanguinette. Paris: Imprimerie Nationale, 1877–93.
Jobson, Richard. *The Golden Trade.* Reprinted from the 1628 edition. London: Penguin Press, 1932.
Kerharo, J., and Bouquet, A. *Sorciers, Féticheurs et Guérisseurs de la Côte d'Ivoire – Haute Volta.* Paris: Vigot Frères, 1950.
Khalīl ibn Ishaq [Khalil ben Ish'āq]. *Abrégé de la loi musulmane suivant le rite de l'Imâm Mâlek.* Trans. Georges H. Bousquet. 4 vols. Paris: A. Maisonneuve, 1956–62.
Krieger, Kurt, and Kutscher, Gerdt. *Westafrikanische Masken.* Berlin: Museum für Völkerkunde, 1960.
Kyerematen, A. A. Y. *Panoply of Ghana.* New York: Praeger, 1964.
Leiris, Michel and Delange, Jacqueline. *African Art.* Trans. Michael Ross. London: Thames and Hudson, 1968.
Levtzion, Nehemiah. *Muslims and Chiefs in West Africa.* Oxford: Clarendon Press, 1968.
Levy, Reuben. *The Social Structure of Islam.* Cambridge: University Press, 1957.
Lewis, I. M. (ed.). *History and Social Anthropology.* London: Tavistock, 1968.
Islam in Tropical Africa. London: Oxford University Press for the International African Institute, 1966.
Macdonald, D. B. *Development of Muslim Theology, Jurisprudence and Constitutional Theory.* New York: Scribner, 1903.
Manoukian, Madeline. *Tribes of the Northern Territories of the Gold Coast.* London: International African Institute, 1951.
Akan and Ga-Adangme Peoples of the Gold Coast. London: Oxford University Press for the International African Institute, 1950.
Marty, Paul. *Etudes sur l'Islam et les tribus de Soudan.* 4 vols. Paris: E. Leroux, 1920–1.
L'Islam en Guinée: Fouta Diallon. Paris: E. Leroux, 1921.
Etudes sur l'Islam en Côte d'Ivoire. Paris: E. Leroux, 1922.
Masterworks of Primitive Art. New York: Aaron Furman Gallery, 1962.
Mauny, Raymond. *Tableau géographique de l'Ouest africain au Moyen Age.* Dakar: Institut Français d'Afrique Noire, 1961.
McCall, D. F. *Africa in Time Perspective.* New York: Oxford University Press, 1969.
Mélanges Louis Massignon. 3 vols. Damascus: Institut Français, 1956–7.
Meyerowitz, Eva L. R. *The Sacred State of the Akan.* London: Faber & Faber, 1951.
Akan Traditions of Origin. London: Faber & Faber, 1952.
The Akan of Ghana. London: Faber & Faber, 1958.
At the Court of an African King. London: Faber & Faber, 1962.

Migeon, Gaston. *Manuel d'art musulman.* Paris: Ricard, 1927.

Monteil, Charles Victor. *Les Bambara du Segou et du Kaarta.* Paris: Emile Larose, 1924.

Monteil, Vincent. *L'Islam noir.* Paris: Editions du Seuil, 1964.

Monti, Franco. *African Masks.* Trans. Andrew Hale. London and New York: Hamlyn, 1969.

Museum of Primitive Art [New York City]. *The John and Domenique de Menil Collection.* New York: University Publishers, 1962.

Nadel, Siegfried Frederick. *A Black Byzantium.* London: Oxford University Press for the International African Institute, 1946.

Nupe Religion. London: Routledge and Kegan Paul, 1954.

Oldman, W. O. *Catalogue of Ethnographic Specimens,* no. 23. London: Brixton Hill, 1905.

Qayrawānī, Ibn Abī Zayd al [Kayrawâni, Ibn Aboû Zaîd el]. *Risâla ou Traité abrégé de droit malékite et morale musulmane.* Ed. and trans. Edmond Fagnan. Paris: Geuthner, 1914.

Qur'ân, The. Trans. E. H. Palmer. Sacred Books of the East, vol. 9. Oxford: Clarendon Press, 1900.

Rattray, Robert S. *Ashanti.* London: Oxford University Press, 1923.

Religion and Art in Ashanti. London: Oxford University Press, 1927.

Ashanti Law and Constitution. London: Oxford University Press, 1929.

Schacht, Joseph. *An Introduction to Islamic Law.* Oxford: Clarendon Press, 1964.

Origins of Muhammadan Jurisprudence. Oxford: Clarendon Press, 1950.

Segy, Ladislas. *African Sculpture.* New York: Dover Publications, 1958.

Sieber, Roy, and Rubin, Arnold. *Sculpture of Black Africa: The Paul Tishman Collection.* Los Angeles: Los Angeles County Museum of Art, 1968.

Smith, Mary F. *Baba of Karo.* New York: Praeger, 1964.

Tauxier, Louis. *Le Noir de Soudan.* Paris: Emile Larose, 1912.

Le Noir de Yatenga. Paris: Emile Larose, 1917.

Le Noir de Bondoukou. Paris: E. Leroux, 1921.

Triande, Toumani. *Masques et sculptures voltaïques.* Ouagadougou: Musée National, 1969.

Trimingham, J. Spencer. *Islam in West Africa.* London: Oxford University Press, 1959.

History of Islam in West Africa. London: Oxford University Press, 1962.

The Influence of Islam upon Africa. New York: Praeger, 1968.

Trowell, Margaret, and Nevermann, Hans. *African and Oceanic Art.* New York: Harry Abrams, 1968.

Underwood, Leon. *Masks of West Africa.* London: Alec Tiranti, 1948.

Von Grunebaum, G. E. (ed.). *Unity and Variety in Muslim Civilization.* Chicago: University of Chicago Press, 1955.

Wensinck, A. J. *A Handbook of Early Muhammadan Tradition.* Leiden: E. J. Brill, 1960.

The Muslim Creed. Cambridge: University Press, 1932.

Westermann, Diedrich, and Bryan, M. A. *Languages of West Africa.* London: Oxford University Press for the International African Institute, 1952.

Bibliography

Wilks, Ivor. *The Northern Factor in Ashanti History*. Legon: Institute of African Studies, 1961.

Willett, Frank. *African Art*. New York: Praeger, 1971.

B. Articles

Ageyeman, E. A. "A Note on the Foundation of the Kingdom of Gyaman," *Ghana Notes and Queries*, 9 (1966): 36–9. (Legon: Historical Society of Ghana.)

Al-Ḥājj, Muḥammad. "A Seventeenth-Century Chronicle on the Origins and Missionary Activities of the Wangarawa," *Kano Studies*, 1, no. 4 (1968): 7–42.

Anderson, J. N. D. "Law as a Social Force in Islamic Culture and History," *Bulletin of the School of Oriental and African Studies*, 20 (1957): 13–40.

Arhin, Kwame. "The Structure of Greater Ashanti," *Journal of African History*, 3, no. 1: 65–85.

Bernus, Edmond. "Kong et sa région," *Etudes Eburnéennes*, 8 (1960): 239–324. (Abidjan: Institut Français de l'Afrique Noire.)

Bivar, A. H. D., and Hiskett, M. "The Arabic Literature of Nigeria to 1804: A Provisional Account," *Bulletin of the School of Oriental and African Studies*, 25, part 1 (1962): 104–48.

Bochet, Gilbert. "Les Masques Sénoufo: de la forme à la signification," *Bulletin de l'Institut Français de l'Afrique Noire*, 27, series B, nos. 3–4: 636–77.

Bravmann, René A. "The Diffusion of Ashanti Political Art" in *Art and Leadership*, eds. Douglas Fraser and H. M. Cole. Madison: University of Wisconsin Press, 1972.

Bravmann, René A., and Mathewson, R. D. "A Note on the History and Archaeology of 'Old Bima,'" *African Historical Studies*, 3, no. 1: 133–49.

Creswell, K. A. C. "The Lawfulness of Painting in Early Islam," *Ars Islamica*, 11–12 (1946): 159–66.

Delafosse, Maurice. "Le Clergé musulman de l'Afrique occidentale," *Revue du Monde Musulman*, 11: 177–206.

"L'Animisme nègre et sa résistance à l'Islamisation en Afrique occidentale," *Revue du Monde Musulman*, 49: 121–64.

Delobsom, A. A. Dim. "Note sur les Yarce au Mossi," *Revue Anthropologique*, 44: 326–33.

Dieterlen, Germaine. "The Mande Creation Myth," *Africa*, 27, no. 2: 124–39.

"Mythe et organisation sociale en Afrique occidentale," *Journal de la Société des Africanistes*, 29: 119–38. (Paris: Musée de l'Homme.)

Dieterlen, Germaine, and Ligers, Z. "Un Objet rituel Bozo: le Maniyalo," *Journal de la Société des Africanistes*, 28: 33–42.

Donne, J. B. "The Celia Barclay Collection of African Art," *The Connoisseur*, June 1972: 88–95.

Ettinghausen, Richard. "The Character of Islamic Art" in *The Arab Heritage*, ed. Nabih A. Faris. Princeton, N.J.: Princeton University Press, 1944.

"Interaction and Integration in Islamic Art" in *Unity and Variety in Muslim Civilisation*, ed. G. E. Von Grunebaum. Chicago: University of Chicago Press, 1955.

"Images and Iconoclasm: Islam" in *The Encyclopedia of Art*, 7: 816–18. New York: McGraw-Hill, 1963.

Farès [Farīs], Bishr. "De la figuration en Islam: un document inédit," *Arts*, March 30, 1951: 3. (Paris.)

"Essai sur l'esprit de la décoration islamique," *Arts*, March 30, 1951: 9, 25–7. (Paris.)

"Philosophie et jurisprudence illustrées par les Arabes: la querelle des images en Islam," *Mélanges Louis Massignon*, 2: 77–109.

Froelich, J. C. "Essai sur les causes et méthodes de l'Islamisation de l'Afrique de l'Ouest du XIe siècle au XXe siècle" in *Islam in Tropical Africa*, ed. I. M. Lewis. London: Oxford University Press, 1966.

Goody, J. R. "A Note on the Penetration of Islam into the West of the Northern Territories of the Gold Coast," *Transactions of the Gold Coast and Togoland Historical Society*, no. 1 (1953): 45–6. (Accra.)

"The Mande and the Akan Hinterland" in *The Historian in Tropical Africa*, eds. J. Vansina, R. Mauny, and L. V. Thomas. London: Oxford University Press, 1964.

"The Akan and the North," *Ghana Notes and Queries*, 9 (1966): 18–24. (Legon: Historical Society of Ghana.)

"The Over-Kingdom of Gonja" in *West African Kingdoms in the Nineteenth Century*, eds. D. Forde and P. M. Kayberry. London: Oxford University Press, 1967.

"Restricted Literacy in Northern Ghana" in *Literacy in Traditional Societies*, ed. the author. Cambridge: University Press, 1968.

Hiskett, M. "An Islamic Tradition of Reform in the Western Sudan from the Sixteenth to the Eighteenth Century," *Bulletin of the School of Oriental and African Studies*, 25, part 3 (1962): 577–96.

Hodgkin, Thomas. "The Islamic Literary Tradition in Ghana" in *Islam in Tropical Africa*, ed. I. M. Lewis. London: Oxford University Press, 1966.

Hunwick, John O. "Ahmad Bābā and the Moroccan Invasion of the Sudan," *Journal of the Historical Society of Nigeria*, 2, no. 3 (1962): 311–28.

"A New Source for the Biography of Ahmad Bābā al-Tinbuktī (1556–1627)," *Bulletin of the School of Oriental and African Studies*, 27, part 3 (1964): 568–93.

"The Influence of Arabic in West Africa," *Transactions of the Historical Society of Ghana*, 7 (1964): 24–41.

"Further Light on Ahmad Bābā al-Tinbuktī," *Research Bulletin*, 2, no. 2 (July 1966): 19–31. (Center of Arabic Documentation, Institute of African Studies, University of Ibadan.)

"Religion and State in the Songhay Empire, 1464–1591" in *Islam in Tropical Africa*, ed. I. M. Lewis. London: Oxford University Press, 1966.

"Notes on a Late Fifteenth-Century Document Concerning 'Al-Takrūr'" in *African Perspectives*, ed. Christopher Allen and R. W. Johnson. Cambridge: University Press, 1970.

'Isā, Aḥmad [Muḥammad]. "Muslims and Taswīr," trans. H. W. Glidden, *The Muslim World*, 45 (1955): 250–68.

Kremitske, John. "Islam" in *The Encyclopedia of Art*, 8: 332–3. New York: McGraw-Hill, 1963.

Bibliography

Last, D. M., and Al-Ḥajj, M. A. "Attempts at Defining a Muslim in Nineteenth-Century Hausaland and Bornu," *Journal of the Historical Society of Nigeria*, 3, no. 2 (1965): 231–40.

Levtzion, Nehemiah. "Salaga: A Nineteenth-Century Trading Town in Ghana," *Asian and African Studies*, 2 (1966): 207–44. (Jerusalem.)

"Arabic Manuscripts from Kumasi of the Early Nineteenth Century," *Transactions of the Historical Society of Ghana*, 8 (1966): 99–119.

Little, Kenneth. "The Mende in Sierra Leone" in *African Worlds*, ed. Daryll Forde. London: Oxford University Press, 1954.

MacDonald, D. B., and Massé, H. "Djinn" in *Encyclopedia of Islam*, new ed., vol. 2. Leiden: E. J. Brill, 1965.

Martin, Bradford G. "Unbelief in the Western Sudan: 'Uthmān dan Fodio's 'Ta'lim al-Ikhwān,'" *Middle Eastern Studies*, 4, no. 1 (1967): 50–97.

Meyerowitz, Eva L. R. "Akan Oral Historical Traditions," *Universitas*, 5, no. 2: 44–9.

Morton-Williams, Peter. "The Fulani Penetration into Nupe and Yoruba in the Nineteenth Century" in *History and Social Anthropology*, ed. I. M. Lewis. London: Tavistock, 1968.

"Nupe (The) of Pategi," *Nigeria Magazine*, no. 50 (1956): 260–79.

Ozanne, Paul. "Seventeenth-Century Wenchi," *Ghana Notes and Queries*, 8 (1966): 16.

Person, Yves. "En quête d'une chronologie ivoirienne" in *The Historian in Tropical Africa*, eds. J. Vansina, R. Mauny, and L. V. Thomas. London: Oxford University Press, 1964.

Prouteaux, Maurice. "Divertissements de Kong," *Bulletin du Comité d'Etudes Historiques et Scientifiques de l'Afrique Occidentale Française* (1925): 605–50. (Dakar.)

"Notes sur certains rites magico-religieux de la Haute Côte d'Ivoire," *L'Anthropologie*, 29: 37–52.

Randau, R. S. "Les Yarce," *Revue Anthropologique*, 64: 324–5.

Shields, C. B. "The Western Gonja (Bole) District," *Geographical Journal*, 67: 421–31.

Smith, H. F. C. "A Neglected Theme of West African History: The Islamic Revolutions of the Nineteenth Century," *Journal of the Historical Society of Nigeria*, 2, no. 2 (December 1961): 169–85.

Trimingham, J. S. "The Phases of Islamic Expansion and Islamic Culture Zones in Africa" in *Islam in Tropical Africa*, ed. I. M. Lewis. London: Oxford University Press, 1966.

Vasilev, Alexander A. "The Iconoclastic Edict of Caliph Yazīd II, A.D. 721," *Dumbarton Oaks Papers*, 9–10: 23–47.

Wensinck, A. J. "Sūra" in *The Encyclopedia of Islām*, 1st edition, vol. 4. Leiden: E. J. Brill, 1934.

Wilks, Ivor. "Abū Bakr al-Siddiq of Timbuktu" in *Africa Remembered*, ed. Philip D. Curtin. Madison: University of Wisconsin Press, 1967.

"Ghana" in *Encyclopedia of Islam*, new ed., vol. 2. Leiden: E. J. Brill, 1965.

"The Growth of Islamic Learning in Ghana," *Journal of the Historical Society of Nigeria*, 2 (December 1963): 409–17.

"The Mande Loan Element in Twi," *Ghana Notes and Queries*, 4 (1962): 26–8.

"A Medieval Trade Route from the Niger to the Guinea Coast," *Journal of African History*, 3, no. 2 (1962): 337–41.

"A Note on the Early Spread of Islam in Dagomba," *Transactions of the Historical Society of Ghana*, 8 (1966): 87–98.

"The Position of Muslims in Metropolitan Ashanti in the Early Nineteenth Century" in *Islam in Tropical Africa*, ed. I. M. Lewis. London: Oxford University Press, 1966.

"The Saghanughu and the Spread of Maliki Law: a Provisional Note," *Research Review*, 2, no. 3: 67–73. (Legon: Institute of African Studies.)

"The Transmission of Islamic Learning in the Western Sudan" in *Literacy in Traditional Societies*, ed. J. R. Goody. Cambridge: University Press, 1968.

Williams, Drid. "The Dance of the Bedu Moon," *African Arts/Arts d'Afrique*, 2, no. 1: 18–21, 72.

C. Unpublished Materials.

Agyeman-Duah, J. A. "Nsumankwa Stool History, A. S. 22." Legon: Institute of African Studies, 1965. (Mimeographed field notes.)

Ameyaw, Kwabena. "Tradition of Bandu: Brong/Ahafo 1." Legon: Institute of African Studies, 1965. (Mimeographed field notes.)

"Hani and Nsawkaw Tradition: Brong/Ahafo 2." Legon: Institute of African Studies, 1965. (Mimeographed field notes.)

"Nwase-Branam Tradition: Brong/Ahafo 3." Legon: Institute of African Studies, 1965. (Mimeographed field notes.)

"Traditions of Wenchi: Brong/Ahafo 4." Legon: Institute of African Studies, 1965. (Mimeographed field notes.)

Ewart, J. H. "Short Report on Mission to Gaman." Accra: National Archives of Ghana, acc. no. 1251/56, 1889.

Fell, T. E. "Notes on the History of Banda." Kumasi: National Archives of Ghana, D216, 1913.

Goody, J. R. *The Ethnography of the Northern Territories of the Gold Coast West of White Volta.* London: Colonial Office, 1954. (Mimeographed.)

Hobbs, H. J. "Notes on the History of Mo." Kumasi: National Archives of Ghana, D216, 1919.

"Notes on the History of Banda." Kumasi: National Archives of Ghana, D216, 1926.

Pitt, W. J. "The Mfantra." Kumasi: National Archives of Ghana, D216, 1925.

Tomlinson, H. H. "The Customs, Constitution, and History of the Gonja People." Institute of African Studies, University of Ghana, 1954. (Mimeographed.)

INDEX

Index